Exchange Rates and the Open Economy

Exchange Rates and the Open Economy

Edited by

K. A. Chrystal
Professor of Economics, University of Sheffield

Robert Sedgwick
Lecturer in Economics, University of Sheffield

WHEATSHEAF BOOKS · SUSSEX

ST. MARTIN'S PRESS · NEW YORK

First published in Great Britain in 1987 by
WHEATSHEAF BOOKS LTD
A MEMBER OF THE HARVESTER PRESS PUBLISHING GROUP
Publisher: John Spiers
16 Ship Street, Brighton, Sussex and in the USA by
ST. MARTIN'S PRESS, INC.
175 Fifth Avenue, New York, NY 10010

British Library Cataloguing in Publication Data
Exchange rates in the open economy
1. Foreign exchange 2. Macroeconomics
I. Chrystal, A. K. II. Sedgwick, Robert
332.4'56 HG3851

ISBN 0–7450–0323–0

Library of Congress Cataloging-in-Publication Data

Exchange rates in the open economy / edited by
A.K. Chrystal, Robert Sedgwick.
p. cm.
"Wheatsheaf books."
Bibliography: p.
Includes index.
ISBN 0–312–01583–6 : $30.00 (est.)
1. Foreign exchange—Congresses.
2. International economic relations—Congresses.
I. Chrystal, A. K. II. Sedgwick, Robert.
HG205.I554E93 1987
332.4'5—dc19
87-28543
CIP

Typeset in Times 11 point by Photo·graphics, Honiton, Devon
Printed and bound in Great Britain by
Billings and Sons Ltd, Worcester

Contents

Contributors

Richard T. Baillie	University of Birmingham
Stanley W. Black	University of North Carolina
Eduard T. Bomhoff	Erasmus University, Rotterdam
K. Alec Chrystal	University of Sheffield
Paul de Grauwe	University of Louvain
Steven Hall	National Institute of Economic and Social Research
Elias Karakitsos	Imperial College, London
Kees G. Koedijk	Erasmus University, Rotterdam
Gene Leon	University of Kent
George McKenzie	University of Southampton
Patrick McMahon	University of Birmingham
Hasan Molana	University of Glasgow
Marc Rosiers	University of Louvain
Michael K. Salemi	University of North Carolina
Robert Sedgwick	University of Sheffield
Steven H. Thomas	University of Southampton
Paul Turner	University of Southampton
Athina Zervoyianni	University of Hull

Preface

This book contains the papers from the tenth annual conference of the International Economics Study Group (IESG). This took place at the University of Sussex Conference Centre, Isle of Thorns, Sussex from 6th to 8th September 1985. The IESG organizes regular seminars in addition to the annual conference. These cover a wide range of topics in both 'real' and 'monetary' aspects of international economics. While membership is mainly of British academics, the IESG encourages the participation of economists in government and business as well as from overseas.

The IESG is supported by a grant from the Economic and Social Research Council. The Group also wishes to express its gratitude to Lloyds Bank and Barclays Bank for additional financial support.

Currently the officers of the IESG are:

Chairman: Professor Alasdair McBean (University of Lancaster)

Secretary: Dr Ed. Kuska (LSE)

Exchange Rates and Open Economy Macroeconomics: An Introduction

K. Alec Chrystal and Robert Sedgwick

The international financial system has experienced a period of rapid change over the last decade. To many the international money markets are a source of great mystery and even greater mistrust. For the economist, however, these developments present a challenge. The challenge is to bring some kind of order to what is going on. Can we establish an intellectual framework within which the evolution of the international monetary system can be understood. The book is part of that process.

TWO QUESTIONS

There are two major question areas in the field of international monetary economics. All of the papers in this collection address at least one of these questions. The first is: how do the international money markets work? The second question is: how does the working of the international money markets impinge upon the macroeconomic system of individual countries? We shall first provide a brief background on these two subject areas before proceeding to summarize the contribution of each of the following papers.

There are many instruments traded in international money markets. For present purposes we are not centrally concerned with international borrowing and lending. Rather the major concern is with exchange rates—the prices at which currencies exchange for each other. Thus it is the foreign exchange markets on which we shall concentrate.

The exchange rate literature has two separate strands. The relationship between them is often far from clear. The first of these we shall call the 'structural approach'. This approach aims to explain exchange rate changes in terms of identifiable macroeconomic changes. One popular model, for example, explains the exchange rate between two currencies in terms of the relative money stocks (for given real incomes and given velocities of circulation). This view could be labelled 'monetarist' since it is consistent with both the quantity theory of money and the classical dichotomy between real and monetary variables. The real economy is independent of money so changes in the money stock influence only the money price level and the exchange rate. Real relative prices are invariant to monetary changes and the exchange rate can either be explained as the ratio of two price levels or as the ratio of two money stocks. The law of one price holds at all times.

A variant of this approach relaxes both the neutrality of money assumption and the law of one price. Nonetheless, it produces testable hypotheses about the determinants of the exchange rate. Typical exchange rate equations would include relative real income and relative interest rates (or inflation rates) in addition to relative money supplies.

While the interest in the exchange rate is as great as ever, the energy being devoted to estimation of structural exchange rate equations has diminished in the last few years. This is because it has been realized that structural equations are little or no use in forecasting the exchange rate. We shall return to this point below.

The second major strand in the exchange rate literature derives from finance theory rather than from macroeconomics or monetary theory. Here the dominant perspective is that of the efficient market. In this respect the foreign exchange market can be treated just like any other financial market. The central question is: does the market price reflect all available information? One way of looking at this is to ask whether there is some forecasting rule which would enable a trader *consistently* to make profit out of speculation.

The most popular way of testing for efficiency in the foreign exchange market has been to test whether the forward exchange rate is an unbiased predictor of the future spot rate. An additional test is whether any data available up to the current time is able to improve the forecast. This is known as the orthogonality test. The forward rate should reflect all available information. So the forecast *error* should be uncorrelated with other variables known at the time the forward rate was set. The forecast error should be white noise.

Early tests of the efficiency hypothesis in foreign exchange markets were unable to reject the hypothesis. However a number of more recent papers using larger data sets and more frequent observations have claimed to reject the hypothesis. These rejections have caused many observers to conclude that the rejections may not be due to a rejection of efficiency *per se* but rather due to a rejection of the implicit assumption that speculators are indifferent to risk. If instead speculators are risk averse, the existing evidence may still be consistent with efficiency. Hence the considerable effort currently being exercised to identify a 'risk premium' in foreign exchange markets.

A word of caution is due at this point. Firstly it would be surprising if there were not some rejections for some periods. The question is: can efficiency be rejected in repeated samples? Secondly, it is not sufficient to reject efficiency within a sample or even within repeated samples. What has to be demonstrated is that the reason for the rejection is *stable*. That is that the extra information can be repeatedly used to improve an out-of-sample forecast. The evidence of Meese and Rogoff suggests this condition is not met (see references to Chapter 2). They show that a random walk model outperforms all other forecasting models out of sample. This raises doubt about the value of all in sample rejections of efficiency. Though it is not necessarily inconsistent with the existence of a time varying risk premium. Thirdly, even if the rejection of market efficiency for a particular period were correct this would not *necessarily* imply either that the market is intrinsically inefficient or that there must be a risk premium. Rather it may simply reflect a significant amount of central bank intervention in *either* the foreign exchange market *or* in domestic money markets or both.

The second major question area concerns how the international money markets impinge upon a macroeconomy. Here there has been much less controversy. Since most macro models incorporate a natural rate in the long run, analysis has concentrated on studying the implications for dynamic adjustment of having one price (the exchange rate) which can jump immediately in response to news and another price (output) which is sticky in the short run. Models in this tradition (which is due to Dornbusch) have pointed to the likelihood of exchange overshooting in response to disturbances. Such overshooting has important implications since it creates swings in the real exchange rate which can have dramatic effects in export or import competing industries.

THE CHAPTERS IN THIS VOLUME

The chapter by De Grauwe and Rosiers straddles both of the two questions discussed above. It is both about how exchange markets work and about how they impinge upon the macroeconomy. The authors study, on an international comparative level, the relationship between monetary disturbances and real exchange rate changes. They model and test the hypothesis that deviations from purchasing power parity can be explained by differences in monetary regimes across countries. They conclude that differences in monetary variability explain only about 40 per cent of differences in real exchange rate variability.

The next three chapters have a closely related theme. Baillie and McMahon present a comprehensive survey of the statistical work relating to the question of efficiency. They also present results of their own which appear to be inconsistent with the hypothesis of efficiency. One of their principal conclusions is that there appears to be a time varying risk premium.

Both Bomhoff and Koedijk and Black and Salemi take on the difficult task of trying to isolate influences due to risk factors. The former consider the variability of interest rates, in a portfolio balance model of the exchange rate. This appears to have significant explanatory power. The latter approach the problem by comparing parameter estimates for a model which is fitted across fixed and floating rate regimes. The parameters are found to shift in the way that would be expected in the presence of a higher risk premium for the floating regime.

Hall, in chapter 5, presents some estimates of a structural exchange rate equation for the UK. He is particularly concerned to find an equation which can be incorporated into the National Institute forecasting model. The evidence he presents appears to be inconsistent with uncovered interest parity. McKenzie and Thomas are also interested in estimating a structural exchange rate model. However, their strategy is quite different from that of Hall. They work from an initial presumption that a wide range of variables may influence the exchange rate. We have no way of knowing *a priori* which of these actually matter in practice. Therefore, they start from a fairly general equation and let the data suggest which is the appropriate functional form. The resulting equations are quite different from those suggested by most of the theoretical exchange rate literature.

The final four chapters are all concerned with more complete models of open economies rather than the exchange rate *per se*. Leon and Molana reconsider the methodology used to estimate parameters of a monetary approach balance of payments model by economists at the IMF. The IMF study involved the pooling of data from a large number of countries, over a short time period, in order to estimate structural equations. By testing many of the implicit restrictions, on a smaller sample of countries over a longer time period, Leon and Molana raise doubts about the value of such exercises.

Karakitsos addresses the central questions of open economy macroeconomics. How does the economy respond to various monetary and fiscal policy shocks. His method of analysis is by simulation using his own fairly complex macro model. He is also able to test his results for sensitivity to assumptions of parameter variations. Most of his results appear to be robust to parameter variation. However, he discovers that the parameter which is crucial is the labour market adjustment speed.

The last two chapters are the only two in this volume to be purely theoretical. Athina Zervoyianni modifies the standard Dornbusch–Buiter–Miller model of an open economy to include the possibility of currency substitution. She shows that currency substitution reduces the variation in the output of a small open economy following unanticipated disturbances to either foreign interest rates or foreign output. She also demonstrates, in a two-country model, that currency substitution may limit the extent of real exchange rate overshooting in response to unexpected disturbances to either the level or the rate of growth of either of the two money supplies.

Finally, Paul Turner analyses the problem of international macroeconomic policy coordination. He distinguishes between inefficiencies due to disagreement about targets and those due to failure to coordinate the adjustment path towards agreed targets.

1 Empirical Regularities in Exchange Rate Behaviour

Richard T. Baillie and Patrick C. McMahon

1. INTRODUCTION

Recent research on exchange rate determination has been characterized by the emergence of the asset market approach as the dominant theory, replacing the Mundell–Fleming trade flow approach. While asset market theory has provided considerable new insights and has been received with understandable enthusiasm by the profession, recent econometric work has shown many of the assumptions and implications of the theory to be incorrect. Furthermore, as has been noted by Mussa (1979) and Frenkel (1981) among others, recent movements of nominal exchange rates have been dominated by volatility, apparently caused by the arrival of 'news' or unanticipated components. Thus models based on fundamentals can typically account for only a small proportion of exchange rate changes. To what extent this fact and the empirical departures from standard assumptions are a problem for the asset market theory is an open question. Certainly departures from some assumptions should lead to fairly straightforward modifications of existing theories although the most appropriate way of modelling risk, for example, is far from clear.

Based on $4\frac{1}{2}$ years of the current float, Mussa (1979) considered some sixteen empirical regularities of the foreign exchange market. In our view, given the benefit of some 12 years of experience of floating and the development of more sophisticated econometric methods, many of these apparent 'regularities' are highly contentious. The purpose of this chapter is to consider the evidence for some of the main assumptions and regularities and to show how they relate to the asset market based theories of exchange rate determination. The next section reviews some of the basic components of the theories and subsequent sections examine the theories of random walk or martingale behaviour of the nominal spot exchange rate, the efficiency of the forward market, the forecasting abilities of the forward rate *vis à vis* a models forecast, interest rate parity and the relationship between forward rates of different maturity times.

2. SOME ASSUMPTIONS AND MODELS

Virtually any asset market approach to exchange rate determination requires the basic assumptions of uncovered interest rate parity

$$E_t s_{t+1} - s_t = r_t - r_t^* \tag{1.1}$$

and unbiased efficient expectations (UEE) of the forward rate with respect to the future spot exchange rate

$$f_t = E_t s_{t+1} \tag{1.2}$$

where f is the logarithm of the forward exchange rate, s is the logarithm of the spot exchange rate, r is the domestic interest rate, r^* is the foreign equivalent and $E_t(\cdot)$ denotes the rational expectation of a random variable conditioned on all relevant and available information at time t. In the following, we use the terminology of UEE, although equivalent and commonly used alternatives would be that the 'forward rate is an unbiased predictor', 'forward market efficiency', or the 'speculative efficiency hypothesis' (Bilson, 1981).

The basic monetary model of exchange rate determination also requires the assumptions of short run purchasing power parity (PPP),

$$s_t = p_t / p_t^* \tag{1.3}$$

and a stable and static demand for real balances in both countries, namely

$$m_t - p_t = \phi y_t - \lambda r_t \tag{1.4}$$

and

$$m_t^* - p_t^* = \phi^* y_t^* - \lambda^* r_t^* \tag{1.5}$$

where m is money stock, p is the price level, and y is real income, all variables are in logarithmic form and asterisks denote corresponding foreign quantities. On imposing the further assumptions of identical real income elasticities and nominal interest rate semi-elasticities, the exchange rate can be expressed as

$$s_t = z_t + \left(\frac{\lambda}{1+\lambda}\right) E_t s_{t+1} \tag{1.6}$$

where z_t is the 'fundamentals' and is given by a linear combination of explanatory variables as

$$z_t = \left(\frac{1}{1+\lambda}\right) \{m_t - m_t^* - \phi(y_t - y_t^*)\}$$

Equation (1.6) is one of the simplest forward-looking rational expectation models and the usual solution is of the form

$$s_t = \left(\frac{1}{1+\lambda}\right) \sum_{j=0}^{\infty} \left(\frac{\lambda}{1+\lambda}\right)^j \mathrm{E}_t z_{t+j} \tag{1.7}$$

Since $\lambda/(1+\lambda) < 1$, convergence is guaranteed subject to z_t being covariance stationary; see Hansen and Sargent (1980).

In Dornbusch's (1976) celebrated 'overshooting' model, equations (1.1), (1.2), (1.4) and (1.5) of the monetary model are retained, while a sticky price equation (1.8) is introduced

$$(p_t - p_t^*) - (p_{t-1} - p_{t-1}^*) = \partial\{(d_t - d_t^*) - (y_t - y_t^*)\} \tag{1.8}$$

where d_t and d_t^* are the domestic and foreign demand for goods, so that equation (1.8) specifies relative price adjustment to be a function of relative excess demand. The model also requires the specification of a demand equation of the form

$$(d_t - d_t^*) = \gamma(y_t - y_t^*) - \sigma(r_t - r_t^*) + \omega(s_t - p_t + p_t^*) \tag{1.9}$$

Originally, Dornbusch's analysis of this model was through imposing a long run equilibrium solution for the exchange rate. However, solution of equations (1.1), (1.2), (1.4), (1.5), (1.8) and (1.9) under rational expectations gives rise to a second-order equation in forward expectations of the form

$$\lambda E_{t-1}s_{t+1} - (\beta_1\lambda+\lambda+\beta_2)\, E_{t-1}s_t+\beta_1\lambda s_{t-1} = E_{t-1}x_t \tag{1.9a}$$

where $\beta_1 = 1+\partial(\omega+\sigma/\lambda)^{-1}$, $\beta_2 = \beta_1\partial\omega$ and x_t is a linear combination of m_t, m_t^*, y_t, y_t^*, m_{t-1}, m_{t-1}^*, y_{t-1}, and y_{t-1}^*. The exact functional form of x_t is unimportant for the present purposes, but is given in Wickens (1984) and Baillie and McMahon (1987, Chapter 3).

The solution of equation (1.9a) is then given by

$$s_t = \xi_1 s_{t-1} - (\lambda\xi_2)^{-1}\sum_{j=0}^{\infty}\xi_2^{-j}E_{t-1}x_{t+j}+\epsilon_t \tag{1.10}$$

where ϵ_t is a white noise process and ξ_1 and ξ_2 are roots of the characteristic equation

$$\lambda F^2 - (\beta_1\lambda+\lambda+\beta_2)F+\beta_1\lambda=0$$

$|\xi_1| <1$, $|j_2| >1$ and $F=L^{-1}$ is the forward operator.

Hence the solution given by equation (1.10) relates the exchange rate to its lagged values plus the discounted future expectations of current and lagged fundamentals. Interestingly enough an extremely similar equation to (1.10) can be derived by other types of simple modifications to the monetary model. For example, Woo (1985) retains equations (1.1), (1.2) and (1.3) of the monetary model but introduces a Goldfeld (1973) type partial adjustment mechanism in the demands for real balances, so that equations (1.4) and (1.5) are replaced by the equation

$$(m_t-m_t^*) - (p_t-p_t^*) = \phi(y_t-y_t^*) + \alpha(m_{t-1}-m_{t-1}^*) - \alpha(p_{t-1}-p_{t-1}^*) - \lambda(r_t-r_t^*) \tag{1.11}$$

The resulting solution of a second-order forward expectations equation again gives a solution of the form of (1.10) where now $x_t = (m_t-m_t^*) - \alpha(m_{t-1}-m_{t-1}^*) - \phi(y_t-y_t^*)$ and

ξ_1 and ξ_2 are the roots of the difference equation $\beta F^2 - (1+\beta)F + \alpha = 0$.

The introduction of further dynamic adjustments to the basic equations of the model also generally implies equations of the form of (1.10) with the possible inclusion of further lagged nominal exchange rate variables.

3. THE RANDOM WALK PROPERTY

In the context of a 'fair game', Fama (1970) has demonstrated that in an efficient market an asset price will follow a martingale or random walk model. By denoting the expected yield as E_tR_{t+1} then $E_ts_{t+1} = (1+E_tR_{t+1})s_t$ and from equation (1.1)

$$\frac{E_ts_{t+1}-s_t}{s_t} = \frac{r_t-r_t^*}{1+r_t^*}$$

or,

$$E_ts_{t+1} = s_t + \frac{r - r_t^*}{1+r_t^*}\,s_t$$

so that the expected yield will be zero only if domestic and foreign securities are identical.

Despite the difficulties associated with translating the random walk model to the foreign exchange market, the view that the spot rate follows such a process is widespread and has received empirical support in studies such as Cornell (1977) and Meese and Singleton (1982). On using the same approach as Meese and Singleton (1982) we took end of month and also weekly data from the New York foreign exchange market between 1973 and 1980. Under the null hypothesis of a random walk

$$s_t = \rho s_{t-1} + \epsilon_t \qquad (1.12)$$

where $\rho=1$ and ϵ_t is an i.i.d. sequence with mean zero and constant variance σ^2. The alternative hypotheses are

$$s_t = \rho s_{t-1} + \epsilon_t \qquad |\rho| < 1 \qquad (1.13)$$

Table 1.1: Tests of unit roots on monthly nominal spot exchange rates

Country	Φ_1	Φ_2
UK	0.000	1.044
France	0.470	1.599
West Germany	0.428	1.752
Italy	0.634	0.847
Canada	0.028	3.082
Japan	1.007	1.511

Table 1.2: Tests of unit roots on weekly nominal spot exchange rates

Country	Φ_1	Φ_2
UK	1.284	1.569
France	0.892	1.029
West Germany	0.987	1.111
Italy	1.281	1.384

and

$$s_t = \alpha + \beta t + \rho s_{t-1} + \epsilon_t \qquad |\rho| < 1 \tag{1.14}$$

Since the usual limiting distribution of the OLS estimate of ρ is not defined when ρ is unity it is necessary to use the unit root test of Dickey and Fuller (1981), who have tabulated the distributions of Φ_1 and Φ_2 which test (1.12) versus (1.13) and (1.12) versus (1.14) respectively. The results are presented in Tables 1.1 and 1.2 and it can be seen that the hypothesis of a unit root cannot be rejected for any of the currencies on either a monthly or weekly basis. However occurrence of a unit root and the possible stationarity of the nominal exchange rate in first difference form, i.e. being cointegrated of order one, does not necessarily imply the validity of the random walk/martingale fair game model. Tables 1.3 and 1.4 present the results of estimating autoregressions for the first differences of monthly and weekly spot exchange rates. While the random

Table 1.3: Autoregressions of differenced monthly nominal spot exchange rates

Country	Constant	$\hat{\alpha}_1$	$\hat{\alpha}_2$	$\hat{\alpha}_3$	$\hat{\alpha}_4$	$\hat{\alpha}_5$	$\hat{\alpha}_6$	LR test of AR(6) model
UK	0.004	0.038	−0.104	−0.074	−0.055	0.011	0.001	7.40
	(0.003)	(0.087)	(0.093)	(0.093)	(0.094)	(0.093)	(0.094)	
France	0.005	−0.095	0.113	−0.066	0.079	0.068	−0.106	15.57
	(0.003)	(0.087)	(0.088)	(0.089)	(0.086)	(0.086)	(0.086)	
West Germany	−0.002	−0.036	0.083	−0.008	−0.091	−0.041	−0.100	21.72
	(0.003)	(0.086)	(0.087)	(0.088)	(0.083)	(0.083)	(0.083)	
Italy	0.009	−0.003	0.68	0.026	−0.076	0.073	−0.039	6.64
	(0.003)	(0.087)	(0.087)	(0.088)	(0.088)	(0.088)	(0.088)	
Canada	0.0025	−0.111	−0.169	0.108	0.024	0.143	−0.092	12.08
	(0.0012)	(0.087)	(0.086)	(0.090)	(0.090)	(0.089)	(0.090)	
Japan	−0.00033	0.053	−0.057	0.128	0.023	0.041	−0.071	3.97
	(0.00028)	(0.087)	(0.087)	(0.087)	(0.087)	(0.087)	(0.087)	

Table 1.4: Autoregressions of differenced weekly nominal spot exchange rates

Country	Var (Δs_t)	$\hat{\phi}_1$	$\hat{\phi}_2$	$\hat{\sigma}^2$	LR
UK	$0.1227\ (10)^{-3}$	0.039	0.165	$0.1198(10)^{-3}$	10.39(.01)
		(0.053)	(0.053)		
West Germany	$0.1334(10)^{-3}$	0.129	0.143	$0.1283(10)^{-3}$	15.65(.00)
		(0.053)	(0.052)		
France	$0.1139(10)^{-3}$	0.118	0.143	$0.1099(10)^{-3}$	14.52(.00)
		(0.053)	(0.052)		
Italy	$0.1243(10)^{-3}$	0.083	0.131	$0.1217(10)^{-3}$	9.41(.01)
		(0.053)	(0.053)		

For each country an AR(2) model $\Delta s_t = \phi_1\, \Delta s_{t-1} + \phi_2\, \Delta s_{t-2} + \epsilon_t$, var $(\epsilon_t) = \sigma^2$ was estimated. Estimates of ϕ_1 and ϕ_2 have standard errors in parentheses below them and LR is the likelihood ratio test that Δs_t is white noise against the alternative that it was AR(2). Significance levels are in parentheses beside each LR statistic.

walk model cannot be rejected for any of the 6-monthly exchange rate series it can be conclusively rejected for all 4-weekly series. A second-order autoregression of the form $\Delta(1+\rho_1 L+\rho_2 L^2)s_t = \epsilon_t$ where L is the lag operator and $\Delta=1-L$ turns out to be appropriate for all four exchange rate series in weekly form. Analysis of weekly data thus indicates significant departures from random walk behaviour and, although low frequency components (corresponding to trend) in the spectra of nominal exchange rates are generally important, they are not the only components of note. Possible departures of the differenced spot exchange rate from normality, the presence of heteroskedasticity and kurtosis are also likely but are not considered in this study.

Since the foreign exchange market does have important differences from most asset markets, it is also of interest to consider under what circumstances random walk behaviour in the nominal spot rate is likely to be apparent. Firstly, consider the monetary model given by equation (1.7) as

$$s_t = \left(\frac{1}{1+\lambda}\right)\sum_{j=0}^{\infty}\left(\frac{\lambda}{1+\lambda}\right)^j E_t z_{t+j} \tag{1.7}$$

and consider the fundamentals z_t to possess an infinite moving average representation given by

$$z_t = \sum_{k=0}^{\infty} \alpha_k \epsilon_{t-k} \tag{1.15}$$

where ϵ_t is an i.i.d. process with mean zero and constant variance σ^2 and

$$\sum_{k=0}^{\infty} \alpha_k^2 < \infty$$

Then

$$E_t z_{t+j} = \sum_{k=0}^{\infty} \alpha_{j+k}\epsilon_{t-k}$$

and on substitution into equation (1.7)

$$s_t = \sum_{j=0}^{\infty} \beta_j \epsilon_{t-j} \tag{1.16}$$

where

$$\beta_j = \left(\frac{1}{1+\lambda}\right)\{\alpha_j + \left(\frac{\lambda}{1+\lambda}\right)\alpha_{j+1} + \left(\frac{\lambda}{1+\lambda}\right)^2 \alpha_{j+2} + \ldots\} \tag{1.17}$$

From (1.16) for s_t to be a random walk, $\beta_j=1$ for $j=0$, 1, 2, . . . and on imposing this restriction and multiplying through β_{j+1} by $(\lambda/1+\lambda)$:

$$\left(\frac{\lambda}{1+\lambda}\right)\alpha_{j+1} + \left(\frac{\lambda}{1+\lambda}\right)^2 \alpha_{j+2} + \ldots = \frac{\lambda}{1+\lambda}$$

on subtraction from (1.17) with $\beta_j=1$; it follows that $\alpha_j = 1/(1+\lambda)$ where $j = 0, 1, 2, \ldots$ and hence

$$z_t = \frac{1}{1+\lambda}\sum_{k=0}^{\infty} \epsilon_{t-k}$$

or $z_t = z_{t-1} + v_t$ where $v_t = [1/(1+\lambda)]\epsilon_t$, so that z_t is also a random walk process. Then $E_t z_{t+j} = z_t$
then

$$s_t = \left(\frac{1}{1+\lambda}\right)\sum_{j=0}^{\infty}\left(\frac{\lambda}{1+\lambda}\right)^j z_t = z_t$$

The implication of this result is that a linear combination of the fundamental variables $(m_t - m_t^*)$ and $(y_t - y_t^*)$ must also follow a random walk. Hence, either or both the money supply differential variable and the real output differential variable must be cointegrated of order at least one.

In Tables 1.5 and 1.6 we present the results of computing Dickey and Fuller (1981) unit root tests for $(m_t - m_t^*)$ and $(y_t - y_t^*)$ based on monthly seasonally unadjusted data from March 1973 to December 1984 inclusive. The money supply series were based on an $M2$ definition which is broadly comparable between countries with the exception of the UK which was based on $M1$, and real incomes or outputs which are measured in terms of indices for industrial production. It can be seen from Tables 1.5 and 1.6 that the unit root restrictions can be strongly rejected for Canada and France money supply differentials and marginally for Japan, *vis á vis* the US, and for all the real output

Table 1.5: Tests of unit roots on money supply differentials

Country	Φ_1	$\hat{\rho}$	Φ_2	Φ_2^*
UK	3.032	0.906	2.058	6.067
France	5.645	0.979	3.731	5.328
West Germany	1.253	0.956	2.430	3.116
Italy	4.494	0.946	2.993	3.316
Canada	11.842	0.984	8.365	n.a.
Japan	0.387	1.007	0.803	6.394

* In this instance the alternative model contained one more lagged differenced dependent variable.

Table 1.6: Tests of unit roots on real output differentials

Country	Φ_1	$\hat{\rho}$	Φ_2
UK	11.065	0.730	11.213
France	30.744	0.387	22.229
West Germany	17.375	0.597	15.260
Italy	17.165	−0.006	47.850
Canada	18.733	0.574	16.982
Japan	13.696	0.669	18.690

differentials series. Hence for two if not three out of the six countries studied there is evidence that neither fundamental variable is cointegrated of higher order than zero. This directly conflicts with the assumption of the monetary model and the random walk behaviour of the spot exchange rate. Tables 1.7 and 1.8 also reveal significant departures from random walk behaviour for all the money supply differential and real output differential series.

4. UNBIASED EFFICIENT EXPECTATION OF THE FORWARD RATE

From equation (1.2) the forward rate is hypothesized to be the unbiased efficient expectation of the future spot exch-

Table 1.7: Autoregressions of differenced money supply differentials

Country	Constant	$\hat{\alpha}_1$	$\hat{\alpha}_2$	$\hat{\alpha}_3$	$\hat{\alpha}_4$	$\hat{\alpha}_5$	$\hat{\alpha}_6$	LR test of AR(6) model
UK	0.011	−0.326	−0.085	−0.116	−0.184	−0.032	0.011	34.03
	(0.022)	(0.088)	(0.092)	(0.097)	(0.091)	(0.092)	(0.022)	
France	0.053	−0.006	−0.008	−0.392	−0.083	−0.031	−0.162	60.23
	(0.027)	(0.087)	(0.087)	(0.085)	(0.084)	(0.085)	(0.085)	
West Germany	−0.032	−0.070	0.417	−0.242	0.064	0.024	−0.454	48.05
	(0.024)	(0.079)	(0.080)	(0.080)	(0.080)	(0.079)	(0.078)	
Italy	0.031	0.047	−0.082	0.001	0.026	−0.054	−0.116	4.70
	(0.023)	(0.090)	(0.090)	(0.090)	(0.090)	(0.090)	(0.090)	
Canada	0.072	0.183	0.198	0.016	0.077	0.071	0.112	35.33
	(0.055)	(0.088)	(0.090)	(0.092)	(0.092)	0.090)	(0.089)	
Japan	−0.026	0.342	0.137	−0.202	0.082	−0.002	−0.015	31.26
	(0.012)	(0.089)	(0.094)	(0.094)	(0.094)	(0.094)	(0.088)	

Table 1.8: Autoregressions of differenced real output differentials

Country	Constant	$\hat{\alpha}_1$	$\hat{\alpha}_2$	$\hat{\alpha}_3$	$\hat{\alpha}_4$	$\hat{\alpha}_5$	$\hat{\alpha}_6$	LR test of AR(6) model
UK	−0.003	−0.103	−0.113	−0.360	0.163	−0.238	−0.311	54.83
	(0.005)	(0.083)	(0.080)	(0.079)	(0.080)	(0.082)	(0.083)	
France	−0.001	−0.418	−0.294	−0.233	−0.248	−0.197	−0.110	37.36
	(0.014)	(0.087)	(0.092)	(0.093)	(0.093)	(0.093)	(0.086)	
West Germany	−0.002	−0.271	−0.282	−0.280	−0.482	−0.042	−0.007	53.70
	(0.006)	(0.088)	(0.091)	(0.083)	(0.084)	(0.092)	(0.089)	
Italy	−0.002	−0.816	−0.638	−0.560	−0.368	−0.239	−0.150	79.52
	(0.020)	(0.087)	(0.111)	(0.120)	(0.121)	(0.114)	(0.098)	
Canada	−0.001	−0.268	−0.457	−0.173	−0.371	−0.066	−0.248	41.97
	(0.004)	(0.085)	(0.088)	(0.091)	(0.092)	(0.089)	(0.086)	
Japan	0.002	−0.830	−0.815	−0.241	−0.021	0.245	0.008	109.60
	(0.004)	(0.088)	(0.113)	(0.134)	(0.135)	(0.115)	(0.090)	

ange rate, i.e. $f_t = E_t s_{t+\ell}$. This hypothesis is well known to imply the existence of rational expectations and risk neutrality on the part of agents in the foreign exchange market. The hypothesis is generally tested by means of taking expectations of equation (1.2) conditioned on information available at time $t-h$, to give

$$E_{t-h}(s_{t+\ell} - f_t) = 0 \tag{1.18}$$

where $h = 0, 1, 2, \ldots$ In order to test the hypothesis, a suitable alternative specification is required and on choosing $\ell=1$ it is usual to test that $(s_{t+1}-f_t) = \boldsymbol{\psi}'\mathbf{x}_{t-h}+\epsilon_{t+1}$ where $\mathbf{x}_{t-h}$ is a vector of explanatory variables known at time $t-h$ and $\boldsymbol{\psi}$ is the corresponding vector of parameters. Then under UEE, $\boldsymbol{\psi}=0$. Initial studies by Cornell (1977), Frenkel (1979, 1980), Bilson (1981) etc. generally chose the data to match exactly the maturity time of the forward contract and conditioned on small sets of information, so that $\mathbf{x}$ contained a constant and possibly the lagged forward rate f_{t-1}. These studies were generally unable to reject the UEE hypothesis.

Analysis of equation (1.18) with overlapping data (i.e. $\ell > 1$) necessitates estimation of models of the form

$$(s_{t+\ell}-f_t) = \boldsymbol{\psi}'\mathbf{x}_{t-h}+u_{t+\ell} \tag{1.19}$$

where $u_{t+\ell}$ is a moving average process of order $\ell-1$ and gives rise to some special econometric problems. Hansen and Hodrick (1980) have considered single equation tests based on (1.19) while Hakkio (1981a) and Baillie *et al.* (1983) have tested (1.18) from cross-equation restrictions. All these tests on overlapping data have tended to reject the UEE hypothesis. In most cases weekly data have been taken on either 4-week (30-day) or 13-week (90-day) forward contracts.

In this section of the paper we present some new results for a generalization of the cross-equation restrictions method. It is useful to consider the spot and forward rates, together with other monetary and real variables, as constituting some joint stochastic process.

From the interest rate parity relationship (1.1) we have

$$(s_{t+\ell}-s_t) = (f_t-s_t) + u_{t+\ell} \tag{1.20}$$

where

$$u_{t+\ell} = (i_{t+\ell} - E_t i_{t+\ell}) + \sum_{j=0}^{\ell-1} \theta_j \epsilon_{t+\ell-j}$$

and ϵ_t are i.i.d. $(0, \sigma^2)$ random variables. Hence $u_{t+\ell}$ will be a moving average process of order $\ell-1$ and equation (1.20) is a convenient way of expressing the actual change in the spot rate in terms of the expected change plus the unanticipated change due to 'news' on the interest rate differential and other random innovations that have entered the market.

Consider a vector of relevant variables given by

$$y_t' = [(s_t - s_{t-\ell})\,(f_t - s_t), y_{3t} \cdot\,\cdot\, y_{gt}] \qquad (1.21)$$

and following the arguments given by Baillie *et al.* (1983), for example, assume we can represent y_t as a linear non-deterministic covariance stationary process with vector autoregressive representation.

$$y_t = \sum_{j=1}^{p} A_j y_{t-j} + \epsilon_t \qquad (1.22)$$

where

$$E(\epsilon_t) = 0 \qquad E(\epsilon_t \epsilon_s') = \begin{cases} \Omega\, s = t \\ 0\, s \neq t \end{cases}$$

and A_j are $g \times g$ coefficient matrices.

The vector of parameters $\boldsymbol{\theta}$ is such that

$$\boldsymbol{\theta}' = \text{vec}\,(N'A)$$

where

$$A = \begin{bmatrix} A_1 & A_2 & . & . & A_p \\ I & . & . & . & . & I\ 0 \end{bmatrix}$$

and $N' = [I{:}0]$

Then the MLE of $\boldsymbol{\theta}$ based on T observations will have the limiting distribution of

$$\sqrt{T}(\hat{\boldsymbol{\theta}} - \boldsymbol{\theta}) \rightarrow N(0, \Omega \times M^{-1})$$

and

$$M = \underset{T\to\infty}{\text{plim}} \frac{1}{T} \sum_{t=1}^{T} y_{t-1}y'_{t-1}$$

The UEE hypothesis embodied in (1.18) can be written as

$$r(\boldsymbol{\theta})' = e'_1 A^{\ell+h} - e'_2 A^h = 0 \qquad (1.23)$$

where e'_j is a *gp* dimensional row vector, full of zeros, save for writing 1 in the *j*th element. Hence the UEE hypothesis as given by (1.23) is seen to place restrictions on the parameters of the model (1.22).

The results of estimating some of the models for 30-day and 90-day forward rates with and without the addition of a third variable in (1.21), namely $y_{3t} = (i_t - i_{t-\ell})$ are presented in Table 1.9. The data used are weekly opening bid prices from the New York foreign exchange market between 1 June 1973 and 8 April 1980 realizing 362 observations. Since the choice of lag length estimation and testing of the restricted and unrestricted models is an extension of the approach developed in Baillie *et al.* (1983) and is described in detail in Baillie and McMahon (1986 Chapter 6) we shall merely state the main results. In general the UEE hypothesis can be rejected for both the 30-day and 90-day results for information dated at times t, $t-1$ and $t-2$, rejections usually being stronger for the 30-day forward rates.

As has been noted by many authors, the UEE hypothesis is closely related to the forecasting ability of the forward rate. Some preliminary results of the forecasting abilities of various forward rates *vis á vis* predictions from vector autoregressions such as (1.22) have also been performed and are reported in Table 1.10. These results are merely within sample comparisons and are thus only suggestive of the efficiencies to be gained through using the vector autoregression rather than the forward rate. It is obviously important eventually to do a detailed out of sample (i.e. ex ante prediction) study. However, preliminary results indicate the 30-day forward rate to be comfortably outperformed by a vector autoregression over 4 weeks and the 90-day forward rate to be only marginally outperformed over a 13-week forecasting horizon.

5. INTEREST RATE PARITY AND THE TERM STRUCTURE OF FORWARD RATES

The covered interest parity equivalent of (1.1) is $f_t - s_t = r_t - r_t^*$ and an actual forward rate which is not compatible with the above should immediately be eliminated through the activities of pure interest arbitrageurs. Apart from domestic and foreign securities by necessity having the same maturity times and degrees of risk, (1.1) also requires the absence of any capital controls, transactions costs and other market imperfections. Then forward rates will be determined by pure interest arbitrageurs possessing an infinitely elastic excess demand curve for foreign exchange. Hence hedging traders and speculators will be unable to determine the forward rate. Many authors have found minor deviations from covered interest parity and Table 1.11 presents some analysis of weekly data where substantial autocorrelation is found for many of the series $f_t - s_t - r_t + r_t^* = \epsilon_t$, which should be expected to be white noise under covered interest parity. Note the above data are recorded at the same instant of time, whereas some authors such as Frenkel and Levich (1977) used data several hours apart. However evidence presented in Baillie and McMahon (1984) has shown that apparent short run deviations of covered interest parity seem to occur but are eliminated within a week. Since the existence of risk does not necessarily involve departures from covered interest parity, the size of transactions costs is the only obvious explanation of this phenomenon. Although statistically significant, such deviations are generally well under 1 per cent of the current spot rate.

Hakkio (1985) and Baillie and McMahon (1985) have also considered a term structure of the forward premium on 30- and 90-day forward rates under rational expectations. Such theories generally require the existence of interest parity and the absence of time-varying liquidity premia in the domestic and foreign bond markets. The above studies

Table 1.9: Summary of VAR models and tests of the UEE hypothesis with 30 day forward rates

Country	Number of equations	Variables	Order of VAR model	Date period	Tests of UEE $h=1$
UK	2	$(s_t - s_{t-4})$ $(f_t - s_t)$	5	April 1973 to June 1980	W=46.54 (0.00) LR=44.93 (0.00)
UK	3	$(s_t - s_{t-4})$ $(f_t - s_t)$ $(i_t - i_{t-4})$	5	April 1973 to June 1980	W=49.31 (0.00) LR=47.50 (0.00)
West Germany	2	$(s_t - s_{t-4})$ $(f_t - s_t)$	5	April 1973 to June 1980	W=48.21 (0.00) LR=46.19 (0.00)
West Germany	3	$(s_t - s_{t-4})$ $(f_t - s_t)$ $(i_t - i_{t-4})$	5	April 1973 to June 1980	W=50.05 (0.00) LR=47.81 (0.00)
France	2	$(s_t - s_{t-4})$ $(f_t - s_t)$	5	April 1973 to June 1980	W=58.21 (0.00) LR=55.01 (0.00)
France	2	$(s_t - s_{t-4})$ $(f_t - s_t)$ $(i_t - t_{t-4})$	5	April 1973 to June 1980	W=59.26 (0.00) LR=55.95 (0.00)
Italy	2	$(s_t - s_{t-4})$ $(f_t - s_t)$	5	April 1973 to June 1980	W=44.04 (0.00) LR=42.18) (0.00)

Table 9 cont.

Country	Number of equations	Variables	Order of VAR model	Data period	Tests of UEE $h=0$	$h=1$	$h=2$
UK	2	$(s_t-s_{t-12}), (f_t-s_t)$	4	April 1973 to January 1980	W=94.15 (0.00) LR=82.70 (0.00)	W=18.31 (0.02) LR=17.95 (0.02)	W=21.30 (0.01) LR=20.85 (0.01)
UK	3	$(s_t-s_{t-12}), (f_t-s_t), (i_t-i_{t-12})$	3	April 1973 to January 1980	W=56.25 (0.00) LR=51.83 (0.00)	W=15.27 (0.08) LR=15.00 (0.08)	W=12.43 (0.19) LR=12.28 (0.19)
West Germany	2	$(s_t-s_{t-12}), (f_t-s_t)$	4	April 1973 to January 1980	W=141.51 (0.00) LR=116.08 (0.00)	W=13.95 (0.08) LR=13.74 (0.08)	W=17.65 (0.02) LR=17.38 (0.02)
West Germany	3	$(s_t-s_{t-12}), (f_t-s_t), (i_t-i_{t-12})$	2	April 1973 to January 1980	W=117.26 (0.00) LR=99.91 (0.00)	W=15.72 (0.20) LR=15.49 (0.20)	W=14.34 (0.28) LR=14.18 (0.28)

Table 1.10: Percentage increase in mse from using the forward rate rather than a bivariate vector AR to predict future spot rates

		% Change in mse	
Country	Order of vector AR	30-day forward rates	90-day forward rates
UK	9	37.30	17.81
West Germany	6	38.43	18.29
France	6	42.84	N.a.
Italy	10	25.30	N.a.
Canada	3	17.09	N.a.
Switzerland	3	21.64	N.a.

Note: these are unconditional forecast mse calculated over entire sample and do not refer to ex post predictions.
N.a. signifies figures not available.

have generally concluded that this theory is inappropriate for the forward premium and have suggested the presence of a time-varying liquidity premium.

6. CONCLUSIONS

(1) Although spot exchange rates appear to exhibit random walk behaviour at a monthly level, at a weekly level they do not.
(2) The time series characteristics of certain fundamentals, such as real output differentials, cast doubt on the validity of the monetary model given the approximate random walk behaviour of monthly nominal exchange rates.
(3) The assumption of UEE of the forward rate is inappropriate and the existence of a time-varying risk premium seems an important part of the forward rate.
(4) Related to the previous point, autocorrelation present in s_t and f_t allows better predictions to be formed of the future spot rate than just considering the current forward rate.
(5) The 90-day forward rate appears a better predict or of the future spot rate than the 30-day forward rate does

Table 1.11: Percentage deviation of the forward rate from interest parity

Year	UK			West Germany			France		
	Mean	Variance	LM(5)	Mean	Variance	LM(5)	Mean	Variance	LM(5)
1973	−0.557	0.0151	5.63 (0.34)	0.0298	0.0825	1.13 (0.95)	0.1607	0.4768	11.06 (0.05)
1974	−0.0709	0.0116	4.20 (0.52)	−0.0593	0.1225	0.22 (0.99)	−0.1908	0.0365	41.78 (0.00)
1975	−0.0634	0.0062	3.33 (0.65)	−0.0110	0.0013	21.14 (0.00)	−0.0520	0.0063	5.79 (0.33)
1976	−0.0990	0.0067	53.90 (0.00)	−0.0058	0.0004	36.94 (0.00)	−0.1072	0.0424	3.82 (0.58)
1977	−0.0245	0.0049	14.98 (0.01)	0.0036	0.0004	8.44 (0.13)	−0.0888	0.0054	16.43 (0.00)
1978	−0.0387	0.0020	11.03 (0.05)	0.0344	0.0010	95.27 (0.00)	−0.0283	0.0045	16.44 (0.00)
1979	−0.0233	0.0225	1.33 (0.93)	0.0322	0.0180	0.73 (0.98)	−0.0067	0.0044	51.71 (0.00)
1980	−0.0409	0.0086	6.06 (0.30)	0.0736	0.0117	36.34 (0.00)	0.0348	0.0076	45.56 (0.00)
Total sample	−0.0530	0.0101	19.33 (0.00)	0.0053	0.0300	1.88 (0.87)	−0.0536	0.0624	97.74 (0.00)

Key: significance levels are shown in parentheses beside test statistics.

of its corresponding future spot rate.
(6) Deviations from covered interest parity have been of a fairly small level, but have persisted for some days.

REFERENCES

Baillie, R. T. and McMahon, P. C. (1984) 'Empirical evidence on interest rate parity', University of Birmingham Discussion Paper, November.

Baillie, R. T. and McMahon, P. C. (1985) 'Estimation and testing of the term structure of the forward premium under rational expectations', *Journal of Macroeconomics*.

Baillie, R. T. and McMahon, P. C. (1987) *The Foreign Exchange Market; Theory and Econometric Evidence*, Cambridge University Press, forthcoming.

Baillie, R. T., Lippens, R. E. and McMahon, P. C. (1983) 'Testing rational expectations and efficiency in the foreign exchange market', *Econometrica,* **51**, 553–563.

Bilson, J. F. O. (1981) 'The speculative efficiency hypothesis', *Journal of Business,* **54**, 435–451.

Cornell, B. (1977) 'Spot rates, forward rates and exchange market efficiency', *Journal of Financial Economics,* **5**, 55–65.

Dickey, D. A. and Fuller, W. A. (1981) 'Likelihood ratio statistics for autoregressive time series with a unit root', *Econometrica,* **49**, 1057–1072.

Dornbusch, R. E. (1976) 'Expectations and exchange rate dynamics', *Journal of Political Economy,* **84**, 1161–1176.

Fama, E. (1970) 'Efficient capital markets: a review of theory and empirical work', *Journal of Finance,* **25**, 383–417.

Frenkel, J. A. (1979) 'Further evidence on expectations and the demand for money during the German hyperinflation', *Journal of Monetary Economics,* **5**, 81–96.

Frenkel, J. A. (1980) 'Exchange rates, prices and money: lessons from the 1920's', *American Economic Review, Papers and Proceedings,* **70**, 235–242.

Frenkel, J. A. (1981) 'Flexible exchange rates, prices and the role of 'news': lessons from the 1970's', *Journal of Political Economy,* **89**, 665–705.

Frenkel, J. A. and Levich, R. M. (1977) 'Covered interest arbitrage: unexploited profits?' *Journal of Political Economy,* **83**, 325–338.

Goldfeld, S. (1973) 'The demand for money revisited', *Brookings Papers on Economic Activity,* **3**, 577–638.

Hakkio, C. S. (1981a) 'Expectations and the forward exchange rate', *International Economic Review,* **22**, 663–678.

Hakkio, C. S. (1981b) 'The term structure of the forward premium', *Journal of Monetary Economics,* **8**, 41–58.

Hakkio, C. S. and Heiderman, H. (1986) 'Intertemporal asset pricing and the term structure of exchange rates and interest rates', *European Economic Review,* **30**, 325–344.

Hansen, L. P. and Hodrick, R. J. (1980) 'Forward exchange rates as optimal predictors of future spot rates: an econometric analysis', *Journal of Political Economy,* **88**, 829–853.

Hansen, L. P. and Sargent, T. J. (1980) 'Formulating and estimating dynamic linear rational expectations models', *Journal of Economic Dynamics and Control,* **2**, 7–46.

Hoffman, D. L. and Schlagenhauf, D. E. (1983) 'Rational expectations and monetary models of exchange rate determination', *Journal of Monetary Economics,* **11**, 247–260.

Meese, R. A. and Singleton, K. J. (1982) 'On unit roots and the empirical modelling of exchange rates', *Journal of Finance,* **37**, 1029–1035.

Mussa, M. L. (1979) 'Empirical regularities in the behaviour of exchange rates and theories of the foreign exchange market', in Brunner, K. and Meltzer, A. H. (eds.) *Policies for Employment, Prices and Exchange Rates*. Carnegie-Rochester Conference Series, **11**. North Holland, Amsterdam.

Wickens, M. R. (1984) 'Rational expectations and exchange rate dynamics', University of Southampton Discussion Paper, December.

Woo, W. T. (1985) 'The monetary approach to exchange rate determination under rational expectations', *Journal of International Economics,* **18**, 1–16.

2 Real Exchange Rate Variability and Monetary Disturbances

Paul de Grauwe and Marc Rosiers

1. INTRODUCTION

There is now a large body of empirical literature documenting and explaining the substantial short-term deviations of the exchange rates from purchasing power parities (PPP) (see e.g. Frenkel, 1981; Kravis, 1984). The most widely accepted explanation of this phenomenon relies on models in which prices are sticky in the short run. In such models exchange rates adjust immediately to new information. As a result, they will tend to fluctuate around PPP.

A phenomenon which is less well understood is the substantial difference in the experience of different countries with widely divergent monetary and inflationary environments. Table 2.1 illustrates these differences. It shows the mean (absolute) monthly change of the real exchange rates of a sample of countries during 1970–1982(1). It is evident that the short term variability of the real exchange rates has been quite different across countries, with some countries experiencing real exchange rate variability which was five times higher than others.

In this chapter we contribute towards an explanation of these differences. The focus of this explanation will be put on the differences in monetary regimes across countries. In addition, we will try to isolate some structural factors. In Section 2 a theoretical model is developed. Section 3 provides the empirical evidence, and Section 4 draws the conclusions.

Table 2.1: Mean absolute monthly change of real effective exchange rates, in percentages (1970–1982)

1. Germany	1.92
2. Switzerland	2.11
3. Austria	1.90
4. Netherlands	1.88
5. Canada	0.82
6. Norway	1.56
7. France	1.70
8. Japan	2.00
9. Denmark	1.91
10. United Kingdom	1.77
11. Italy	1.41
12. Spain	1.51
13. Greece	1.75
14. Turkey	2.88
15. Venezuela	0.47
16. Indonesia	1.65
17. Nigeria	1.98
18. Bolivia	3.03
19. Peru	1.80
20. Brazil	1.08
21. Argentina	5.81
22. Malaysia	1.19
23. Singapore	1.36
24. Thailand	0.77
25. India	1.41
26. Pakistan	1.17
27. Philippines	1.38
28. Korea	1.26
29. Burma	2.77
30. South Africa	1.13
31. Morocco	1.58
32. Tunisia	1.70
33. Keyna	1.28
34. Ivory Coast	2.81
35. Malawi	2.24
36. Senegal	2.60
37. Israel	2.10
38. Upper Volta	4.30
39. Zaire	5.19

Source: IMF, International Financial Statistics.

2. THE MODEL

In this section we develop a model which endogenizes the short term deviations of the exchange rate around its PPP value. The model draws heavily on Aizenman (1984) and extends it so as to derive testable propositions. The model is based on two strands of economic thinking about exchange rates, one is the sticky price model (Dornbusch, 1976), the other is the 'news' model of exchange rate determination (Frenkel, 1976; Mussa, 1976).

Consider a small open economy with perfect capital mobility. Money market equilibrium is obtained when the demand for money (m^d) equals the supply (m^s). The money demand function is specified in log-linear form, i.e.

$$m_t^d = p_t + y_t - \alpha r_t \tag{2.1}$$

where m_t^d is the log of the demand for money in period t, p_t is the log of the price level in period t, y_t is the log of the output level in period t and r_t is the domestic interest rate in period t. Note that for the sake of convenience we have assumed that the income elasticity of the demand for money is equal to one. Money market equilibrium implies

$$m_t^d = m_t^s = m_t \tag{2.2}$$

or

$$m_t = p_t + y_t - \alpha r_t \tag{2.3}$$

The domestic interest rate is assumed to be determined by uncovered interest parity

$$r_t = r_t^* + E_t e_{t+1} - e_t \tag{2.4}$$

where r_t^* is the foreign interest rate, and $E_t e_{t+1}$ is the expectation in period t of next period's exchange rate. Note that we disregard here the existence of risk premia.

We now introduce the idea that there is some form of price stickiness. In a first step we just assume price stickiness, in a second step the degree of price stickiness is made endogenous by explicitly specifying the nature of the transactions cost in the goods market. Suppose that the price of the domestic good in period t is set at the end of period $t-1$ on the basis of expectations which then prevail about the PPP level in period t. Thus

$$P_t = E_{t-1}(p_t^* + e_t) \qquad (2.5)$$

The implicit assumption of this price setting behaviour is that transactions costs are high enough to prevent a flow of goods from (or to) the world, which would equalize goods prices during period t. We will relax this assumption later.

Substituting (2.5) into (2.3), and (2.4) into (2.3) yields an expression for the exchange rate, i.e.

$$e_t = \frac{1}{\alpha}[m_t - y_t + \alpha r_t^*] - \frac{1}{\alpha}[E_{t-1}(p_t^* + e_t)] + E_t e_{t+1} \qquad (2.6)$$

We can now contrast the exchange rate obtained in (2.6) with the exchange rate obtaining assuming complete price flexibility. The latter implies that

$$p_t = p_t^* + e_t \qquad (2.7)$$

that is, the domestic price level adjusts instantaneously to its PPP level.

Substituting (2.7) into (2.3) and using the notation $\bar{e}_t$ and $\bar{p}_t$ to indicate that this is the solution under price flexibility yields

$$\bar{e}_t = \frac{1}{\alpha}[m_t - y_t + \alpha r_t^*] - \frac{1}{\alpha}[p_t^* + \bar{e}_t] + E_t\bar{e}_{t+1} \qquad (2.8)$$

Subtracting (2.8) from (2.6) yields

$$e_t - \bar{e}_t = \frac{1}{\alpha}[\bar{e}_t + p_t^* - E_{t-1}(p_t^* + e_t)] + E_t e_{t+1} - E_t\bar{e}_{t+1} \qquad (9)$$

The rational expectations solutions of (2.6) and (2.8) are given by[1]

$$e_t = \frac{1}{1+\alpha}\sum_{k=0}^{\infty} E_t B_{t+k}\left(\frac{\alpha}{1+\alpha}\right)^k$$

$$+ \frac{1}{\alpha}\left[\frac{1}{1+\alpha}\sum_{k=0}^{\infty} E_t B_{t+k} - E_{t-1}B_{t+k}\left(\frac{\alpha}{1+\alpha}\right)^k\right] \qquad (2.10)$$

and

$$\bar{e}_t = \frac{1}{1+\alpha}\left[\sum_{k=0}^{\infty} E_t B_{t+k}\left(\frac{\alpha}{1+\alpha}\right)^k\right] - \frac{p_t^* - E_{t-1}p_t^*}{1+\alpha} \qquad (2.11)$$

where

$$B_t = E_{t-1}e_t - \alpha E_t e_{t+1} + \alpha e_t;\ B_t = m_t + \alpha r_t - y_t - E_{t-1}p_t^*.$$

From (2.10) and (2.11) it follows that in both pricing regimes $E_t e_{t+1} = E_t \bar{e}_{t+1}$ so that (2.9) reduces to

$$e_t - \bar{e}_t = \frac{1}{\alpha}\left[\bar{e}_t + p_t^* - E_{t-1}\left(\bar{e}_t + p_t^*\right)\right] \qquad (2.12)$$

or

$$e_t - \bar{e}_t = \frac{1}{\alpha}\left[\bar{p}_t - E_{t-1}\bar{p}_t\right] \qquad (2.13)$$

Equation (2.13) tells us that the exchange rate under the preset price rule will deviate from the exchange rate under price flexibility to the extent that economic agents make errors in forecasting the price level (i.e. the world price and the exchange rate).

Using (2.5) and (2.7), we can rewrite equation (2.13) as follows

$$\theta_t \equiv e_t + p_t^* - p_t = \left(1 + \frac{1}{\alpha}\right)\left[\bar{p}_t - E_{t-1}\bar{p}_t\right] \qquad (2.14)$$

where θ_t is the percentage deviation from PPP. According to (2.14) deviations from PPP in period t increase with the size of the unanticipated price disturbances.

The model discussed here has a simple graphical representation (see Figure 2.1). The *aa* line is the asset market equilibrium line (equations (2.3) and (2.4)). It is given for a given foreign interest rate and the expectations prevailing in period t about the future exchange rate. The PPP line represents equation (2.7).

We can now use the model to analyse the effects of exogenous disturbances. The major focus of this analysis is the question of how the size of the disturbances affects the

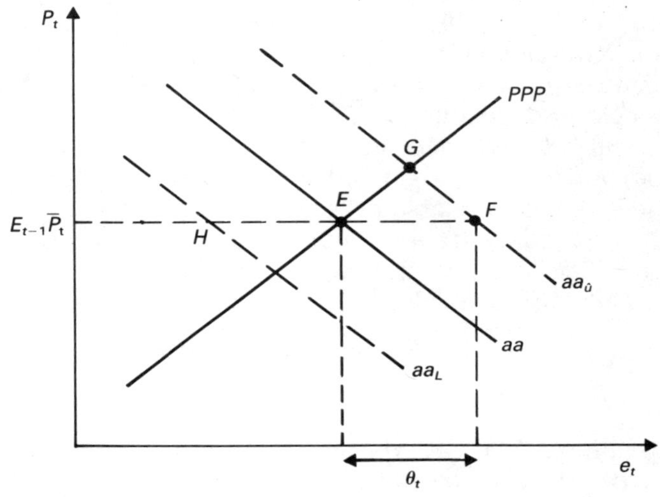

Figure 2.1: The model with price stickiness

workings of the model. Here we consider only stochastic (unanticipated) disturbances, and assume that these disturbances are a random variable in the money market equilibrium condition (2.3).

In terms of Figure 2.1 we now obtain random movements of the *aa* line. Depending on the size of the stochastic disturbances the *aa* line will be displaced between the limits set by aa_L and aa_U. In the sticky price version of the model this implies that as the price level is preset at $E_{t-1}\bar{p}_t$ the (unanticipated) nominal and real exchange rates will fluctuate between the limits set by points *H* and *F* and will be perfectly correlated. To give an example, suppose that an unanticipated disturbance has shifted the *aa* line in period *t* to aa_U. As the price level cannot change in period *t*, the short term equilibrium point is *F*. (The equilibrium point under price flexibility is at *G*.) The deviation from PPP is measured by the distance *EF*.

When the underlying stochastic disturbances increase, the band given by aa_L and aa_U increases so that the short term deviations from PPP also increase.

The next step in the analysis consists in making the nature of the transaction costs (which explain price stickiness) explicit. This then allows us to make the degree of price stickiness endogenous.

It will be assumed here that transactions costs are proportional. They originate from transporting goods across borders. Thus, we assume that there are no transaction costs involved in trading domestic goods in the domestic market. The per unit transaction cost is C. We then have the following price rule:

$$\text{if } |\theta_t| < C \rightarrow p_t = E_{t-1}(e_t + p_t^*) \tag{2.15}$$

$$\text{if } |\theta_t| \geqslant C \rightarrow p_t = p_t^* + \bar{e}_t \pm C \tag{2.16}$$

Equation (2.15) says that if the deviation from PPP (Θ_t) is smaller than the cost of transporting goods (C), the price of the domestic good is not influenced by $p^* + e$, (i.e. it will not be profitable during period t to ship goods across borders in order to profit from a differential between the domestic and foreign price). In this case the price is preset at its expected PPP level. Thus, we also assume that there are no domestic forces tending to change the price during period t. If, however, the deviations from PPP exceed transport costs (equation (2.16)), goods arbitrage will be undertaken during period t because it is profitable. Put differently, if $p_t > p_t^* + \bar{e}_t + C$ the foreign good will be imported forcing p_t to equal $p_t^* + \bar{e}_t + C$. If $p_t <$ $p_t^* + e_t - C$ *the domestic good will be exported forcing* p_t *to equal* $p_t^* + \bar{e}_t - C$.

The effect of transaction costs as specified in equations (2.15) and (2.16) on the working of the model is also represented in Figure 2.2. The existence of transaction costs now introduces a band around the PPP line within which price stickiness will occur.

It can easily be shown that the degree of price stickiness depends on the size of the stochastic disturbances in the *aa* line. If these are small compared to the transaction cost band around PPP, prices will be sticky in the short run. We will observe points on the line segment *AB*. One implication of this is that there will be a perfect correlation between

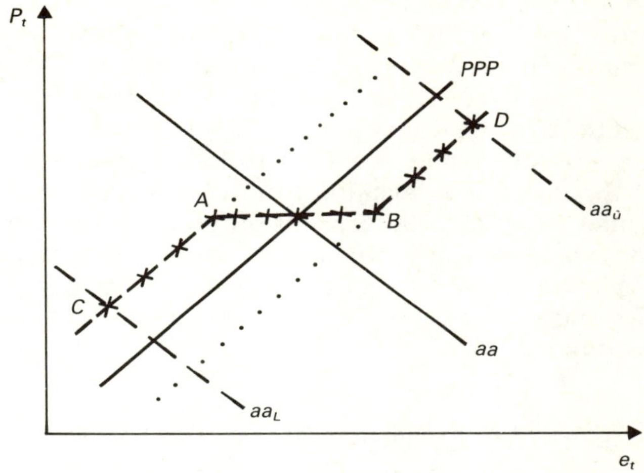

Figure 2.2: The model with endogenous price stickiness

the nominal (e_t) and the real exchange rate (θ_t). If the stochastic disturbances increase in size, say between the limits given by aa_L and aa_U, we will observe points on the line segments *CABD*. Thus the price level becomes flexible, preventing the exchange rate to deviate from PPP by more than $\bar{\theta}$. One implication is that the correlation between the nominal and the real exchange rate declines. In the limit when the stochastic disturbances in the *aa* line become very large relative to the transactions band around PPP the correlation between the nominal and the real exchange rate tends to zero. By the same token the correlation between the nominal exchange rate and the price level increases when the size of the monetary disturbances increases. In the limit this correlation tends to 1 when the monetary disturbances become very large relative to the transactions band.

The theoretical model discussed here also allows us to analyse the importance of structural factors, such as the openness of the economy and the proximity to foreign markets, for the movements of the real exchange rate.

In more open economies the cost of shipping goods across borders will generally be lower than in relatively closed economies or in economies with a large degree of protection. Thus, in open economies with liberal trade policies the transaction cost band around the PPP line will be smaller than in less open and more protected economies. As a result, the maximum deviation from PPP will be smaller in the former than in the latter. This difference, however, will become apparent only when the size of the monetary disturbances is large enough to produce real exchange rate changes that hit the ceiling imposed by the transaction cost band around PPP.

3. EMPIRICAL EVIDENCE

The theory developed in the previous section allows us to derive the following testable propositions:

(1) When the size of monetary disturbances increases, the variability of the real exchange rate increases. Thus, we expect a positive correlation between monetary variability and the variability of the real exchange rate.

(2) The relation between monetary variability and real exchange rate variability is non-monotonic (i.e. when monetary variability becomes large enough relative to the transaction cost band exchange rate variability stops increasing).

(3) With low monetary variability the correlation between nominal and real exchange rates is high. When the size of monetary disturbances increases the correlation between nominal and real exchange rates declines and the correlation between the nominal exchange rates and the price level increases. These propositions are another way to formulate the non-linear relationship between monetary and real exchange rate variability.

(4) The size of real exchange rate variability declines with the degree of openness of a country.

In order to test these propositions it is important to have a sample of countries with divergent monetary regimes. We selected a sample of thirty-nine countries during the period 1970–1982.[2] This sample includes both industrialized countries and developing countries, and countries with low and high inflationary experiences.

3.1 Monetary Variability and Real Exchange Rate Variability

In order to test the first proposition, regressions were performed using this cross-section of countries. As explanatory variables two measures of monetary variability are selected. One is the mean absolute monthly change of the money stock ($M2$), the other is the standard deviation of the monthly change of the money stock.

The estimated equations were specified as follows:

$$\log \overline{R}_i = \alpha + \beta \log \overline{M}_i + u_i \tag{2.17}$$

and

$$\log \overline{R}_i = \alpha' + \beta' \log \sigma_{M_i} + v_i \tag{2.18}$$

where $\overline{R}_i$ = the mean absolute *rate of change* of the real exchange rate of country i relative to the dollar, during 1970–1983.

$\overline{M}_i$ = the mean absolute monthly *growth rate* of the money stock ($M2$) of country i during 1970–1983.

σ_{M_i} = the standard deviation of the monthly *growth rate* of $M2$ of country i during 1970–1983.

It should be pointed out here that we use measures of unconditional variability of the growth rate of the money stock, although the results of the theoretical model are formulated in terms of conditional variability. We do this because we feel that, in this cross-section analysis, it is difficult to obtain reliable estimates of the conditional variability of the growth rate of the money stock. This choice, however, may lead to problems as to the interpretation of the results. We return to these problems in Section 3.3.

The results of the estimation are given in Table 2.2. They indicate that the size of monetary variability (measured by $\overline{M}_i$ or σ_{M_i}) had a significant positive effect on the short term real exchange rate change during 1970–1983. Note that the results are better when we use the standard deviation of money growth as proxy for monetary variability. Thus, the results confirm that countries which experienced a higher variability of the money growth also experienced higher real exchange rate variations than countries with lower monetary variability.

The next step in the analysis was to test for non-linearity of the relationship between real exchange rate change and the size of the monetary shocks. From the theory derived in the previous section, one expects that as the size of monetary disturbances continues to increase the size of the real exchange rate movements tends to level off. At a certain point (as determined by the transaction costs band) further increases in the size of monetary disturbances does not increase the real exchange rate variability. To test for this proposition a non-linear (logistic) curve was specified as follows:

$$R_i = C + \exp\left(a - \frac{b}{X_i}\right) \tag{2.19}$$

where X_i represents the monetary variability, which is $\overline{M}_i$ and σ_{M_i} alternatively.

The result of the estimation of this equation is presented in Table 2.3.

Table 2.2: Estimates of regression equation (2.17) and (2.18)

Equation (2.17)	α	β	R^2	SER
	0.59)	0.59	0.39	0.86
	(1.87)	(4.90)		
Equation (2.18)	α'	β'	R^2	SER
	0.60	0.66	0.51	0.77
	(2.41)	(6.27)		

Note: The numbers between brackets are *t*-statistics; SER is the standard error of the regression.

Table 2.3: Estimates of regression equation (2.19)

	C	a	b	SER
$X_i = \overline{M}_i$	1.56 (8.11)	2.91 (5.05)	10.48 (3.43)	0.84
$X_i = \sigma_{M_i}$	1.49 (8.22)	2.60 (7.32)	7.88 (4.38)	0.75

These results suggest a small improvement of the non-linear specification. The standard error of the regression is reduced, although only marginally, and the significance of the coefficients is enhanced. As these improvements of the non-linear specification turn out to be relatively small we do not want to draw strong conclusions at this stage. We take up this problem of non-linearity in the next section where we present evidence on the correlation between nominal and real exchange rate changes.

3.2. Nominal Exchange Rates, Real Exchange Rates and the Price Level

The theory developed in Section 2 allowed us to derive two testable propositions concerning the correlation pattern between nominal and real exchange rates, and between nominal exchange rates and price levels. In this section the empirical evidence is presented.

The empirical tests were devised as follows. First, the correlations between the monthly changes of the real and of the nominal exchange rates were computed for each of the thirty-nine countries in the sample during 1970–1983. The theory predicts that in countries with low monetary variability this correlation coefficient will be high, and *vice versa*.

Therefore, in the second step these correlation coefficients were related to the size of the monetary disturbances of each country during the same period, as measured by the mean absolute monthly change of the money stock.

In a similar way the correlation coefficients between price changes and changes in the nominal exchange rates were

Table 2.4: Correlation coefficients between nominal and real exchange rates changes and between nominal exchange rate and price level changes

Country	$Cor(p_i, e_i)$	$Cor(R_i, e_i)$	M_i	σ_{M_i}
1. Germany	0.11	0.97	1.16	0.95
2. Switzerland	0.05	0.97	1.27	2.42
3. Austria	0.03	0.96	1.04	0.90
4. Netherlands	0.06	0.95	1.14	0.94
5. Canada	0.04	0.88	1.35	0.87
6. Norway	0.14	0.93	2.55	2.18
7. France	0.22	0.98	1.55	1.26
8. Japan	0.06	0.90	1.54	1.17
9. Denmark	0.13	0.92	1.68	1.29
10. United Kingdom	0.15	0.87	1.47	1.21
11. Italy	0.31	0.92	1.74	2.24
12. Spain	0.15	0.90	1.71	1.38
13. Greece	0.23	0.67	1.94	1.99
14. Turkey	0.43	0.91	3.32	3.00
15. Venezuela	0.08	0.36	2.43	2.26
16. Indonesia	0.04	0.87	2.65	2.10
17. Nigeria	0.16	0.25	3.24	2.71
18. Bolivia	0.49	0.93	3.39	3.49
19. Peru	0.19	0.83	3.40	2.78
20. Brazil	0.69	0.72	4.28	2.92
21. Argentina	0.37	0.86	6.73	7.03
22. Malaysia	0.13	0.89	1.55	1.19
23. Singapore	0.23	0.75	1.46	1.18
24. Thailand	0.12	0.68	1.53	1.02
25. India	0.20	0.67	1.58	1.18
26. Pakistan	0.01	0.99	1.75	1.74
27. Philippines	0.01	0.94	2.25	1.99
28. Korea	0.14	0.92	2.24	1.45
29. Burma	0.08	0.67	1.79	1.77
30. South Africa	0.11	0.95	1.51	1.05
31. Morocco	0.21	0.82	1.50	1.25
32. Tunisia	0.20	0.83	1.86	1.57
33. Kenya	0.05	0.74	2.08	1.48
34. Ivory Coast	0.00	0.55	3.52	2.76
35. Malawi	0.00	0.43	3.22	2.72
36. Senegal	0.01	0.44	3.54	3.99
37. Israel	0.60	0.82	4.17	3.21
38. Upper Volta	0.05	0.18	2.61	2.12
39. Zaire	0.23	0.76	3.67	3.67

computed for each country during 1970–1983. These correlation coefficients were then related to the same measures of monetary variability. From the theory one expects that countries with low monetary variability are countries where the correlation between price changes and nominal exchange rate changes is low, and *vice versa*.

The regression equations were specified as follows:

$$Cor(R_i, e_i) = a + b\overline{M}_i \tag{2.20}$$

$$Cor(R_i, e_i) = a' + b'\sigma_{M_i} \tag{2.21}$$

$$Cor(p_i, e_i) = c + g\overline{M}_i \tag{2.22}$$

$$Cor(p_i, e_i) = c' + g'\sigma_{M_i} \tag{2.23}$$

where Cor( ) is the correlation coefficient between the two variables in the bracket; $\overline{M}_i$ is the mean absolute monthly change of the money stock of country *i* during 1970–1982, σ_{M_i} is the standard deviation of the monthly growth rate of the money stock of country *i* during 1970–1982, R_i is the percentage change of the real effective exchange rate of country *i*, and e_i is the percent change of the nominal exchange rate of country *i*.

The results of these empirical tests are presented in Tables 2.4 and 2.5. Table 2.4 shows the correlation coefficients between nominal and real exchange rate changes, and between price changes and changes in the nominal exchange rates. We have also added a column with the mean absolute monthly change of the money stock for each country, and one with the standard deviation of the same variable. Table 2.5 then presents the results of regressing equations (2.20) to (2.23). These results confirm the theoretical predictions (i.e. the coefficient of the monetary variability variable has the correct and significant negative sign in the regression explaining the correlation between nominal and real exchange rates, and the coefficients of the monetary variability variable in the regression explaining the correlation between nominal exchange rates and prices are have the expected positive sign). Thus, countries which experienced relatively little variability in the money stock are also the countries where the correlation between nominal and real exchange

Table 2.5: Results of estimating equations (2.20) to (2.23)

	a	b	a'	b'	R^2	SER
Equation (2.20)	0.91	−0.05			0.09	0.20
	(12.40)	(−1.87)				
Equation (2.21)			0.87	−0.04	0.05	0.20
			(13.0)	(1.44)		
	c	g	c'	g'	R^2	SER
Equation (2.22)	0.003	0.070			0.25	0.14
	(0.06)	(3.55)				
Equation (2.23)			0.51	0.06	0.17	0.15
			(1.05)	(2.77)		

rate changes is high. On the other hand, as the regression coefficients of the monetary variable in equations (2.22) and (2.23) indicate, these same countries experienced low correlations between price changes and changes in the nominal exchange rate. The opposite holds for countries experiencing high monetary variability. In these countries the correlation between nominal and real exchange rate changes tended to be lower, and the correlation between price changes and changes in the nominal exchange rates tended to be higher.[3]

This evidence also provides indirect confirmation of the theoretical proposition concerning the non-monotonic relation between monetary variability and real exchange rate changes.

3.3 Conditional and Unconditional Variability

The results reported in the previous sections used measures of unconditional variability of the growth rate of the money stock. The theoretical model, however, led to predictions about the relation between the conditional (unanticipated) variability of money growth and of real exchange rate changes. This leads to a problem. For it can be shown that if the growth rate of the money stock is not a white noise process, as we have implicitly assumed, the empirical results discussed in the previous sections can also be consistent with the simple Dornbusch model without the transactions cost complication. This can be shown as follows.

Suppose the money stock follows the stochastic process described by:[4]

$$m_t = \rho m_{t-1} + u_t \tag{2.24}$$

Using equation (2.6), which is the Dornbusch version of the model, and assuming, for simplicity, all exogenous variables to be zero, except m_{t-1} and u_t, yields the following solution for the exchange rate, e_t.

$$e_t = \frac{\rho}{1+\alpha(1-\rho)} m_{t-1} + \left(\frac{1}{\alpha} + \frac{\rho}{(1+\alpha(1-\rho)}\right) u_t \tag{2.25}$$

It follows that

$$p_t = \frac{\rho}{1+\alpha(1-\rho)} m_{t-1} \tag{2.26}$$

and

$$e_t - p_t = \left(\frac{1}{\alpha} + \frac{\rho}{1+\alpha(1-\rho)}\right) u_t \tag{2.27}$$

We can now calculate the (*unconditional*) correlation between the nominal exchange rate (e_t) and the real exchange rate ($e_t - p_t$) to show that in the simple Dornbusch model this correlation will generally not be equal to 1. We find that

$$Corr(e_t, e_t - p_t) = \frac{\frac{1}{\alpha} + \frac{\rho}{1+\alpha(1-\rho)}}{\left[\left(\frac{\rho}{1+\alpha(1-\rho)}\right)^2 \left(\frac{1}{1-\rho^2}\right) + \left(\frac{1}{\alpha} + \frac{\rho}{1+\alpha(1-\rho)}\right)^2\right]^{1/2}} \tag{2.28}$$

It can be seen that this correlation is less than 1, whereas the conditional correlation is always equal to 1 (because the conditional variance of m_{t-1} is zero). Note also that if $\rho =$ 0 (money is white noise), the correlation is also equal to 1, and that as ρ increases the correlation tends to decline below 1.

Now we also have that

$$var\,(m) = \frac{1}{1-\rho^2}\,var\,(u) \qquad (2.29)$$

so that for any given conditional variance of the money stock (var (u)), the unconditional variance (var (m)) rises as ρ increases from 0. Thus, it follows that our main empirical result (i.e. a high variance of money growth is associated with a low correlation between nominal and real exchange rate changes) is also consistent with the simple Dornbusch model. Put differently, to the extent that differences in the variance of the money stock across countries are due not to differences in the unconditional variances of m, but to differences in ρ, our central empirical result is consistent with the Dornbusch model without the Aizenman twist.

In order to check for this possibility, the following test was devised. First, we estimated the following money supply process for each country in our sample

$$M_{t,i} = \mu_i + \rho_i\, M_{t-1,i} + u_{t,i} \qquad (2.30)$$

where $M_{t,i}$ and $M_{t-1,i}$ are the growth rate of the money stock of country i in period t and $t{-}1$; μ_i is a constant expressing the mean growth rate of the money stock of country i. The estimates of μ_i and ρ_i are presented in Table 2.6.

Next we checked whether the observed differences in the variability of the growth rates of the money stock across countries is related to differences in the ρ_i's. If it is, our results can be explained by the Dornbusch model without the Aizenman complication. In order to do so, the following regressions were estimated

$$\overline{M}_i = f + h\rho_i \qquad (2.31)$$

Table 2.6: Estimates of M_i and ρ_i

Country	μ_i	(*t*-value)	ρ_i	(*t*-value)
1. Germany	0.00713	(5.83)	−0.0174	(−21)
2. Switzerland	0.00728	(3.35)	−0.237	(− 3.0)
3. Austria	0.0121	(10.8)	−0.187	(− 2.26)
4. Netherlands	0.0069	(5.9)	0.273	(3.47)
5. Canada	0.01027	(7.9)	0.122	(1.53)
6. Norway	0.0174	(8.9)	−0.706	(−12.0)
7. France	0.0149	(9.7)	−0.327	(− 4.3)
8. Japan	0.0136	(8.85)	−0.239	(− 3.01)
9. Denmark	0.0095	(5.6)	−0.070	(− 0.8)
10. United Kingdom	0.112	(4.9)	0.205	(2.4)
11. Italy	0.0177	(7.9)	−0.252	(− 3.0)
12. Spain	0.0205	(12.4)	−0.388	(− 5.12)
13. Greece	0.0228	(10.7)	−0.336	(− 4.3)
14. Turkey	0.0354	(10.1)	−0.286	(3.6)
15. Venezuela	0.0164	(6.0)	−0.037	(0.46)
16. Indonesia	0.0279	(9.6)	−0.091	(1.1)
17. Nigeria	0.0206	(6.0)	−0.010	(0.12)
18. Bolivia	0.0224	(5.7)	0.161	(1.9)
19. Peru	0.0302	(8.4)	−0.0426	(− 0.5)
20. Brazil	0.0362	(8.61)	−0.0877	(− 1.1)
21. Argentina	0.407	(2.9)	0.660	(6.9)
22. Malaysia	0.0137	(8.6)	0.0744	(0.9)
23. Singapore	0.0099	(6.6)	0.199	(2.45)
24. Thailand	0.0089	(6.4)	0.402	(5.2)
25. India	0.0177	(11.7)	−0.355	(− 4.6)
26. Pakistan	0.011	(5.6)	0.134	(1.66)
27. Philippines	0.018	(7.8)	0.025	(− 3.2)
28. Korea	0.0234	(10.8)	−0.089	(1.1)
29. Burma	0.0069	(3.8)	0.284	(3.9)
30. South Africa	0.0128	(8.6)	−0.049	(0.6)
31. Morocco	0.0134	(8.5)	−0.068	(0.8)
32. Tunisia	0.018	(9.2)	−0.242	(− 2.98)
33. Kenya	0.176	(6.4)	0.013	(0.15)
34. Ivory Coast	0.126	(3.6)	0.291	(3.7)
35. Malawi	0.105	(2.6)	0.239	(2.9)
36. Senegal	0.143	(3.2)	0.111	(1.3)
37. Israel	0.117	(2.8)	0.709	(12.2)
38. Upper Volta	0.183	(5.2)	−0.095	(1.1)
39. Zaire	0.245	(4.1)	0.0214	(0.2)

Table 2.7: Results of estimating equations (2.31) and (2.32)

	f	h	f'	h'	R^2	SER
Equation (2.31)	2.38	1.25			0.08	1.13
	(13.1)	(1.7)				
Equation (2.32)			2.10	1.06	0.05	1.16
			(11.2)	(1.4)		

$$\sigma_{M_i} = f' + h'\rho_i \qquad (2.32)$$

where $\overline{M}_i$ and σ_{M_i} have been defined on p. 39.

The results are presented in Table 2.7. Although the coefficients of ρ_i have the expected positive sign they are not statistically significant at the 95 per cent confidence interval. In addition, only 5 to 8 per cent of the difference in the variability of the growth rates of the money stocks across countries can be explained by differences in the ρ's across countries. Thus, these results suggest that, in order to understand the empirical evidence presented in the previous sections it is useful to add transactions costs to the Dornbusch model, as was done by Aizenman. It should be stressed here, however, that we have used relatively simple stochastic processes of the money stock. Further research will be needed to see whether this conclusion stands when using more complicated processes.

3.4. The Importance of Structural Factors

The theoretical model predicts that when transaction costs involved in trading goods internationally are low the variability of real exchange rates will tend to be low, *ceteris paribus*.

In order to test for this hypothesis we need proxies that indicate the extent to which transactions costs differ across countries. Two proxies were selected. The first one is the degree of openness (the share of exports in GDP). In general one expects that in more open economies the cost of transacting with other countries will be smaller than in more closed economies. This proxy measures the average degree of openness of a country during the sample period. A second proxy is the growth rate of exports relative to GDP. This measure can be interpreted as the marginal degree of openness of a country. One expects that in a growing world those countries that have a relatively liberal trading system (with low impediments to trade, and thus low transactions cost) experience a faster growth of the share of exports in GDP than countries with a less liberal trading system. Thus a country which experienced a growth rate of its export share in GDP above the average in the sample during 1970–1983 is a country in which economic agents faced relatively low transactions cost when trading internationally.

Similar equations as (2.17) and (2.18) were estimated adding these two proxies of transactions costs (called D_1 and D_2 respectively). The results are presented in Table 2.8.

The results of Table 2.8 tend to confirm the theoretical hypothesis. Both proxies of transactions costs have the expected negative sign. However, the coefficient of the first proxy (D_1) is not significantly different from zero. The second proxy (D_2) has a coefficient significantly different

Table 2.8: Estimates of regression equations (2.17) and (2.18) with proxies for openness

Equation (2.17)	α	β	D_1	D_2	R^2	SER
	0.67	0.59	−0.003		0.39	0.87
	(1.44)	(4.75)	(−0.24)			
	1.79	0.56		−0.009	0.45	0.83
	(2.62)	(4.78)		(1.95)		
Equation (2.18)	α'	β'	D_1	D_1	R^2	SER
	0.66	0.66	−0.002		0.52	0.78
	(1.67)	(6.10)	(−0.17)			
	1.57	0.63		−0.008	0.55	0.75
	(2.54)	(5.99)		(1.70)		

Note : *D_1 is the average openness variable; D_2 is the marginal openness variable.*

Table 2.9: F-test for difference between DCs and LDCs

Equation (2.17)	*F*-ratio
Marginal openness	1.43
Average openness	0.86
Equation (2.18)	
Marginal openness	1.56
Average openness	0.80

from zero. This suggests that countries which experienced a high growth rate of exports relative to GDP (and which we interpret as reflecting relatively small transactions cost) were countries facing small short term real exchange rate variability (for a given monetary variability) compared with other countries.

Other structural factors might influence the size of real exchange rate variability. In particular, we want to test whether there could be a difference between developed and developing countries. Therefore, the equations were run separately for the developed countries (DCs) and the less developed countries (LDCs), and the *F*-ratio was computed to test for the significance of the difference in the estimated equations. These *F*-ratios are shown in Table 2.9.
It can be seen that the *F*-ratios fall short of the critical *F*-value, which is 3.25. Thus, the hypothesis of structural differences between DCs and LDCs must be rejected.

4. CONCLUSION

The short term deviations from PPPs have been substantial since the advent of floating exchange rates. In addition, the experience of different countries has been quite different in this area.

In this paper we used and extended a model endogenizing short term real exchange rate variations. The thrust of the model is that real exchange rate variability increases with the size of monetary disturbances. However, as the degree of price flexibility is itself a positive function of the size of monetary disturbances, this relation between monetary and real exchange rate variability is a non-linear one. That is, when monetary disturbances increase beyond a certain level it will be worthwhile for economic agents to make quicker price adjustments, thereby limiting further deviations of the exchange rate from PPP. The theory, however, does not allow one to conclude that PPP holds better in a hyperinflationary environment. In fact, deviations from PPP achieve their highest level in such an environment.

The theoretical model was tested with a sample of countries during 1970–1983. In general, the results were favourable. In addition, the theory allowed us to explain why the correlation pattern between nominal and real exchange rate changes, and between changes in the price level and the nominal exchange rate diverge between countries with high and low monetary disturbances.

Much of the theorizing about the determinants of exchange rates has been influenced by 'stylized facts' observed during the seventies and the early eighties for the major currencies. These stylized facts are the strong positive correlation between nominal and real exchange rate changes in the short run, and the weak correlation between price changes and nominal exchange rate changes in the short run. This has contributed to the popularity of the sticky price models of exchange rate determination.

In this paper we stressed that these stylized facts are not universal phenomena. They are not found in countries with monetary regimes which are drastically different from those prevailing in the industrialized countries. The model developed here allowed us to understand better the divergent exchange rate experiences of a large sample of countries.

To conclude, the limitations of the present study should be stressed. Differences in monetary variability explain about 40 per cent of the cross-country differences in real exchange rate variability. There is thus a lot more to be explained. It is clear that further work will have to focus on structural and 'real' variables (e.g. terms of trade changes, supply shocks, etc.)

ACKNOWLEDGEMENT

We are grateful to Joshua Aizenman for his suggestions.

NOTES

1. We assume that the information set includes knowledge of the current shocks. Also we disregard the bubble component of the solution. *See also* Aizenman (1984), p. 178.
2. All the data are from the IFS tape. Only thirty-nine countries could be selected. For the other countries in the IFS database monthly data on prices and exchange rates are lacking. The list of countries selected is presented in Table 2.1.
3. In another paper these correlations were analysed for the German hyperinflation; *see* P. De Grauwe *et al.* (1984). It was found that in this situation of extreme monetary disturbances, the correlation between nominal and real exchange rate changes is close to zero, whereas the correlation between the price changes and the changes in the nominal exchange rates was close to one.
4. Note that in the empirical analysis all variables (including the money stock) are expressed in *growth rates*.

REFERENCES

Aizenman, J. (1984) 'Modeling deviations from purchasing power parity', *International Economic Review,* **25**(1), February.

De Grauwe, P., Janssens, M. and Leliaert, H. (1984) 'Real exchange rate variability during 1920–26 and 1973–82', unpublished, University of Louvain, June.

Dornbusch (1976) 'Expectations and exchange rate dynamics', *Journal of Political Economy*, December, 1161–1176.

Frenkel, J. A. (1976) 'A monetary approach to the exchange rate, doctrinal aspects and empirical evidence', Frenkel, J. and Johnson, H. (eds.) in *The Economics of Exchange Rates.* Addison-Wesley, Reading, Mass. 1978. *Scandinavian Journal of Economics* 78 (May), 145–165. Reprinted.

Frenkel, J. A. (1981) 'The collapse of purchasing power parities during the 1970s', *European Economic Review*, May, 145–165.

Kravis, Irving, B. and Lipsey, Robert E. (1983) 'Toward an explanation of national price levels', *Princeton Studies in International Finance*, no. 52, November.

Kravis, Irving, B. (1984) 'Comparative studies of national incomes and prices', *Journal of Economic Literature*, March, 1–39.

Mussa, M. (1976) 'The exchange rate, the balance of payments and monetary and fiscal policy under a regime of controlled floating', *Scandinavian Journal of Economics*, May, 229–248.

3 A Portfolio Balance Model of Bilateral Exchange Rates

Eduard J. Bomhoff and Kees G. Koedijk

1. INTRODUCTION

In this chapter we try to investigate movements in three bilateral dollar exchange rates. The basic framework is familiar from many other recent studies of bilateral exchange rates

$$e - f_{-1} = \text{'news'} + \text{'risk'} \qquad (3.1)$$

Here, e represents the natural logarithm of the spot exchange rate, f the corresponding value of the forward rate as observed one period earlier, so that $e - f_{-1}$ would stand for the forecast error in the current exchange rate if the forward rate were an unbiased predictor of the future spot rate. In that case it would be sufficient to explain the discrepancies of $e - f_{-1}$ as functions of relevant news which occurred between the observations on each f and the subsequent observations on the corresponding values of e.

A number of recent empirical studies have rejected the hypothesis that the forward rate is an unbiased predictor of the future spot rate (Hansen and Hodrick, 1983; Cosset, 1984; Korajczyk, 1985). On the assumption that the spot and forward markets in foreign exchange are efficient, it follows that non-zero risk premia must be present in the market.

Thus one obtains the well-known regression specification: $e - f_{-1}$ = 'news' + 'risk', where 'news' refers to unexpected changes in the fundamental determinants of the exchange rate which occur during the current period and 'risk' refers to all economic factors which make f unequal to the rational expectation of next period's e. The existence of risk factors can be investigated without specifying explicitly the preferences of risk-averse investors in the two countries. Evidence against the null hypothesis of no risk premium is already obtained if one finds statistically significant serial correlation in the time series for $e-f_{-1}$ or if a regression of $e-f_{-1}$ on news factors shows a significant constant term or significant serial correlation in the residuals. This statistical approach is unable, however, to deliver positive insights about the sources of risk in international investment or normative statements which could be useful for international investors or political authorities.

Potentially stronger tests of the null hypothesis that no significant risk premium comes between the forward rate and the expected future spot rate can be conducted by inserting empirical proxies for risk factors in equation (3.1). Hansen and Hodrick (1983) use the forward premium, and Korajczyk (1985) works with an approximation of the current difference between the real rates of interest in the two countries. In both cases, the 'risk' variable concerned belongs in the information set at the time when expectations about the future spot rate have to be formed, so that the conclusion follows that the forward rate differs intentionally from the expected future spot rate. For agents would have been capable of reducing the discrepancies between the future spot rate and the forward rate but decided not to put the forward rate equal to the expected future spot rate.

The format of the statistical tests in the present chapter is quite similar to that of Hansen and Hodrick, and Korajczyk, but we have attempted to start our theoretical analysis at the level of investor preferences for a given stochastic structure of the world economy. Working in the tradition of the finance literature, we have specified stochastic processes for the forcing variables that drive the two respective economies and assumed that risk-averse investors can augment their domestic portfolios by engaging in open positions in the foreign exchange market. Using a simple mean-variance model we then derive a condition for the required risk premium in the foreign exchange market which relates this risk premium to the covariability between the unexpected part of the return on the domestic portfolio and the unexpected change in the exchange rate. This theoretical analysis is contained in Section 2 of the chapter.

In Section 3 we discuss a reduced-form equation for the difference between the log of the current spot rate and the log of the lagged forward rate, which combines the mean-variance model of Section 2 with the general notion that spot rates differ from lagged forward rates due to a combination of news and risk. Some additional structure is helpful here; we follow Isard (1983) and connect the current real exchange rate through its expected future rate of change to the long term real exchange rate in equilibrium.

In Section 4 we present some preliminary statistical results. The empirical findings suggest that at least some of the proxies for risk factors which follow from our theoretical model do contribute towards an explanation of the discrepancies between the spot rate and the lagged forward rate. Thus, the paper provides some additional evidence against the hypothesis that the forward rate is an unbiased predictor of the future spot rate. Moreover, the principal variable suggested by our theoretical model as a risk factor, namely the variability of interest rates, does appear to be important. Clearly, considerable additional work on other currencies will be required before one can make confident statements about the main sources of risk in the foreign exchange markets. This preliminary investigation cannot be more than suggestive.

The chapter concludes with a technical appendix which provides information about the data sources and the ways in which the explanatory variables in the regression equations have been computed.

2. THE RISK PREMIUM IN A BILATERAL EXCHANGE RATE

In this section we apply a basic model from the theory of finance to a simple international setting. We attempt to extend the standard mean-variance framework and derive the corresponding formula for a two-country world, in our case the United States and Germany. Similar models will be implemented empirically for the dollar/pound and the dollar/yen.

Let q_{US} represent the required return on the portfolio of a representative investor in the United States. We assume that the representative investor has the opportunity to bet with a representative investor in Germany about next period's exchange rate by way of assuming uncovered positions in the foreign exchange market.[1] The two parties use these bets in order to improve the risk–return characteristics of their total portfolios, according to equations (3.2) and (3.3).

US investors maximize

$$_tE\{q_{US} - X(e_{t+1} - f_t) - K.var[q_{US} - X(e_{t+1} - f_t)]\} \tag{3.2}$$

with respect to X. German investors maximize

$$_tE\{q_D + Y(e_{t+1} - f_t) - K.var[q_D - Y(e_{t+1} - f_t)]\} \tag{3.3}$$

with respect to Y. Here X and Y indicate the extent to which the two representative investors wish to engage in betting on the forward exchange rate. X equals the number of dollars which the US investor sells in the forward currency market today to obtain forward marks for each dollar in his domestic portfolio.

Similarly, Y indicates the number of marks with which the German investor goes to the forward currency market for each mark in his domestic German portfolio on which he expects to earn a return of q(D).

K represents the degree of risk aversion, assumed to be equal for both representative investors.

If the representative US investor was constrained to invest in the US market portfolio, he could look forward to an expected return of q_{US} and a variation in his returns equal to var[q_{US}]. Each bet which he places with the German investor produces an uncertain pay-off of $-(e_{t+1} - f_t)$, where e_{t+1} is the logarithm of next period's exchange rate, defined as the price of one dollar in terms of the Deutsche mark and f_t is the logarithm of the corresponding forward rate. Similarly, the representative German investor can alter his expected real rate of return through engaging in bets with his US counterpart. Each bet produces an uncertain return of $(e_{t+1} - f_t)$, which is positive if the US dollar appreciates between today and the next period.

Equilibrium in the international capital market requires that both representative investors are satisfied with the volume of betting in each period. Formally, two first-order conditions have to be satisfied, and the total sum of bets as measured in a common currency has to be equal in both countries:

$$-{}_tE\,(e_{t+1} - f_t) - 2KX.var(e) + 2K.cov(q_{US},e) = 0 \quad (3.4)$$

$${}_tE(e_{t+1} - f_t) - 2KY.var(e) - 2K.cov(q_D,e) = 0 \quad (3.5)$$

$$W_{US}.X.e = W_D.Y$$

where $var(e)$ = the expected value at time t of $(e_{t+1} - f_t)^2$ (3.6)

$cov(q_{US},e)$ = expected value at time t of the covariance between the unexpected part in the total return on one unit of the US portfolio and the unexpected change in the (log of the) exchange rate between the current and next periods.

$cov(q_D,e)$ = estimated value at time t of the covariance between unexpected changes in the total return on one unit of the German market portfolio and the unexpected movement of the (log of the) exchange rate.

W_{US}, W_D = scale factors in equation (3.6), to be chosen such that $(W_{US}.e/W_D)$ represents the ratio of total wealth in a common currency in the two countries.

Equations (3.4)–(3.6) can be solved for the three unknowns

$${}_tE(e_{t+1} - f_t),\ X \text{ and } Y.$$

The solution for ${}_tE(e_{t+1} - f_t)$ is

$$ {}_{t}E(e_{t+1} - f_t) = 2K[w_{US}.cov(q_{US},e) + w_D.cov(q_D,e)] \tag{3.7} $$

In equation (3.7) w_{US} and w_D are defined as follows

$$ w_{US} = W_{US}.e/(W_{US}.e + W_D) \tag{3.8} $$

$$ w_D = W_D/(W_{US}.e + W_D) \tag{3.9} $$

The two weights w_{US} and w_D add up to 1, so that the expected value of the difference between next period's nominal rate of exchange and the current forward rate is equal to two times the risk-aversion parameter K multiplied by a weighted average of the covariance terms $cov(q_{US},e)$ and $cov(q_D,e)$.

3. TESTABLE IMPLICATIONS

Equation (3.7) relates the risk premium in the foreign exchange market to the weighted average of two covariance terms. Since the risk premium can not be observed in isolation, one has to embed one's model for the risk premium in a testable specification for one or more observable variables. Single-equation tests for risk premia in the foreign exchange market usually consist of reduced-form equations for the differences between the (logs of the) spot rate and the corresponding forward rate. Such tests decompose the difference $(e_{t+1} - f_t)$ as follows

$$ e_{t+1} - f_t = (e_{t+1} - e^e_{t+1}) + (e^e_{t+1} - f_t) \tag{3.10} $$

[log spot rate − log lagged forward rate = news + risk premium]

Our application of the basic relationship starts from the concept of a long term equilibrium real exchange rate, *er*. Agents hold homogeneous views on this long term real exchange rate ('the anchor') and on the speed at which the current real exchange rate will move towards its long term value ('the rope') (illuminating metaphors taken from Isard, 1983). We postulate that the difference between the log of the current real exchange rate and the log of its expected long term value is a linear function of the differential between the two current *ex ante* real interest rates on the one hand and the current assessment of the risk premium on the other hand

$$e_t - p_D + p_{US} - A(r_{US} - r_D) + B.\,{}_tE(e_{t+1} - f_t) = {}_tE(er) \qquad (3.11)$$

er_t	real interest differential	risk premium	long-term real exchange rate

with $A,\ B > 0$.

The formulation in equation (3.11) is appropriate if agents expect both the real interest differential and the current risk premium to converge towards zero. We do not impose the restriction that the real interest rate differential and the risk premium disappear with the same speed. In our empirical work we shall find some weak evidence for an effect of changes in the variability of interest rates on the risk premium, and there is no *a priori* reason why such a risk factor would have to disappear over time at the same speed with which any current real interest rate differentials converge towards zero (see Korajczyk, 1985, for a different approach).

The relationship between the current real exchange rate, the real interest rate differential, the risk premium and the long term equilibrium real exchange rate must hold also in terms of the expectations of these four quantities as held by economic agents during the period preceding period t. Rewriting equation (3.11) in terms of these expectations and subtracting we obtain

$$\begin{aligned} e_t - e_t^e = {} & p_D^{ue} - p_{US}^{ue} + A(r_{US}^{ue} - r_D^{ue}) \\ & - \mathrm{B}[{}_tE(e_{t+1} - f_t) - {}_{t-1}E_tE(e_{t+1} - f_t)] \\ & + {}_tE\,er - {}_{t-1}Eer \end{aligned} \qquad (3.12)$$

Here p_D^{ue} represents the unexpected change in the current German price level. It may be advantageous in practical applications to define the current price level in this context as the equilibrium value of the price level which corresponds to the current values of its macroeconomic determinants; p_{US}^{ue} represents the unexpected change in the US price level. Similarly, r_{US}^{ue} represents the unanticipated change in the real rate of interest in the US and r_D^{ue} stands for the unexpected change in the German real rate of interest. The remaining two terms in equation (3.12) refer to revisions of expected values. Using some obvious new notation, we may rewrite equation (3.12) as

$$e_t - e_t^e = p_D^{ue} - p_{US}^{ue} + A(r_{US}^{ue} - r_D^{ue}) - B.rp^{ue} + er^{ue} \tag{3.13}$$

We now combine equation (3.13) with equation (3.7)

$$_tE(e_{t+1} - f_t) = 2K\{w_{US}.cov(q_{US},e) + w_D.cov(q_D,e)\}$$

Shifting equation (3.7) one period backwards in time and adding it to equation (3.13) will give

$$e_t - f_{t-1} = p_D^{ue} - p_{US}^{ue} + A(r_{US}^{ue} - r_D^{ue}) - Brp_t^{ue} + rp_{t-1} + er^{ue} \tag{3.14}$$

where *rp* represents the risk premium as defined on the right-hand side of equation (3.6).

Equation (3.14) has the observable difference between the log of the current spot rate and the log of last period's forward rate on the left-hand side and a combination of 'news' and 'risk' on the right-hand side. Note that changes in the risk premium multiplied by *B* are one element in the 'news' of the current period. Since *B* is a positive constant, the unexpected change in the assessment of the risk premium and last period's estimated risk premium have different signs in this expression for $e_t - f_t$. In our view this is one fundamental reason why it is so difficult to test empirically hypotheses about risk premia in the foreign exchange market. Formally, the situation where both the level and the first difference of an unobservable variable are important, but affect the dependent variable in different directions, is similar to the determination of share prices if we make the simplifying assumption that the shareholder gets his return in the form of capital gains. If the required real return on a share is high, share prices may be expected to increase rapidly. If, however, the required real rate of return increases unexpectedly without a corresponding change in the expected stream of future earnings, current share prices have to fall. Returning to the foreign exchange market, a high positive risk premium on our definition implies a weak dollar, because the dollar is expected to appreciate a little more each period than would be indicated by the forward premium. A low initial value of the dollar is then required. If the risk premium increases unexpectedly the dollar has to depreciate further in order to be able to reach its expected long term equilibrium real value on a rational expectation path. It follows that the expected value of $e_t - f_{t-1}$ is positive if there is no change in the assessment of the risk premium, but the *ex post* realization may be strongly negative if there is a strong increase in the risk premium. If the empirical counterparts to the risk premium incorporate measurement errors or are included with inappropriate lags then statistical tests will be strongly biased towards no rejection of the null hypothesis of a negligible risk premium.

We assume that the dynamics of the price level in both countries are given by

$$\Delta p_{US} = (1 - \theta_{US} B)\, u_{p,US} \tag{3.15}$$

$$\Delta p_D = (1 - \theta_D B)\, u_{p,D} \tag{3.16}$$

Here, B is the lag operator, familiar from Box–Jenkins modelling, and θ_{US}, θ_D are positive parameters. From equations (3.15) and (3.16) it follows that

$$\Delta_t E\hat{p}_{US} = (1 - \theta_{US}) p_{US}^{ue} \tag{3.17}$$

$$\Delta_t E\hat{p}_D = (1 - \theta_D) p_D^{ue} \tag{3.18}$$

For convenience, define

$$\psi_{US} = (1 - \theta_{US})^{-1} \tag{3.19}$$

$$\psi_D = (1 - \theta_D)^{-1} \tag{3.20}$$

It follows that

$$p_{US}^{ue} = \psi_{US} \Delta_t E\hat{p}_D \tag{3.21}$$

$$p_D^{ue} = \psi_D \Delta_t E\hat{p}_D \tag{3.22}$$

In addition to news regarding the domestic and foreign price levels, equation (3.14) includes also news about the domestic and foreign real rates of interest, news about the risk premium in the foreign exchange market and news about the future equilibrium value of the real exchange rate.

We assume that news about the nominal interest rates can be represented adequately by the first difference of $i_{\mathrm{US}}(t)$ and $i_{\mathrm{D}}(t)$ respectively. Since the long term equilibrium value of the real exchange rate is an unobservable variable, any assumptions regarding its stochastic behaviour and its macroeconomic determinants have to be tested jointly with the other assumptions embedded in the exchange rate model. We hypothesize that the real exchange rate in future equilibrium is a function of the long run differences in inflation and economic growth between the two countries. If rates of inflation and economic growth converge over the long run, then the long run value of the real exchange rate should correspond to purchasing power parity. However, if the long run characteristics of the countries differ in important respects there may be persisting capital flows. In such a case, the real exchange rate would settle at a level which would induce a long run capital flow and a corresponding non-zero value for the current account.

Unfortunately, there is no direct evidence to bear on these assumptions regarding the determinants of the long run real exchange rate. Also, we do not know with what speed the real exchange rate moves towards its long run equilibrium value. We therefore opt for a flexible specification in which the coefficients A and B are proportional to the 'length' of the 'rope' and the movements in the 'anchor' are described by

$$\Delta er_\infty = C(\Delta_t E\hat{y}_{\mathrm{US}} - \Delta_t E\hat{y}_{\mathrm{D}} - \mathrm{D}(\Delta_t E\hat{p}_{\mathrm{US}} - \Delta_t E\hat{p}_{\mathrm{D}}) + u_e \tag{3.23}$$

This implies that all movements in the equilibrium long term value of the real exchange rate are unexpected.

Substitution of (3.21), (3.22) and (3.23) into (3.14) and some rearrangement gives

$$\begin{aligned} e - f_{-1} = {} & A(\Delta i_{US} - \Delta i_D) + (-A - D - \psi_{US}) \\ & \Delta_t E\hat{p}_{US} + (A + D + \psi_D)\, \Delta_t E\hat{p}_D \\ & + C\Delta_t E\hat{y}_{US} - C\Delta_t E\hat{y}_D \\ & + rp_{-1} - Brp^{ue} + u_e \end{aligned} \tag{3.24}$$

For convenience we assume that the first differences in each country in interest rates, expected rates of inflation and expected future rates of economic growth are independent. Statistical tests of this hypothesis show that the assumption of statistical independence does not need to be rejected for either country.

It now remains to specify the causes in q_{US} and q_D. In selecting the determinants of the expected return on the market portfolio, we follow Fama and Gibbons (1982) who found that the expected return on bonds and stocks is negatively correlated with the expected inflation rate and positively correlated with real activity represented by the expected growth rate;

$$\begin{aligned} \Delta q_{US} = {} & \epsilon(q_{US}, i_{US})\Delta i_{US} + \epsilon(q_{US}, p_{US})\Delta_t E\hat{p}_{US} \\ & + \epsilon(q_{US}, y_{US})\Delta_t E\hat{y}_{US} + u_{q,US} \end{aligned} \tag{3.25}$$

$$\begin{aligned} \Delta q_D = {} & \epsilon(q_D, i_D)\Delta i_D + \epsilon(q_D, p_D)\Delta_t E\hat{p}_D \\ & + \epsilon(q_D, y_D)\Delta_t E\hat{y}_D + u_{q,D} \end{aligned} \tag{3.26}$$

All terms are elasticities. Unexpected rates of return decrease if interest rates or expected rates of inflation go up, and increase or remain unchanged if the expected future rate of economic growth increases.

In order to obtain an expression for $cov(q_{US},e)$ and $cov(q_D,e)$ we have to multiply equation (3.24) and equation (3.25) and (3.26). We assume that the exogenous variables are not serially correlated. Next, we substitute this expression in equation (3.24). It shows that movements in the (co)variances of the US and German interest rates, the (co)variances in the inflation differential and the (co)variances of the growth differential are the main determinants of the risk premium.

4. EMPIRICAL EVIDENCE

In the previous section we discussed a reduced-form framework for the spot rate minus the lagged forward rate. We have tested our model using monthly data on the dollar/Deutsche mark, dollar/pound and dollar/yen exchange rates. Although the results are far from definitive they seem to confirm in the case of the United Kingdom and Japan earlier evidence against the hypothesis of no risk premium in the forward rate.

Our analysis starts in November 1979, just after the change in US monetary policy, and ends in December 1984.

In trying to implement our theoretical model we have tried to incorporate in every equation the determinants of the long run real exchange rate—the expected growth differential and the expected inflation differential—as well as the real interest differential between the US and the foreign countries. For econometric reasons we inserted the nominal interest rate and the expected inflation separately. However, imposing equal but opposite coefficients on the forward premium and the proxy for the expected inflation does not result in a significant loss in explanatory power according to the usual F-test.

In addition to these factors we have tested for all the risk factors that follow from our model: the variance of the change in the short term interest rate, the variance of the change in expected inflation and the variance of the change in the expected growth rate. For each bilateral exchange rate this implies a total of six potential risk variables. The risk factors were modelled separately for each country, since according to equation (3.7) the weights differ.

The results are shown in Table 3.1 and Table 3.2. Table 3.1 shows ordinary least squares estimates, while the equations in Table 3.2 have been estimated with the seemingly unrelated regressions method (SUR). Contemporaneous values only have been tested for the news variables, and 1-month lagged values for all risk factors. All the variables with t-values of less than one have been left out. All the signs of the coefficients of the explanatory

Table 3.1: OLS estimates 1979:11–1984:12

Germany

$$e - f_{-1} = \underset{(2.56)}{14.73} + \underset{(2.28)}{5.94}\,\Delta FP - \underset{(-2.10)}{5.09}\,\Delta(\hat{p}^e_{US} - \hat{p}^e_D)$$
$$- \underset{(1.01)}{0.91}\,\text{VRUS}(-1) + \underset{(0.92)}{0.87}\,\text{VPUS}(-1)$$

$R^2_c = 0.11$ DW = 1.72 SEE = 37.31

United Kingdom

$$e - f_{-1} = \underset{(2.69)}{14.96} + \underset{(2.04)}{4.15}\,\Delta FP - \underset{(-1.33)}{2.20}\,\Delta(\hat{p}^e_{US} - \hat{p}^e_{UK})$$
$$- \underset{(-1.78)}{1.49}\,\text{VRUS}(-1) - \underset{(-1.60)}{0.10}\,\text{UVYK}(-1)$$
$$+ \underset{(1.06)}{0.95}\,\text{VPUS}(-1)$$

$R^2_c = 0.16$ DW = 1.84 SEE = 34.12

Japan

$$e - f_{-1} = \underset{(1.00)}{6.51} + \underset{(1.12)}{3.38}\,\Delta FP - \underset{(-1.24)}{2.46}\,\Delta(\hat{p}^e_{US} - \hat{p}^e_J)$$
$$- \underset{(-1.92)}{1.92}\,\text{VRUS}(-1) + \underset{(1.47)}{1.57}\,\text{VPUS}(-1)$$

$R^2_c = 0.06$ DW = 1.86 SEE = 41.53

variables agree without exception with our theoretical model. Since the forward premium is measured at an annual rate, the logs of e and f are multiplied by 1200. All the SEEs may be divided by twelve to give the average residual error as a number of percentage points for the exchange rate.

Table 3.1 gives three OLS equations. Table 3.2 shows SUR estimates. Equation 1, the equation for the dollar–Deutsche mark, shows a constant term, which partly reflects risk factors which are not captured by our measures, the change in the 1-month forward premium (ΔFP), the change

Table 3.2: SUR estimates 1979:11–1984:12

Germany

$$e - f_{-1} = \underset{(2.70)}{14.88} + \underset{(2.39)}{5.56}\,\Delta FP - \underset{(-2.06)}{4.23}\,\Delta(p^e_{US} - p^e_D) - \underset{(-1.04)}{0.89}\,\text{VRUS}(-1) + \underset{(0.94)}{0.85}\,\text{VPUS}(-1)$$

DW = 1.76 SEE = 35.34

United Kingdom

$$e - f_{-1} = \underset{(2.97)}{15.54} + \underset{(1.58)}{2.85}\,\Delta FP - \underset{(1.48)}{2.09}\,\Delta(p^e_{US} - p^e_{UK}) - \underset{(-1.94)}{1.53}\,\text{VRUS}(-1) - \underset{(2.29)}{0.12}\,\text{VYUK}(-1) + \underset{(1.15)}{0.97}\,\text{VPUS}(-1)$$

DW = 1.93 SEE = 32.58

Japan

$$e - f_{-1} = \underset{(1.06)}{6.56} + \underset{(1.03)}{2.77}\,\Delta FP - \underset{(-1.49)}{2.48}\,\Delta(\hat{p}^e_{US} - \hat{p}^e_J) \underset{(-2.06)}{-1.96}\,\text{VRUS}(-1) + \underset{(1.53)}{1.57}\,\text{VPUS}(-1)$$

DW = 1.87 SEE = 39.83

in the expected inflation differential ($\Delta(\hat{p}^e_{US} - \hat{p}^e_D)$ and two risk factors, the lagged variance of the change in the US short term interest rate ($VAR(i_{US})$, and the lagged variance of the expected inflation in the United States ($VAR(\hat{p}^e_{US})$.

The equation for the United Kingdom contains also a constant term the change in 1-month forward premium, the lagged variance of the change in the short term US interest rate, the change in the expected inflation differential between the United States and the United Kingdom ($\Delta(\hat{p}^e_{US} - \hat{p}^e_{UK})$ the lagged variance of the change in the expected inflation in the United States and the lagged variance of the change in expected growth in the United Kingdom ($VAR\ \hat{y}^e_{UK}$).

The equation for Japan shows a constant term, the change in the 1-month forward premium, the change in the expected

Table 3.3

	New factors	Risk factors
Germany	4.87**	0.78
UK	3.46**	2.64*
Japan	1.50	2.48*

** = significant at 95% level.
* = significant at 90% level.

inflation differential between the United States and Japan, $(\Delta(\hat{p}^e_{US} - \hat{p}^e_J)$ the lagged variance of the change of the short term US interest rate and the lagged variance of the change in the expected inflation in the United States. We have tested every equation for joint significance of the news factors and the joint significance of the risk factors. The results are presented in Table 3.3.

The change in the 1-month forward premium and the change in the expected inflation differential between the United States and Germany proved to be statistically significant at 0.05 level. Taken together, these variables reflect the real interest rate differential between the US and Germany.

The results confirm findings by others that the strong appreciation of the dollar *vis-à-vis* the Deutsche mark was largely caused by real interest rate differentials. The results in Table 3.3 show that risk factors played only a minor role in the dollar/Deutsche mark case.

The lagged variance of the change in the US short term interest rate and the lagged variance of the change in expected growth in the United Kingdom, two important risk factors from our theoretical model, added significantly to the explanation of the difference between the dollar/pound spot rate and its lagged forward rate. In the case of Japan we also found that the lagged variance of the US short term interest rate was a significant risk factor explaining movements in the dollar/yen spot rate.

The economic interpretation of our model is straightforward and well worth spelling out. If—as the results seem to confirm—the movements in the US interest rate are a major source of uncertainty and do affect the real rates of return on domestic and overseas investments in the same direction, the required real rate on these overseas holdings will be higher for a US-based investor. The market provides this required rise in the real rates by pushing up the value of the dollar to a point where some further depreciation should be thought of as more likely than further appreciation. Thus the strong dollar makes overseas investments more attractive to US-based investors, since they have the perspective of some future appreciation of the value of their overseas holdings. According to our results this effect did play an important role in the appreciation of the dollar since 1980. We should emphasize, however, that the results are still preliminary and that much more theoretical and empirical work is required before we can speak about the role of risk in the determination of exchange rates with the same degree of confidence which shows through in discussions of the risk–return relationship in the context of the national stock markets.

APPENDIX: SYMBOLS, DATA SOURCES AND COMPUTATIONAL METHODS

e : logarithm of the spot rate (end of period)
price of one US dollar in Deutsche marks
Source: Federal Reserve Bank of St Louis

f : logarithm of the 1-month forward rate (end of period)
Source: Federal Reserve Bank of St Louis

fp : 1-month forward premium ($fp = e - f$)

y : Real gross national product
Source: Federal Reserve Bank of St Louis

p : consumer price index
Source: Federal Reserve Bank of St Louis

i_k : short term interest rate (representative money market rates end of month)
Source: World financial markets (Morgan Guaranty)

A circumflex ($\hat{}$) indicates a rate of growth, the superscript (^{e}) an expected value. First differences are indicated by Δ.

All expectations were derived with a Multi-State Kalman Filter, as explained in Kool (1982).

The expressions for the variances were obtained by calculating the product of the first difference

R_c^2 = coefficient of determination, after correction for degrees of freedom.

DW = Durbin–Watson coefficient for first-order serial correlation.

t-statistics are presented in parentheses.

ACKNOWLEDGEMENTS

We are grateful to Stanley Black, Paul de Grauwe, Clemens Kool, Patrick Minford and participants in Seminars at the Universities of Leuven, Siegen and Sussex for their comments. An earlier version of this paper was presented at the 1984 Meetings of the Western Economic Association. Wouter den Haan provided valuable research assistance.

NOTES

1. The model is inspired by Conroy and Rendleman.

REFERENCES

Bomhoff, E. J. (1982) 'Predicting the price level in a world that changes all the time', in: Brunner, K. and Meltzer, A. H. (eds.): Economic policy in a world of change, *Carnegie-Rochester Conference Series on Public Policy*, 17, autumn, 7–38.

Bomhoff, E. J. (1983) *Monetary Uncertainty*, North-Holland, Amsterdam.

Bomhoff, E. J. and Korteweg, P. (1983) 'Exchange rate variability and monetary policy under rational expectations: some Euro-American experience 1973–1979', *Journal of Monetary Economics,* **11** (2), March, 169–206.

Conroy, R. M. and Rendleman, R. J. (1983) 'Pricing commodities when both price and output are uncertain', *The Journal of Futures Markets,* **3** (4), winter.

Cosset, J. C. (1984) 'On the presence of risk premiums in foreign exchange markets', *Journal of International Economics,* **16** (1/2), February, 139–154.

Fama, E. F. and Gibbons, M. R. (1982) Inflation, real returns and capital investment, *Journal of Monetary Economics,* **9** ( ), May, 297–323.

Frenkel, J. A. (1979) 'The diversifiability of exchange risk', *Journal of*

International Economics, 379–393.

Frenkel, J. A. (1981) 'Flexible exchange rates, prices, and the role of "news": lessons from the 1970's'. *Journal of Political Economy,* **89**, (4), August, 665–705.

Hansen, L. P. and Hodrick, R. J. (1983) 'Risk averse speculation in the foreign exchange market: An econometric analysis of linear models', in: Frenkel, J. A. (ed.) *Exchange Rates and International Macroeconomics*, Chicago and London, University of Chicago Press.

Isard, P. (1983) 'An accounting framework and some issues for modelling how exchange rates respond to the news', in Frenkel, J. A. (ed.) *Exchange Rates and International Macroeconomics*, Chicago and London, University of Chicago Press.

Kool, C. J. M. (1982) 'The multi-state Kalman Filter method', in Brunner, K. and Meltzer, A. H. (eds.), Economic Policy in a World of Change, *Carnegie-Rochester Conference Series on Public Policy,* **17**, autumn, 39–55.

Korajczyk, R. A. (1985) 'The pricing of forward contracts for foreign exchange', *Journal of Political Economy,* **93** (2), April, 346–368.

Mascaro, A. and Meltzer, A. H. (1983) Long- and short-term interest rates in a risky world', *Journal of Monetary Economics,* **12**, (3), November, 485–518.

Mussa, M. (1979) 'Empirical regularities in the behavior of exchange and theories of the foreign exchange market', in: Brunner, K. and Meltzer, A. H. (eds.) Policies for employment, prices and exchange rates, *Carnegie-Rochester Conference Series on Public Policy,* **11**, autumn, 9–57.

Meese, R. A. and Rogoff, K. (1983a) 'Empirical exchange rate models of the Seventies: Do they fit out of sample?', *Journal of International Economics,* **14**, (1), 3–24.

Meese, R. A. and Rogoff, K. (1983b) 'The out-of-sample failure of empirical exchange rate, models: sampling error of misspecification', in Frenkel, J. A. (ed.): *Exchange Rates and International Macroeconomics*, Chicago and London, University of Chicago Press.

4 Government Policy and the Risk Premium in Foreign Exchange Markets

Stanley W. Black and Michael K. Salemi

1. INTRODUCTION

Following a period of ambitious efforts to understand the determinants of foreign exchange rates utilizing relatively simple monetary or portfolio balance theories, economists have recently been forced to admit that reality is more complex than these simple models suggest. The exhaustive tests of the forecasting ability of alternative methods performed by Meese and Rogoff (1983) led them to conclude that the models could have broken down either because of time-varying risk premia, variations in long run equilibrium real exchange rates, poor measurement of inflationary expectations, or instability in money demand functions. Our own empirical work with monetary policy and exchange rate intervention policy reaction functions in different countries (Black, 1983) has suggested that there are important shifts in such policies at different times. It takes but a short step to hypothesize that changes in policy regimes may have been an important factor causing the coefficients of exchange rate model to be unstable.

Specific theoretical examples of such changes in regime have been worked out by Black (1984a) in the case of exchange rate policy and by Walsh (1984) in the case of monetary policy. Each paper shows that an exogenous change in the form of a policy rule that affects variances in a stochastic model will change the optimizing behaviour of risk-averse private agents.

Suppose we derive the interest responsiveness of the

demand to hold foreign assets from a portfolio model as $\beta = (\phi\sigma^2_{e,1})^{-1}$, where ϕ is the coefficient of risk aversion and $\sigma^2_{e,1}$ is the conditional variance of the exchange rate. In a model with rational expectations, this conditional variance will depend, in turn, on the parameters describing the government's exchange rate intervention policy. In a partial equilibrium setting, Black (1984a) demonstrates the existence of the 'Harrod effect': an increase in the strength of government intervention that does not aim at an inappropriate target will reduce the conditional variance of the exchange rate and increase the responsiveness of the demand to hold foreign assets. Thus stabilizing government intervention policy induces stabilizing private activity.

This type of interaction between government policy and private behaviour could easily lead to a time-varying risk premium in the foreign exchange market and coefficient instability in simple models of exchange rate determination. Some preliminary tests of a time-varying coefficient model by Black (1984b) suggested that the coefficients of an exchange rate equation did vary systematically with the residual variance in the equation, in a manner consistent with theoretical predictions. However, these results were not based on a structural estimation technique and could have reflected sampling error as well as changes in policy rules. Another approach to the problem of time-varying risk premia has been followed by Hansen and Hodrick (1980, 1983) and Salemi (1983), who find direct evidence for a time-varying risk premium in the forward market. The latter approach, while paying close attention to estimation technique, has not exploited the theoretical arguments suggesting that policy changes could affect the risk premium.

The papers by Black and Walsh take the policy regime as exogenous, and ask what effects on private behaviour can be expected if the policy regime changes unexpectedly. In Flood and Garber (1983), the regime change is anticipated with a probability that increases through time. In the literature on credibility of monetary policy, the announcement of a regime change may not lead the private sector to believe in it until its permanence has been demonstrated

(Fellner, 1976; Cukierman and Meltzer (1984). Finally, the analyses of Barro and Gordon (1983) and Canzoneri (1985) focus on the question of whether the government's announced policy is time consistent or whether the authorities have an incentive to misrepresent their actual policy.

In the context of these various efforts to understand both changing risk premia and changing policy regimes, this chapter has one major objective, which is to perform a structural test of the effect of a change in policy regime on the behaviour of the private sector. We wish to confront the Black–Walsh hypothesis with the data. Credibility itself is not the main issue of this chapter, although a lag in the credibility of a change in policy regime would certainly affect the estimates of structural change that we are trying to obtain.

From a broader perspective, however, the essence of the credibility problem is the interaction of government policy choices and private behaviour in models with rational expectations. By testing for the existence of a particular type of interaction, we hope to throw light on its importance for understanding exchange market behaviour. In Section 2 of the chapter, we set out a structural mode of exchange rate determination that will allow such tests to be made, taking account of the restrictions implied by assuming rational expectations. At this stage in our work, we restrict ourselves to a model of a small open economy for computational reasons. The model is constructed so that it is easy to generalize to two interacting countries, an approach we intend to pursue in the near future. In Section 3 we obtain the solution of a smaller, partial equilibrium submodel of the exchange rate and demonstrate its properties graphically.

After obtaining the solution of the model, we turn in Section 4 to describing and implementing a technique for estimating its parameters across different policy regimes, allowing specific parameters to vary according to the Black–Walsh theory of changing coefficients. Section 4 provides some preliminary estimates of the model for the case of West Germany using quarterly data over the period 1963–1983, allowing for tests of several changes in regime.

2. AN OPEN ECONOMY MODEL WITH MONETARY AND EXCHANGE RATE POLICY

The model we use to test for the effects of changes in policy regime must have several characteristics. It should be small, to minimize the number of parameters to be estimated by maximum likelihood methods. It must explain output, the price level, the interest rate and the exchange rate, since the hypothesized effects work through changing the variability of the exchange rate and the interest rate. The model should assume imperfect substitutability of assets denominated in different currencies, or equivalently risk-averse private agents, since exchange rate intervention and monetary policy are assumed to be separate policy instruments.

The smallest model with these features has equations for aggregate supply and demand for goods, supply and demand for money, and current and capital accounts of the balance of payments. Extensions of the model to make it more realistic will be considered at a later stage.

For aggregate supply, we assume a Lucas-type response to price surprises, allowing for a distributed lag to accommodate cyclical behaviour

$$y_t = \bar{y} + \alpha(p_t - E_{t-1}p_t) + \upsilon(y_{t-1} - \bar{y}) + z_t, \qquad (4.1)$$

where y and p are the logarithms of output and the price level, z is a random disturbance, and $E_{t-1}p_t$ represents the expectation of price in period t, conditional on information available in period $t-1$. This type of supply response can be justified, as in Gray (1976), by assuming that workers negotiate wage contracts based on information available in period $t-1$, and that the contracts are not indexed for current inflation. Allowing indexation would put the terms of trade into the supply function, as the product real wage responds to changes in the price of imported goods. For simplicity, this effect is ignored. Since Flood and Marion (1982) have shown that the optimal degree of wage indexation changes with changes in the monetary policy regime, this assumption leaves out a change in private behaviour that should be investigated in future work.

The aggregate demand for goods is assumed to depend on the logarithm of the terms of trade $e + p^* - p$, the nominal interest rate r, and foreign output y^*, as well as a random disturbance u,

$$y_t = \bar{y} + \eta(e_t + p_t^* - p_t) - \delta r_t + \mu y_t^* + u_t \qquad (4.2)$$

A more realistic specification depending on the real interest rate will be considered in future work. The primary effect of adding the expected rate of inflation to the *IS* curve would be to convert the price level from an endogenous non-state variable to a non-predetermined state variable, in Blanchard and Kahn (1980) terminology. This would add an additional unstable root to the system of stochastic difference equations.

The money demand function is assumed for simplicity to have unitary income elasticity. This has the effect of deleting the absorption price deflator $\tilde{p}$ from the equation.

$$m_t^{\mathrm{d}} = \tilde{p}_t + (p_t + y_t - \tilde{p}_t) - \lambda r_t + v_t. \qquad (4.3)$$

The supply of money is assumed to follow a path $\bar{m}_t$ specified by the authorities, modified by an interest-elastic supply response.

$$m_t^{\mathrm{s}} = \bar{m}_t + \gamma r_t \qquad (4.4)$$

Equating (4.3) and (4.4), we have the equation of the *LM* curve

$$\bar{m}_t = p_t + y_t - (\lambda + \gamma) r_t + v_t. \qquad (4.5)$$

Equations (4.1), (4.2) and (4.5) enable us to determine p, y and r for a given exchange rate e. To find the exchange rate, we turn to the balance of payments. Equation (4.6) shows the accumulation of private foreign assets to depend on the current account, less the government's purchases of foreign exchange for intervention purposes, Δg

$$\Delta f_t = \eta(e_t + p_t^* - p_t) - \mu(y_t - y_t^*) + x_t - \Delta g_t \qquad (4.6)$$

The current account balance depends on the terms of trade $e + p^* - p$, the relative pressure of demand at home and abroad $y - y^*$, and a random shock x_t. In this formulation,

f_t is treated as the *net* stock of foreign assets, that is, foreign assets owned by domestic residents less domestic assets owned by foreign residents. We assume that foreign assets are denominated in foreign currency and domestic assets are denominated in domestic currency.

Government intervention policy is assumed to include components for both leaning against the wind and aiming at a target exchange rate $\bar{e}$

$$\Delta g_t = -\theta_0 \Delta e_t - \theta_1 (e_t - \bar{e}) \tag{4.7}$$

The demand to hold net foreign assets f_t will be derived in two parts, considering separately the domestic demand to hold foreign assets k_t and the foreign demand to hold domestic assets h_t^*. We define the level of the spot price of foreign currency as ϵ_t, so that $e_t = \log(\epsilon_t)$ and net foreign assets are $f_t = k_t - h_t^*/\epsilon_t$. The domestic-currency rate of return in period $t+1$ on foreign assets $\epsilon_t k_t$ and domestic assets $W_t - \epsilon_t k_t$, given non-monetary wealth W_t is then

$$\pi_{t+1} = \frac{\epsilon_t k_t}{w_t}(e_{t+1} - e_t + r_t^*) + \left(1 - \frac{\epsilon_t k_t}{W_t}\right) r_t \tag{4.8}$$

The representative domestic agent is assumed to choose k_t to maximize $U = E_t \pi_{t+1} - \phi/2\, V_t \pi_{t+1}$, where ϕ is a measure of relative risk aversion, $E_t \pi_{t+1}$ is the conditional expectation of π_{t+1} given information available in period t and $V_t \pi_{t+1}$ is its conditional variance. This leads to an optimal portfolio allocation of

$$\frac{\epsilon_t k_t}{W_t} = \frac{1}{\phi \sigma_{e,1}^2}(E_t e_{t+1} - e_t + r_t^* - r_t) \tag{4.9}$$

where $\sigma_{e,1}^2$ is the conditional variance of the (log of the) future spot exchange rate, given information available at time t.

The representative foreign agent's return on his holdings of domestic and foreign assets, given non-monetary wealth $W_t^* = k_t^* + h_t^*/\epsilon_t$, is

$$\pi_{t+1}^* = \frac{h_t^*}{\epsilon_t} W_t^* (e_t - e_{t+1} + r_t) + \left(1 - \frac{h_t^*}{\epsilon_t W_t^*}\right) r_t^* \tag{4.10}$$

A similar optimization leads to the portfolio share

$$\frac{h_t^*}{\epsilon_t W_t^*} = \frac{1}{\phi\, \sigma_{e,1}^2}(e_t - E_t e_{t+1} + r_t - r_t^*) \tag{4.11}$$

Since $f_t = k_t - h_t^*/\epsilon_t$, subtraction and simplification leads to an expression for the *net* demand for foreign assets

$$f_t = \frac{\overline{W}_t}{\phi\, \sigma_{e,1}^2}(E_t e_{t+1} - e_t + r_t^* - r_t) + w_t, \tag{4.12}$$

where $\overline{W}_t$ is world wealth holding $W_t/\epsilon_t + W_t^*$ and w_t is a random disturbance. Thus we conclude that the net demand to hold foreign assets depends on the expected return with a coefficient that depends on the degree of risk aversion of international asset holders and the perceived degree of risk as measured by the conditional variance of the exchange rate.

Since our model does not describe wealth accumulation except through the current account, we take world wealth $\overline{W}$ as constant.

Another form in which equation (4.12) can be written indicates how our model suggests the risk premium will change over time

$$r_t^* - r_t + E_t e_{t+1} - e_t = \frac{\phi \sigma_{e,1}^2}{\overline{W}}(f_t - w_t) = \frac{1}{\beta}(f_t - w_t) \tag{4.13}$$

In equation (4.13), the risk premium is seen to depend on the net stock of foreign assets held f_t and the perceived degree of risk $\sigma_{e,1}^2$. Our major hypothesis is that changes in government policy that affect the perceived degree of risk will have substantial effects on the risk premium. Our model enables us to see how changes in policy rules will affect the conditional variance.

The short run asset market equilibrium of this model can be derived from the market equilibrium equation for foreign assets $\overline{k}_t = k_t + k_t^* + g_t$ and domestic assets $\overline{h}_t = h_t + h_t^* + h_t^b$, where g_t and h_t^b are domestic central bank holdings of each asset. These equations, together with (4.9) and (4.11), imply (4.12), with $f_t = \overline{k}_t - g_t - W_t^*$.

Combining equations (4.6), (4.7) and (4.12), we have an equation for the balance of payments

$$\eta(e_t + p_t^* - p_t) + \mu(y_t^* - y_t) + x_t + \theta_0 \Delta e_t + \theta_1(e_t - \bar{e})$$
$$= \beta\Delta r_t^* - \beta\Delta r_t + \beta(E_t e_{t+1} - e_t - E_{t-1}e_t + e_{t-1}) + \Delta w_t . \tag{4.14}$$

The solution of our model for a given policy regime can be found in either of two equivalent ways. A policy regime is given by a set of parameters for monetary policy, $\bar{m}_t$ and γ in equation (4.4), and a set of parameters for exchange rate policy, θ_0 and θ_1 in equation (4.7). The Blanchard–Kahn (1980) form of the solution is found by taking the exchange rate e_t and the net stock of foreign assets f_{t-1} as non-predetermined and predetermined state variables respectively, and using equations (4.6) and (4.12) to determine their evolution over time. Equations (4.1), (4.2) and (4.5) suffice, as noted earlier, to determine the current values of p, y and r needed for (4.6) and (4.12). This result is a second order stochastic difference equation with two real roots, one stable root corresponding to the backward-looking variable f_{t-1}, and one unstable root corresponding to the forward-looking variable e_t.

For econometric reasons a slightly different but equivalent solution technique will be adopted here. Define the vector $\mathbf{X}_t = (f_t, e_t, p_t, y_t, r_t)'$ of endogenous variables, the vector $\mathbf{Z}_t = (p_t^*, y_t^*, r_t^*, \bar{m}_t, \bar{y}_t, \bar{e}_t)'$ of exogenous variables, and the vector $\mathbf{U}_t = (x_t, w_t, u_t, v_t, z_t)'$ of random disturbances to the equations above. Equations (4.6), (4.13), (4.1), (4.2) and (4.3) may then be expressed in matrix form as

$$A_1 E_t \mathbf{X}_{t+1} + A_2 \mathbf{X}_t + A_3 E_{t-1} \mathbf{X}_t + A_4 \mathbf{X}_{t-1} = B\mathbf{Z}_t + \mathbf{U}_t \tag{4.15}$$

where the matrices A_i, B have as elements simple functions of the underlying parameters of the model. We also assume that the 'rest of the world' variables, p^*, y^*, r^* and the exogenous variables $\bar{m}_t$, $\bar{y}_t$ and $\bar{e}_t$ evolve independently from the endogenous variables according to a stationary Markov process.

$$Z_t = D\mathbf{Z}_{t-1} + \mathbf{V}_t, \qquad (4.16)$$

where $\mathbf{V}_t$ is a vector of six random shocks to these variables.

To express the solution of (4.15) and (4.16) jointly, we stack the endogenous and exogenous variables in the vector $\mathbf{Q}_t = (\mathbf{X}_t, \mathbf{Z}_t)'$ and the disturbances in the vector $\mathbf{R}_t = (\mathbf{U}_t, \mathbf{V}_t)'$. We assume the existence of a solution of the form $\mathbf{Q}_t = C(L)\mathbf{R}_t)$, where $C(L)$ is a matrix polynomial in the lag operator $L\mathbf{X}_t = \mathbf{X}_{t-1}$. In this notation, the conditional expectation is $E_t\mathbf{Q}_{t+1} = [C(L) - C^0]L^{-1}\mathbf{R}_t$, where we delete the one-period-ahead disturbances by omitting the first term C^0 from $C(L)$. We substitute this expression and its lagged value for the conditional expectations in (4.15) and collect terms involving C^0 on the right-hand side. The method of undetermined coefficients applied to (4.15) and (4.16) jointly then leads to the following expression

$$\begin{bmatrix} A_1L^{-1} + (A_2+A_3) + A_4L & -B \\ 0 & I-DL \end{bmatrix}\mathbf{Q}_t$$

$$= \begin{bmatrix} I+C^0_{11}(A_1L^{-1}+A_3) & C^0_{12}(A_1L^{-1}+A_3) \\ 0 & 1 \end{bmatrix}\mathbf{R}_t \qquad (4.17)$$

or

$$H(L)\mathbf{Q}_t = J(L)\mathbf{R}_t \qquad (4.18)$$

The unknown coefficients C^0_{11}, C^0_{12} in $J(L)$ are determined from the condition that the solution $\mathbf{Q}_t$ not explode as t goes to infinity. The solution to equation (4.18) depends on finding the roots of the determinant polynomial det $H(\rho) = 0$, where $H(\rho) = A_1\rho^2 + (A_2 + A_3)\rho + A_4$. We find for our model that

$$det\, H(\rho) = -p^3(\rho-\upsilon)\left[\rho^2 - \left(2 + \frac{\theta_0+\theta_1}{\beta}\ \frac{\eta(1+\delta/\beta)}{\eta\lambda+\delta}\right)\rho\right.$$

$$\left. + \left(1 + \frac{\theta^0}{\beta} + \frac{\eta}{\eta\lambda+\delta}\right)\right]$$

There are three zero roots, corresponding to the non-state variables p, y and r, a stable root $0 < \upsilon < 1$ coming from the lag in the aggregate supply equation, and one stable and one unstable root corresponding to the predetermined and non-predetermined variable f and e respectively. Thus the model satisfies the condition for a unique solution, that there exist as many unstable roots as non-predetermined state variables.

Since our focus is on the determinants of the risk premium, we wish to examine the conditional variance of the exchange rate, defined as $\sigma^2_{e,1} = E_{t-1}(e_t - E_{t-1}e_t)^2$. We can write this as $\sigma^2_{e,1} = C_2^{0\prime}SC_2^0$, where C_2^0 is the second row of the zero-order component of the matrix polynomial $C(L)$ and $S = EU_t'U_t)$ is the covariance matrix of the disturbances to the system.

A change in regime that results in different values of the monetary policy and exchange rate policy parameters will lead to a new stochastic process for the exchange rate and a new value of the conditional variance. Our empirical work will attempt to test for such effects, taking account of the restrictions implied by equation (4.17).

3. A PARTIAL EQUILIBRIUM MODEL

This stage in our work focuses on the dollar–Deutsche mark exchange rate and treats West Germany as a small economy relative to the United States. We further simplify the model by considering a partial equilibrium version which uncouples the exchange market from the macroeconomy by omitting the exchange rate from the *IS* curve in equation (4.2). In addition, we add the lagged real exchange rate to the current account equation (4.6). Our simplified model can then be written in terms of the (log of the) real exchange rate $q_t = e_t + p^* - p_t$ and the differential in expected real interest rates $s_t = r_t - E_t\pi_{t+1}$ and s_t^*, defined similarly, where $E_t\pi_{t+1} = E_t p_{t+1} - p_t$ is the expected inflation rate. Using the modified equations (4.6) and (4.13), we have

$$\Delta f_t = \eta_0 q_t + \eta_1 q_{t-1} + \theta_0 \Delta e_t + \theta_1(q_t - \bar{e}_t + p_t - p_t^*) + \mu(y_t^* - y_t) + x_t \qquad (4.20)$$

$$E_t q_{t+1} = q_t + \beta^{-1} f_t + s_t - s_t^* - \beta^{-1} w_t. \qquad (4.21)$$

If inflation rates at home and abroad diverge, then the target nominal exchange rate $\bar{e}_t$ must crawl. During the pegged exchange rate period, US and German average inflation rates hardly differed, although they varied from year to year. Thus we can simplify by taking $\bar{e}_t$ constant during the pegged rate period.

The model may be written in Blanchard–Kahn format as

$$\begin{bmatrix} 1 & 0 & 0 \\ -\beta^{-1} & 1 & 0 \\ 0 & 0 & 1 \end{bmatrix} \begin{bmatrix} f_t \\ E_t \quad q_{t+1} \\ q_t \end{bmatrix} = \begin{bmatrix} 1 & \tilde{\eta} & h_1-\eta_1^{-\theta_0} \\ 0 & 1 & 0 \\ 0 & 1 & 0 \end{bmatrix} \begin{bmatrix} f_{t-1} \\ q_t \\ q_{t-1} \end{bmatrix} + \begin{bmatrix} u_t \\ v_t \\ C \end{bmatrix} \tag{4.22}$$

where $\tilde{\eta} = \eta_0 + \underline{\theta}_0 + \theta_1$, $u_t = x_t + \mu(y_t^* - y_t) + \theta_0(\Delta p_t - \Delta p_t^*) - \theta_1(e + p_t^* - p_t)$, and $v_t = s_t - s_t^* - \beta^{-1}w_t$. Equivalently

$$\begin{bmatrix} f_t \\ E_t q_{t+1} \\ q_t \end{bmatrix} = \begin{bmatrix} 1 & \eta & \eta_1-\theta_0 \\ \beta^{-1} & 1+\beta^{-1}\tilde{\eta} & \beta^{-1}(\eta_1-\theta_0) \\ 0 & 1 & 0 \end{bmatrix} \begin{bmatrix} f_{t-1} \\ q_t \\ q_{t-1} \end{bmatrix} \begin{bmatrix} u_t \\ v_t+\beta^{-1}u_t \\ 0 \end{bmatrix}. \tag{4.23}$$

The roots of this system are $\rho_3 = 0$ and $\rho_{1,2} = 1 + 0.5\tilde{\eta}\beta^{-1}(1+\Delta)$, where $\Delta = \sqrt{1+4\beta\tilde{\eta}^{-2}\eta^*}$, defining $\eta^* = \eta_0 + \eta_1 + \theta_1$. Let us assume that the exogenous variables are all zero and that the disturbances are uncorrelated over time. Then the solution of the system is

$$f_t = \rho_1 f_{t-1} + \frac{\eta^*}{\rho_2\eta^* + \eta_1 - \theta_0} u_t - \frac{\tilde{\eta}}{\rho_2} v_t - \frac{\eta_1-\theta_0}{\rho_2} v_{t-1} \tag{4.24}$$

$$q_t = -\frac{1-\rho_1-\beta^{-1}(\eta_1-\theta_0)}{\eta^*}\mathrm{f}_{t-1} - \frac{\rho_2-1}{\rho_2\tilde{\eta}+\eta_1-\theta_0} u_t - \frac{1}{\rho_2} v_t + \frac{(\rho_2-1)(\eta_1-\theta_0)}{\rho_2\beta\eta^*} v_{t-1} \tag{4.25}$$

This implies that the conditional variance of the (nominal and real) exchange rate is

$$\sigma^2_{e,1} = \frac{(\rho_2 - 1)^2 \sigma^2_u}{[\rho_2 \tilde{\eta} + \eta_1 - \theta_0]^2} + \frac{\sigma^2_v}{\rho^2_2} \qquad (4.26)$$

assuming $\sigma_{uv} = 0$. Therefore changes in policy regime that affect any of the elements of (4.26) will give rise to a potential 'Harrod' effect. In particular, we expect changes in the exchange rate regime to change the value of $\tilde{\eta} = \eta_0 + \theta_0 + \theta_1$. Likewise, we expect changes in the monetary policy regime to affect the variance of v by affecting the variability of the interest differential. Our empirical work endeavours to test for the implied changes in β and in the conditional variance, since β should vary inversely with the conditional variance, according to (4.12).

The Harrod effect can be demonstrated graphically as follows. Equations (4.20) and (4.21) can be regarded as equations of state for q and f, leading to the phase diagram shown in Figure 4.1.

The *FF* curve represents equation (4.20) and is horizontal at the level $q = e + p^* - p = 0$. Above it, the private sector

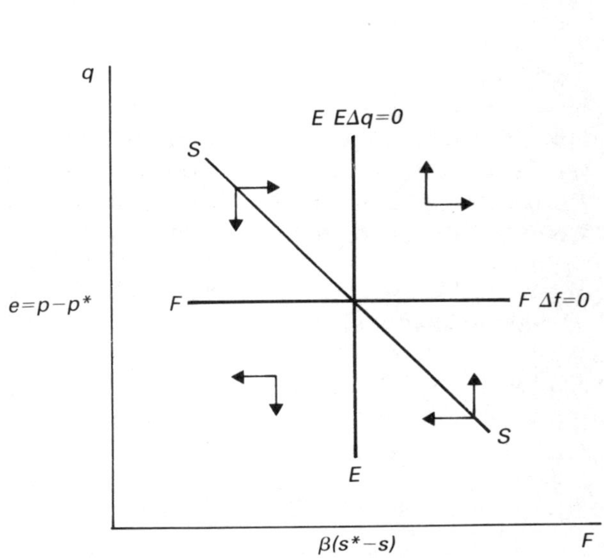

Figure 4.1

is accumulating, foreign assets and vice versa below it. The *EE* curve represents equation (4.21) and is vertical at the level $\beta(s^* - s)$. To its right, foreign assets exceed the level justified by the real interest differential, requiring an expected appreciation of the foreign currency as well, vice versa to the left. The slope of the saddle path *SS* is given by the eigenvector associated with the stable root ρ_1, and is equal to $\{-0.5\ \tilde{\eta}[1 + \sqrt{(1+4\beta\eta^*\tilde{\eta}^{-2})}]\}^{-1}$. From this expression it can be seen that a decline in β steepens the (negative) slope of the saddle path, while a rise in $\theta_0+\theta_1$ will flatten it.

Suppose that the equilibrium is repeatedly displaced by interest rate fluctuations, raising the variability of the exchange rate and its conditional variance. Then β will decline, leading to a steeper saddle path, further raising the variability of the exchange rate. Alternatively, suppose that intervention policy is used to flatten the saddle path. Then the conditional variance will fall, β will rise, and the slope of the saddle path will again become flatter. This is the 'Harrod' effect.

4. ESTIMATION

Our empirical work on the partial equilibrium model is based on OLS estimation of the vector autoregressive solution for the endogenous variables *e* and *f*. We assume that the (exogenous) variables for the interest differential, relative price, and relative real income follow first-order autoregressive processes as in (4.16), with the diagonal matrix *D* having diagonal elements (γ, α, δ). Define the vectors $\mathbf{X}_t = (f_t, e_t)'$, $\mathbf{Z}_t = (r_t - r_t^*, p_t - p_t^*, y_t - y_t^*)'$, and $\mathbf{U}_t = (x_t, v_t)'$, where $v_t = -\beta^{-1}w_t$. Equation (4.15) can then be written as

$$\begin{bmatrix} 0 & 0 \\ 0 & -1 \end{bmatrix} E_t\mathbf{X}_{t+1} + \begin{bmatrix} 1 & -\eta \\ \beta^{-1} & 1 \end{bmatrix} \mathbf{X}_t + \begin{bmatrix} -1 & \theta_0 - \eta_1 \\ 0 & 0 \end{bmatrix} \mathbf{X}_{t-1} =$$

$$\begin{bmatrix} 0 & \eta_0 & \mu \\ -1 & 0 & 0 \end{bmatrix} \mathbf{Z}_t + \begin{bmatrix} 0 & \eta_1 & 0 \\ 0 & 0 & 0 \end{bmatrix} \mathbf{Z}_{t-1} + \mathbf{U}_t. \qquad (4.27)$$

We assume that the disturbance x_t is uncorrelated, but that v_t has first-order autocorrelation, $v_t = d_2 v_{t-1} + \omega_t$, where the coefficient β^{-1} has been absorbed into the definition of v_t. Also, let $\mu = 0$, since empirically income effects do not appear significant.

Under these assumptions, the solution of (4.27), using the methods of Section 2, is

$$
\begin{bmatrix} f_t \\ e_t \end{bmatrix} = \begin{bmatrix} \dfrac{\eta^* + (\rho_2 - 1) d_2 \tilde{\eta}}{\lambda} & \dfrac{\eta^*(\eta^* - \tilde{\eta} + d_2 \tilde{\eta})}{\lambda} \\ \dfrac{-(\rho_2 - 1)(1 - d_2)}{\lambda} & 1 - \dfrac{(\rho_2 - d_2)}{\eta^* \lambda} \end{bmatrix} \begin{bmatrix} f_{t-1} \\ e_{t-1} \end{bmatrix}
$$

$$
+ \begin{bmatrix} -\dfrac{\tilde{\eta}}{\rho_2 - \gamma} & -\eta_0 + \dfrac{\beta^{-1} \tilde{\eta}(\rho_2 \eta_0 + \eta_1)}{(\rho_2 - 1)(\rho_2 - \alpha)} \\ -\dfrac{1}{\rho_2 - \gamma} & \dfrac{(\rho_2 - 1)(\rho_2 \eta_0 + \eta_1)}{\lambda(\rho_2 - \alpha)} \end{bmatrix} \begin{bmatrix} r_t - r_t^* \\ p_t - p_t^* \end{bmatrix}
$$

$$
+ \begin{bmatrix} \dfrac{\tilde{\eta} d_2}{\rho_2 - \gamma} & -\dfrac{\eta_1 \eta^*}{\lambda} + \dfrac{\tilde{\eta}(\rho_2 - 1)(\alpha \eta_0 + \eta_1) d_2}{\lambda(\rho_2 - \alpha)} \\ \dfrac{d_2}{\rho_2 - \gamma} & \dfrac{(\rho_2 - 1)[\eta_1(\rho_2 \alpha) + d_2(\alpha \eta_0 + \eta_1)]}{\lambda(\rho_2 - \alpha)} \end{bmatrix} \begin{bmatrix} r_{t-1} - r_{t-1}^* \\ p_{t-1} - p_{t-1}^* \end{bmatrix} + \begin{bmatrix} x_t \\ \varphi_t \end{bmatrix}, \tag{4.28}
$$

where λ is defined as $\eta^* + (\rho_2 - 1)\tilde{\eta} > 0$ and ρ_2 is the root previously given as greater than unity following equation (4.23). In our empirical study, we simply try to determine whether the shift from a pegged exchange rate for the Deutsche mark over the period 1963–1969 to more flexible rates during 1970–1983 has had the predicted effects on variances and the values of the parameter β and the roots of the system.

We expect the coefficients to change as shown in Table 4.1, since an increase in σ_ω^2 causes β to fall, ρ_1 to fall, and ρ_2 to rise. In general, we expect coefficients to become smaller in absolute value in the floating rate period, with one exception in the last column of the first row of Table 4.1. Since the residual variances are expected to increase from the first regime to the second, weighted least squares

Table 4.1: Expected changes in coefficients

		Dependent variable			
		f_t		e_t	
Independent variable	Regime	Peg	Float	Peg	Float
f_{t-1}		++	+	−	−−
e_{t-1}		++	+	++	+
$r_t - r_t^*$		−−	−	−−	−
$p_t - p_t^*$		?	?	+	+
$r_{t-1} - r_{t-1}^*$		++	+	++	+
$p_{t-1} - p_{t-1}^*$		?	?	−	−

was used to improve the efficiency of estimation. Careful analysis of preliminary OLS results showed that the shift in variances occurs in two steps, the first in 1969 when the mark began to float and the second in 1973 when generalized floating began. Thus it seemed appropriate to test for shifts at both points.

The quarterly data for this test cover the period 1963–1983. The end-of-period dollar exchange rate of the mark, relative Treasury bill rates, and relative consumer price indexes were taken from the International Financial Statistics tape. The net stock of German foreign assets was calculated by cumulating the current account less the official settlements balance, data being obtained from the Monthly Bulletin of the Deutsche Bundesbank.

Table 4.2 shows weighted least squares results based on changes in the variances occurring in 1973. Coefficients are allowed to change with the regime change in 1973, except that the coefficient of the lagged exchange rate also is allowed to change in 1969, when the mark first floated temporarily. Allowing for this coefficient, Table 4.1 predicts the signs of twenty-two coefficients, of which fifteen have

*Table 4.2: Weighted least squares regressions**

	Dependent variable			
	f		e	
Independent variables Regime	Peg	Float**	Peg	Float**
f_{t-1}	0.531 (3.16)	0.833[b] (1.63)	−0.057(−02) (−0.16)	−0.414(−02)[b] (−0.90)
e_{t-1}	6.777 (1.84)	7.149[a]1.066[b] (0.48) (1.18)	0.994 (9.23)	0.935[a]0.753[b] (3.44) (1.67)
$r_t - r_t^*$	1.329 (1.41)	−0.599[b] (−1.52)	0.238(−01) (1.64)	−0.426(−1)[b] (−2.98)
$p_t - p_t^*$	65.6 (0.44)	−147.1[b] (−0.97)	−2.45 (1.07)	1.50[b] (1.00)
$r_{t-1} - r_{t-1}^*$	−1.156 (−1.14)	−0.132[b] (0.79)	−0.064(−01) (−0.40)	0.198(−01)[b] (1.17)
$p_{t-1} - p_{t-1}^*$	−260.7 (−1.91)	130.4[b] (1.94)	0.574 (0.26)	−1.042[b] (−0.43)
Residual variance	16.69	34.12	0.353(−02)	1.41(−02)
$\bar{R}^2$	0.918		0.997	
Q_{24}	24.4		35.2	
$F_{7,57}$	3.57		3.19	

* Each regression contained a constant term, three seasonal dummies and the oil price. *t*-ratios are shown in parentheses below the coefficients, scaling factors behind them. *Q* is chi-squared test for autocorrelated residuals

** The *t*-ratios for the floating period test for the *difference* between the pegged and floating period coefficients.

[a] Semifloating period 1969:3–1973:1.

[b] Floating period 1973:2–1983:2.

the predicted sign in Table 4.2. In the floating-rate period, all but one of the signs is correct. The *Q*-test for autocorrelated residuals is not significant in the equation for the stock of foreign assets but is significant at the 7 per cent level in the exchange rate equation, suggesting perhaps some further omitted variables.

The central issue is, of course, the changes in the coefficients between the pegged and floating-rate period. As noted earlier, most coefficients are expected to be smaller in absolute value, with the exception of the lagged stock of foreign assets in the exchange rate equation. In some, but not all, cases this is fulfilled. Among the lagged endogenous variables, only the lagged stock of foreign assets in the foreign asset equation moves counter to the predicted direction, and that not significantly so. In the other three cases the direction of movement is as predicted. In particular, the coefficient of the lagged exchange rate in the exchange rate equation drops significantly below unity in the floating-rate period. Using the Dickey–Fuller (1981) test for a unit root, $\phi_1 = 4.11$ rejects the random walk hypothesis at the 10 per cent level.

Among the coefficients of the current and lagged relative prices and interest rates, sign changes between the two periods are frequently found, although only two of these are statistically significant. Thus the evidence of predicted changes in coefficients is less impressive here, perhaps because of the weakness of the underlying exogeneity hypothesis.

The *F*-tests for joint significance of the changes in coefficients are both highly significant, showing that coefficient changes indeed occurred. Based on these results, which do not impose all of the cross-equation restrictions implicit in the solution (4.28), we would argue that there is favourable evidence of coefficient shifts of the type we hypothesize, but that further work taking account of those restrictions is required to confirm this evidence.

NOTES

This is a revised version of a paper prepared for the AEA Meetings, Dallas, 28 December 1984. This research has been supported by an experimental study grant in International Economic Policy awarded to the Brookings Institute by the National Science Foundation. Computational assistance was provided by Brian Cody.

REFERENCES

Barro, R. J. and Gordon, D. (1983) 'A positive theory of monetary policy in a natural-rate model', *Journal of Political Economy,* **91** (August), 589–610.

Black, S. W. (1983) 'The use of monetary policy for internal and external balance in ten industrial countries', in Frenkel, J. A. (ed.) *Exchange Rates and International Macroeconomics*. U. of Chicago Press for NBER, Chicago, pp. 189–225.

Black, S. W. (1984a) 'The effect of alternative intervention policies on the variability of exchange rates: the Harrod effect', in Bhandari, J. S. (ed.) *Exchange Rate Management Under Uncertainty*. MIT Press, Cambridge, pp. 73–82.

Black, S. W. (1984b) 'Changing causes of exchange rate fluctuations', *Brookings Discussion Papers in International Economics,* No. 12 (January).

Blanchard, O. J. and Kahn, C. M. (1980) 'The solution of linear difference models under rational expectations', *Econometrica,* **48** (July), 1305–1311.

Canzoneri, M. B. (1985) 'Monetary policy games and the role of private information', *American Economic Review,* **75**, 1056–1070.

Cukierman, A. and Meltzer, A. H. (1984) 'A positive theory of credibility and monetary inflation', presented at December meeting, American Economic Association, Dallas.

Dickey, D. A. and Fuller, W. A. (1981) 'Likelihood ratio statistics for autoregressive time series with a unit root', *Econometrica,* **49**, 1057–1072.

Fellner, W. (1976) *Towards a Reconstruction of Macroeconomics: Problems of Theory and Policy*. American Enterprise Institute, Washington.

Flood, R. P. and Garber, P. M. (1983) 'A model of stochastic process switching', *Econometrica,* **51** (May), 537–551.

Flood, R. P. and Marion, N. P. (1982) 'The transmission of disturbances under alternative exchange rate regimes with optimal indexing', *Quarterly Journal of Economics,* **97**, 43–66.

Gray, J. A. (1976) 'Wage indexation: a macroeconomic approach', *Journal of Monetary Economics,* **2**, 221–235.

Hansen, L. P. and Hodrick, R. J. (1980) 'Forward exchange rates as optimal predictors of future spot rates: an econometric analysis', *Journal of Political Economy,* **88**, 829–853.

Hansen, L. P. and Hodrick, R. J. (1983) 'Risk averse speculation in the forward foreign exchange market: an econometric analysis of linear models', in Frenkel, J. A. (ed.) *Exchange Rates and International Macroeconomics*. U. of Chicago Press for NBER, Chicago, pp. 113–42.

Meese, R. and Rogoff, K. (1983) 'The out-of-sample failure of empirical exchange rate models: sampling error or misspecification?', in Frenkel, J. A. (ed.) *Exchange Rates and International Macroeconomics*. U. of Chicago Press for NBER, Chicago, pp. 65–105.

Salemi, M. K. (1983) 'Time-varying risk premia and the forward foreign exchange market', presented at the Winter Meeting of the Econometric Society, 28–30 December, San Francisco.

Walsh, Carl (1984) 'Interest rate volatility and monetary policy', *Journal of Money, Credit, and Banking,* **16** (May), 133–150.

5 An Empirical Model of the Exchange Rate Incorporating Rational Expectations

S. G. Hall

This chapter outlines a simple framework for testing some of the underlying concepts which form the basis of a number of recent models of exchange rate determination. Much of this work (e.g. Frenkel, 1979; Dornbusch, 1976; Buiter and Miller 1981) has proceeded by setting out small but complete macro models and solving the model for a reduced form exchange rate equation. It is this reduced-form equation which is then estimated and tested. One problem with this approach is that it is difficult, if not impossible, to isolate which part of the model has failed in the cases when the reduced-form equation has been rejected. So we are unable to say whether the problem actually lies in the exchange rate section of the model or if the false hypothesis lies elsewhere, for example the money demand function. This chapter will concentrate solely on the structural exchange rate equation and will not work through reduced-form equations of the whole economy.

Apart from the obvious desire to test some generally accepted assumptions about asset and foreign exchange markets, a secondary reason for concentrating on the structural level is that the final estimated equation may be incorporated into the National Institute Model 8.

A GENERAL BACKGROUND

The foreign exchange markets are perhaps the closest real work example of a perfect market; the exchange rate fluctuates continually so that the market actually does clear continuously. So at any point in time we know that

$$E_0 = \frac{\Delta A_D + X}{\Delta A_F + M} \tag{5.1}$$

where ΔA_F is the foreign price flow of assets into this country, M is the foreign price value of imports, ΔA_D is the domestic price flow of assets leaving this country and X is the domestic price value of exports. All that equation (5.1) says is that the exchange rate is the ratio of foreign currency coming on to the market to be exchanged for sterling to the amount of sterling coming to be exchanged for foreign currency. This equation is an identity and has no behavioural significance except that it reveals immediately an important division in the possible approaches to the exchange rate. This division is between asset market models and trade models. It is often assumed that asset markets are more flexible and adjust more quickly and so it is the relative flows of assets which determine short run movements in exchange rates. However, as in the long run the trade balance must be in balance, the long run determinant of the exchange rate is the trade terms.

Many models are based around the open arbitrage condition, which suggests simply that assets will move so as to maximize the expected value of the asset stock. If we consider the problem of allocating a stock of assets, A, between domestic assets, A_1, and foreign assets, A_2, when domestic assets yield a return of r_D and foreign assets yield r_F, then we can maximize the value of total assets in the next period subject to a constraint on the quantity of total assets available. This may be formulated in the following Lagrangian function

$$\text{Max } V = A_1(1 + r_D) + A_2\frac{E_0}{E_1}(1 + r_F) + \lambda(A_1 + A_2 - A) \tag{5.2}$$

this will yield

$$(1 + r_D) + \lambda = 0$$

$$\frac{E_0}{E_1}(1 + r_F + \lambda = 0$$

$$A_1 + A_2 = A \qquad (5.3)$$

as the first-order conditions. The first two may be used to derive the open arbitrage condition

$$\frac{r_D - r_F}{1 + r_F} = \frac{E_0}{E_1} - 1 \qquad (5.4)$$

In this simple form the model will not have an internal solution, but if the flow of assets which results when (5.4) is not satisfied causes a change in E_0 the model will have an internal solution. This model implies, however, that when the exchange rate is at its equilibrium level ($E_0 = E_1$) all interest rate differentials are zero and it assumes that when there is no zero interest rate differential the flow of assets is always sufficient to move the exchange rate sufficiently to maintain (5.4). A slightly more general model would be one which allows for an equilibrium determination of asset stocks for any given interest rate differential. Perhaps the main way of deriving this result is by allowing for the effect of risk in the maximization of equation (5.2).

We might therefore restate (5.2) as

$$\text{Max } V = A_1(1 + r_D) + A_2\frac{E_0}{E_1}(1 + r_F) + \frac{b}{2}A_1^2V_D$$

$$+ \frac{b}{2}A_2^2V_F + \lambda(A_1 + A_2 - A) \qquad (5.5)$$

where V_D, V_F are the variances of the yields on domestic and foreign investment in domestic currency, $b < 0$ is the loss of welfare due to the riskiness of the assets. This will yield

$$(1 + r_D) + bA_1V_D + \lambda = 0$$

$$\frac{E_0}{E_1}(1 + r_F) + bA_2V_F + \lambda = 0$$

$$A_1 + A_2 = A \qquad (5.6)$$

This yields a generalization of the open arbitrage equation as follows

$$\frac{r_D - r_F + b(A_1V_D - A_2V_F)}{1 + r_F} = \frac{E_0}{E_1} - 1 \tag{5.7}$$

This suggests that uncertainty will drive a variable wedge into the open arbitrage equation. It further suggests that the flow of funds across the exchange market will not continue indefinitely while an interest rate differential exists as the variable wedge will move to make (5.7) hold.

It is now also possible to solve (5.6) for a determinate demand function for the relative asset stocks. The general demand function for A_2 is

$$A_2 = \frac{r_D - r_F + bAV_D - (1 + r_F)\left(\dfrac{E_0}{E_1} - 1\right)}{b(V_D + V_F)} \tag{5.8}$$

and for the special case where $E_0 = E_1$

$$A_2 = \frac{r_D - r_F + bAV_D}{b(V_D + V_F)} \tag{5.9}$$

Equation (5.1) derives the current exchange rate as a function of the change in asset stocks, so we may differentiate (5.8) with respect to $(r_D - r_F)$ and E_0/E_1 to give

$$dA_2 = \frac{1}{b(V_D + V_F)} d(r_D - r_F) + \frac{(1 + r_F)}{bV_D + bV_F} \cdot \frac{E_0}{E_1^2} dE_1 \tag{5.10}$$

So as

$$b < 0, \frac{\delta A_2}{\delta(r_D - r_F)} < 0, \frac{\delta A_2}{\delta E_1} < 0$$

or in general notation in discrete time

$$\Delta A_2 = f_1[\Delta(r_D - r_F), (E_1 - E_0)] \text{ where } f_1^1 < 0, f_1^2 < 0$$

Similarly by an analogous argument

$$\Delta A_1 = f_2[\Delta(r_D - r_F), (E_1 - E_0)] \text{ where } f_2^1 > 0, f_2^2 > 0$$

So we may restate (5.1) as

$$E_0 = \frac{f_2\,(\Delta(r_D - r_F); E_1 - E_0) + X)}{f_1(\Delta(r_D - r_F); E_1 - E_0 + M)} \tag{5.11}$$

On the basis of equation (5.11) I now posit a log linearization on the assumption that asset stocks are sufficiently dominant to remove any role for trade.

$$\text{Log}(E_0^*) = \alpha(r_{Dt} - r_{Ft}) + B(r_{Dt-1} - r_{Ft-1}) + \phi\log(E_1) \tag{5.12}$$

where E_0^* is the exchange rate which the market would set in the absence of any government intervention or any form of adjustment costs. In (5.12) if $B = 0$, $\alpha > 0$ and $\phi = 1$, then the equation is simply the open arbitrage equation set out in (5.4). If $-B = \alpha > 0$ then it is a pure difference term in the real interest rate differential and it suggests an asset stock model in which assets fully adjust to a change in interest rates within the time period.

Equation (5.12) is not, however, the whole story; such equations give no role for the lagged exchange rate, which is typically found to be the most important explanatory variable. Given equation (5.12) we would also tend to see very large jumps in the exchange rate; the exchange rate, however, seems not to move in large discrete jumps but instead it follows clear trends, either rising or falling for many months at a time. One reason for this may be that governments perceive considerable costs associated with large or erratic movements in the exchange rate. While government action may not be able to alter the long term level of the exchange rate radically, it does seem likely that government has the power to smooth out fluctuations in the exchange rate and that they actually use this power in practice (the famous 'leaning into the wind' practice). A useful way of formalizing this notion is to set up a cost minimization problem for the central authorities where there are costs attached both to a divergence between the actual exchange rate and E_0^* and to the rate at which the exchange rate changes.

So let (now defining E_t to be the log of the exchange rate)

$$C = \sum_{t=0}^{T} \frac{a}{2}(E_t - E_t^*)^2 + \frac{d}{2}(E_t - E_{t-1})^2 \qquad (5.13)$$

where $E_t = g(I_t)$. I represents government intervention, either through official financing flows on the foreign exchange market or through direct intervention in the markets.

If we maximize this expression with respect to I we get the following set of first-order conditions

$$ag'[g(I_t) - E_t^*] + dg'[g(I_t) - g(I_{t-1})] - dg'[g(I_{t+1}) - g(I_t)] = 0 \qquad (5.14)$$

$t = 0 \ldots T - 1$

with a special form of this equation for T.

Dividing through by g' equation (5.14) will yield

$$E_t = \frac{a}{a + 2d} E_t^* + \frac{d}{a+2d}(E_{t-1} + E_{t+1}) \qquad (5.15)$$

and using (5.12)

$$E_t = \frac{a}{a + 2d}[\alpha(r_{Dt} - r_{Ft}) + B(r_{Dt-1} - r_{Ft-1}) + \phi E_{t+1}] + \frac{d}{a + 2d}(E_{t-1} + E_{T+1}) \qquad (5.16)$$

So

$$E_t = \frac{a}{a + 2d}[\alpha(r_{Dt} - r_{Ft}) + B(r_{Dt-1} - r_{Ft-1})] + \frac{\phi a+d}{a+2d} E_{t+1} + \frac{d}{a + 2d} E_{t-1} \qquad (5.17)$$

Equation (5.17) offers an interesting general equation to begin estimation from. If $B = 0$, $\phi = 1$ and $d = 0$ the equation reduces to the open arbitrage equation but if any of these restrictions are violated the simple open arbitrage model is rejected in preference for a more complex one. The coefficients on E_{t+1} and E_{t-1} should both be greater than or equal to zero and they shoud sum to close to unity. (If $\phi = 1$ then they sum to exactly unity.)

ESTIMATION AND RESULTS

The estimation will be carried out over the period 1973 third month to 1984 sixth month using monthly data (see appendix for definition). The term in the expected exchange rate will be estimated using the Wickens (1982) errors in variable technique and an equation will also be specified for the interest rate differential so as to allow for the possible endogeneity of interest rates. The whole of equation (5.17) will be specified in real terms, that is real exchange rates and real interest differentials.

The Wickens technique is an implementation of the rational expectations hypothesis, which allows us to use actual lead data as a measure of expected future variables. The outturns are then taken to be an estimate of expectations, where the data are subject to a white noise measurement error. The model is estimated by a systems estimation technique (either three-stage least squares (3SLS) or full information maximum likelihood (FIML)) where an equation is specified for each of the expectations terms. These equations will generally be an unrestricted reduced form of the model. Specifying these reduced form equations for expectations corrects for the bias produced by the measurement error and the Wickens estimates are shown to be consistent. As the expectations equations do not exploit the structure of the model this technique will not generally be fully efficient.

Before examining the system estimations a useful point of departure is the OLS results. These results are obviously inconsistent but it is useful to have them as a guide to the effect of the systems estimation.

OLS estimates of (5.15)

$$\begin{aligned} E_t = & \underset{(0.5)}{-0.016} + \underset{(18)}{0.52}\, E_{t-1} + \underset{(16.2)}{0.48}\, E_{t+1} - \underset{(4.1)}{0.003}\,(r_{Dt} - r_{Ft}) \\ & + \underset{(3.6)}{0.003}\,(r_{Dt-1} - r_{Ft-1}) \end{aligned} \qquad (5.18)$$

$$\Sigma e^2 = 0.014;\ \mathrm{DW} = 2.6;\ \mathrm{SEE} = 0.010;\ \bar{R} = 0.994$$

This is a well-fitting equation but it violates many of the main conditions of (5.17). For example, if $\phi = 1$ then as $(a+b) > b$ (for a, $b > 0$), the coefficient on E_{t+1} must be greater than the coefficient on E_{t-1}. This is not true of equation (5.18). Also this parameter on the current interest rate term is significant but carries the wrong sign. This is a common finding in exchange rate equations (see Hall, 1983), so the OLS estimates seem to reject the general theory outlined in (5.15).

Happily this need not be the end of the story. There are at least two main problems with the OLS results; the first, highlighted by Haache and Townend (1981) and Hall (1983), is that interest rates are endogenous and so are subject to simultaneous equation bias. The second problem is that the expected exchange rate term cannot be validly modelled simply by using the forward actual exchange rate. In order to cope with both these problems a three-equation model has been estimated using 3SLS and FIML where both the forward exchange rate and the interest rate differential are specified as endogenous in addition to the exchange rate. The expected exchange rate equation will not be reported as this equation has no structural significance within the Wickens framework.

In this paper the interest rate equation is not the prime concern so a specific conceptual model will not be developed for it. Instead a fairly simple specification will be used which makes interest rates a function of the endogenous exchange rate, two lagged dependent variables and two terms in the rate of change of relative inflation (ΔP_t). The lagged dependent variables may be thought of as correcting a non-white-noise error process induced by some missing explanatory variables. In this interpretation part of the equation is a simple time series model of interest rate movements. If we view the exchange rate term as a government reaction term (i.e. the famous 'leaning into the wind' policy) then we would expect a negative coefficient. The sign of this effect becomes ambiguous, however, if we interpret the term as a market response to the overall expected return on assets.

Table 5.1: The unrestricted exchange rate and interest rate equation

	Dependent variable E_0			
Independent variable	3SLS		FIML	
Constant	−0.04	(1.2)	−0.05	(1.1)
E_{-1}	0.35	(5.7)	0.22	(7.2)
E_{+1}	0.65	(10.2)	0.79	(26.8)
$(r_D - r_F)_t$	0.0005	(0.3)	0.0024	(2.1)
$(r_D - r_F)_{t-1}$	−0.0009	(0.6)	−0.0031	(2.7)
	$\Sigma e^2 = 0.019$		$\Sigma e^2 = 0.0286$	
	DW = 2.3		DW = 1.96	
	Dependent variable $(r_D - r_F)_t$			
Constant	0.34	(1.2)	0.48	
$(E_t - E_{t-1})$	−21.8	(1.7)	−1.8	(0.21)
ΔP_t	−51.2	(5.0)	−56.5	(4.3)
ΔP_{t-1}	48.0	(4.6)	51.6	(3.8)
$(r_D - r_F)_{t-1}$	0.96	(13.2)	0.96	(10.8)
$(r_D - r_F)_{t-2}$	0.006	(0.08)	−0.03	(0.4)
	$\Sigma e^2 = 170.1$		$\Sigma e^2 = 185.6$	
	DW = 1.93		DW = 1.9	
	3SLS Minimand = 36.6		Log likelihood function = 515.6	

The results for the unrestricted model are reported in Table 5.1; the picture presented for the exchange rate equation is now radically different. In the 3SLS estimates the term on the future exchange rate is now much larger than the lagged exchange rate, as equation (5.15) would suggest. The two parameters still sum close to unity, and the current real interest rate terms are now positive but not significant. The real interest rate equation is fairly well determined with correctly signed parameters. The FIML estimates are perhaps even more satisfactory than the 3SLS estimates. The expected exchange rate term has an even larger parameter, while the interest rates are now both correctly signed and significant.

Table 5.2 shows the effect of imposing the following restrictions on the expected and lagged exchange rate terms

$$\alpha(E_{-1}) + (1 - \alpha)E_{+1}$$

A likelihood ratio test of the imposed restriction in Table 5.2 gives a test statistic of 1.6 (the 95 per cent significance level for the chi-squared (1) distribution is 3.4), so the restriction is easily accepted by the data. The Table 5.2 results differ from those in Table 5.1 with respect to the

Table 5.2: Imposing the unit restriction on the model

	Dependent variable E_0			
Independent variable	3SLS		FIML	
Constant	−0.0009	(0.82)	0.0013	(1.3)
α	0.38	(6.5)	0.246	(8.2)
$(r_D - r_F)_t$	−0.00009	(0.06)	0.0024	(2.3)
$(r_D - r_F)t_{-1}$	−0.0003	(0.8)	−0.0029	(1.3)
	$\Sigma e^2 = 0.017$, DW = 2.3		$\Sigma e^2 = 0.0267$, DW = 2.0	
	Dependent variable $(r_D - r_F)_t$			
Constant	0.34	(1.2)	0.49	
$(E_t - E_{t-1})$	−21.9	(1.7)	−2.5	(0.3)
ΔP_t	−51.4	(5.0)	−56.2	(4.3)
ΔP_{t-1}	48.2	(4.1)	51.1	(3.8)
$(r_D - r_F)_{t-1}$	0.96	(13.2)	0.958	(11.0)
$(r_D - r_F)_{t-2}$	0.007	(0.1)	−0.029	(0.4)
	$\Sigma e^2 = 170.1$		$\Sigma e^2 = 184.6$	
	DW = 1.93		DW = 1.9	
	3SLS Minimand = 38.66		Log likelihood function = 514.8	

interest rate effects, the FIML estimates now look much more like a difference term. A further restriction on the model was therefore imposed to see if the interest rate effect could be reparameterized as a difference term. These results are reported in Table 5.3.

The likelihood ratio test of this restriction against the model in Table 5.2 is 4.2 which would reject the restriction. The likelihood ratio test of both restrictions jointly (the model in Table 5.3 as a restricted version of Table 5.1) is 5.8, which is just within the critical limit of 5.99. It would seem, therefore, that we can comfortably accept the restriction that the parameters on the expected and lagged exchange rate term sum to one. The interest rate terms,

Table 5.3: A restricted interest rate effect

	Dependent variable E_0	
Independent variable	3SLS	FIML
Constant	−0.001 (0.1)	−0.0002 (0.2)
α	0.41 (7.4)	0.242 (8.7)
$(r_D - r_F)_t - (r_D - r_F)_{t-1}$	0.0002 (0.1)	0.0042 (3.9)
	$\Sigma e^2 = 0.017$	$\Sigma e^2 = 0.031$
	DW = 2.4	DW = 2.03
	Dependent variable $(r_D - r_F)t$	
Constant	0.32 (13.3)	0.56 (1.9)
$(E_t - E_{t-1})$	−23.2 (1.9)	−0.3 (0.04)
ΔP_t	−46.4 (4.6)	−48.0 (3.9)
ΔP_{t-1}	42.9 (4.2)	41.7 (3.3)
$(r_D - r_F)_{t-1}$	0.93 (13.3)	0.91 (11.5)
$(r_D - r_F)_{t-2}$	0.01 (0.17)	−0.02 (0.3)
	$\Sigma e^2 = 172.6$	$\Sigma e^2 = 191.9$
	DW = 1.9	DW = 1.82
	3SLS Minimand = 43.08	Log likelihood function = 512.7

however, may not form a simple difference. One problem with both the models outlined in Tables 5.1 and 5.2 is that, although the current interest rate term is positive, the net effect is negative and so an increase in interest rates will lower the exchange rate. This is not the case for the restricted model in Table 5.3. To accept the model set out in Table 5.2 would therefore be to reject the underlying theory. However, one explanation of the results is that stocks do adjust to a new equilibrium level but they take more than a month to do it. In order to allow for this a slightly more general restriction was included; this took $B(r_D - r_F)t + \phi(r_D - r_F)_{t-1} - (B + \phi)(r_D - r_F)_{t-2}$. So adjustment may be spread over 2 months but the whole term represents an exact difference none the less. This produced a likelihood ratio test statistic of this restriction (against Table 5.2) of 1.8, which is easily accepted. The full set of results is presented in Table 5.4.

It is interesting that throughout this series of estimations the FIML results have been uniformly more acceptable than the 3SLS results. On the bases of the FIML results we can conclusively reject the simple open arbitrage equation on two grounds. First, the results indicate that stocks of assets will reach an equilibrium even in the presence of a non-zero interest rate differential. Second, there is a significant effect from the lagged exchange rate so that the exchange rate will not move by discrete jumps but will follow a more gradual path.

As an illustration of this point Figure 5.1 shows the step responses of the exchange rate equation. In Figure 5.1b the interest rate is raised in the initial period of the solution; this causes an immediate jump in the exchange rate which then falls smoothly back to its original level. In Figure 5.1a the interest rate is raised in period 8 of the solution. This causes a rise in the exchange rate in anticipation of the move in interest rates; as soon as interest rates do rise, however, the exchange rate falls back to its long run level. The example in (a) corresponds to an anticipated change in interest rates while (b) represents an unanticipated rise. The effect in (a) is particularly interesting. The actual rise in interest rates in period 8 appears to lead to a fall in the

Table 5.4: The preferred, fully restricted model

	Dependent variable E_0	
Independent variable	3SLS	FIML
Constant	−0.0001 (0.1)	−0.0002 (0.2)
α	0.42 (7.5)	0.265 (9.4)
B	0.00015 (0.1)	0.003659 (3.5)
ϕ	−0.00053 (0.3)	−0.003657 (3.0)
	$\Sigma e^2 = 0.0166$	$\Sigma e^2 = 0.028$
	DW = 2.5	DW = 2.1
	Dependent variable $(r_D - r_F)_t$	
Constant	0.35 (1.2)	0.49 (1.6)
$(E_t - E_{t-1})$	−20.94 (1.6)	1.0 (0.1)
ΔP_t	−51.82 (5.0)	−52.6 (4.2)
ΔP_{t-1}	47.82 (4.6)	47.1 (3.6)
$(r_D - r_F)_{t-1}$	0.95 (13.0)	0.93 (10.5)
$(r_D - r_F)_{t-2}$	0.004 (0.06)	−0.03 (0.3)
	$\Sigma e^2 = 170.2$	$\Sigma e^2 = 192.1$
	DW = 1.92	DW = 1.86
	3SLS Minimand = 40.15	Log likelihood function = 513.9

exchange rate, although in fact it is a fall from a high level where the high exchange rate is actually caused by the increase in interest rates. The apparent correlation between a rise in interest rates and a fall in the exchange rate offers an explanation of the common finding of a highly significant negative effect of interest rates on the exchange rate, which contradicts all our normal theoretical models.

So far this analysis has been based around equation (5.17), which assumed that asset markets were sufficiently strong and flexible that they would completely dominate exchange rate movements. This assumption will now be relaxed and a possible effect from trade movements will be

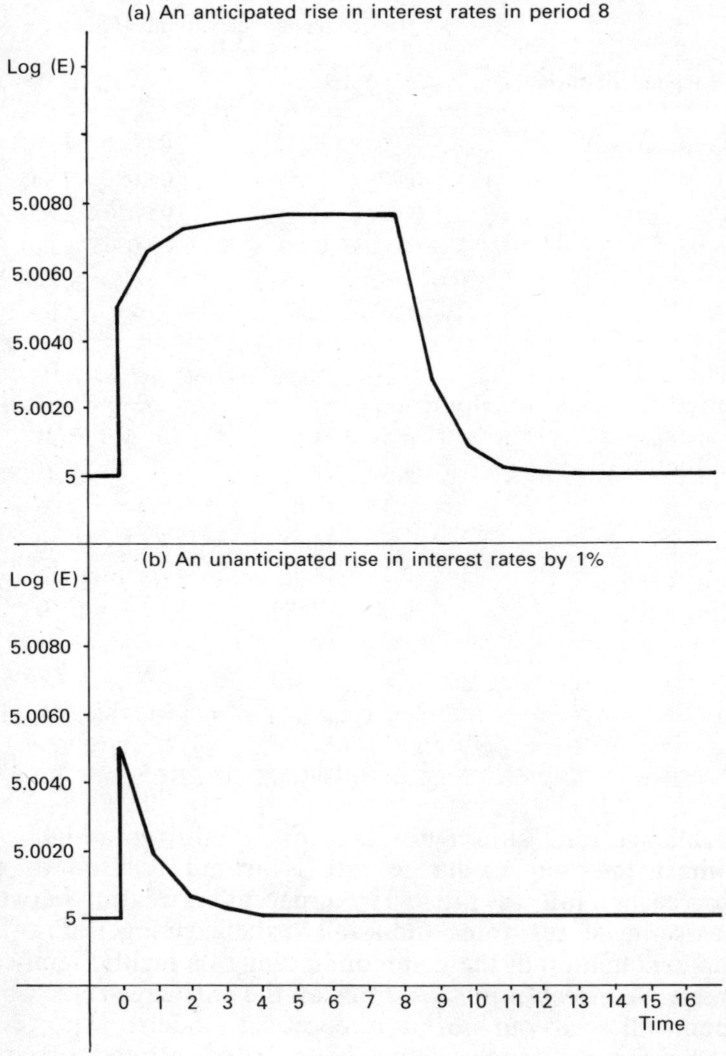

Figure 5.1: Step responses of the exchange rate equation

investigated. A common approach here would be to include a term in the current balance in the exchange rate equation. This, in fact, is not quite correct, if we are estimating a log-linear model. If we consider a log version of the underlying structural equation (5.11) this will be made clear

$$\log(E_0) = \log\{f_2[\Delta(r_D - r_F), \Delta E_1] + X\}$$
$$- \log\{f_2[\Delta(r_D - r_F), \Delta F_1] + M\}$$

Formally, it is not possible to separate out exports from asset outflows or imports from asset inflows. If, however, we make a linearization assumption we may state that

$$\log(E_0) = \alpha\Delta(r_D - r_F) + \beta\log E_1 + \mu\log(X/M)$$

The current balance actually appears as a ratio of foreign price exports to domestic price imports. By following through the earlier arguments we arrive at an equation much like (5.17) but including this term in the ratio of exports to imports.

By the following the same nesting-down procedure as outlined earlier I arrive at a model similar to that presented in Table 5.4 but including a term in the ratio of exports to imports (*LXM*). This model is presented in Table 5.5.

The addition of *LXM* has produced a dramatic increase in the log likelihood function, the parameter on *LXM* in the exchange rate equation is correctly signed with a *t* value of close to two for both the 3SLS and FIML results. The coefficient on the change in the exchange rate in the interest equation has now taken its expected negative sign in the FIML results. It is interesting that despite the obvious improvement in the likelihood function the 3SLS minimand has risen. This is caused by the addition of LXM to the instrument set in the 3SLS estimation process.

To conclude this section. An exchange rate equation has been estimated using the Wickens technique which rejects the open arbitrage condition in three important ways. First, it finds a significant role for the lagged exchange rate, suggesting that the exchange rate cannot jump sufficiently freely to meet the open arbitrage condition. Second, it finds that asset stocks seem to reach equilibrium before the

Table 5.5: A fully restricted version with trade effect

	Dependent variable E_0	
Independent variable	3SLS	FIML
Constant	0.0017 (1.4)	0.0015 (0.9)
α	0.40 (6.8)	0.19 (6.5)
β	−0.0008 (0.5)	0.0044 (3.9)
ϕ	0.0006 (0.4)	−0.0041 (3.2)
LXM	0.016 (2.2)	0.016 (1.95)
	Σe^2 = 0.015	Σe^2 = 0.032
	DW = 2.3	DW = 1.89
	Dependent variable $(r_D - r_F)_t$	
Constant	0.184 (0.7)	0.44 (1.6)
$(E_t - E_{t-1})$	−43.3 (3.9)	−10.56 (1.3)
ΔP_t	−44.0 (4.4)	−48.8 (4.1)
ΔP_{t-1}	43.0 (4.4)	43.9 (3.6)
$(r_D - r_F)_{t-1}$	0.98 (14.0)	0.93 (11.1)
$(r_D - r_F)_{t-2}$	0.03 (0.5)	−0.01 (0.2)
	Σe^2 = 189.9	Σe^2 = 176.89
	DW = 1.92	DW = 1.88
	3SLS Minimand = 45.7	Log likelihood function = 523.242

interest rate differential is removed, so that a non-zero differential does not lead to a constantly changing exchange rate. Finally, it finds a significant role for the current balance in exchange rate determination, thereby rejecting the assumption that in the short run the asset markets completely dominate exchange rate determination.

A QUARTERLY MODEL

The above analysis has been carried out using monthly data. The larger sample this provides is very important when

Table 5.6: The quarterly model (FIML estimates)

	The exchange rate equation	
Constant	0.0004	(0.06)
α	0.1	(1.3)
B	0.009	(2.5)
	$\Sigma e^2 = 0.08$ DW = 2.1	
	The interest rate equation	
Constant	0.8	(1.0)
$(E_t - E_{t-1})$	7.5	(0.69)
ΔP_t	−13.5	(2.8)
ΔP_{t-1}	0	(0)
$(r_D - r_F)_{t-1}$	0.85	(7.7)
$(r_D - r_F)_{t-2}$	−0.23	(2.1)
	$\Sigma e^2 = 270.4$ DW = 1.7	
	Log likelihood function = 78.2	

systems estimation, such as FIML, is being used. It is hoped, however, that an equation of this type will be used in the National Institute's quarterly model, so a quarterly version must be derived. This could be done simply by trying to apply some aggregation procedure but a more satisfactory approach seems to be to re-estimate the model on quarterly data.

The set of results presented below is for an identical model to that presented in Table 5.4 except that some of the data definitions have been altered to correspond with the NIESR model and the two-period lag on the interest rates was found to be unnecessary in the case of quarterly data. This is not surprising; if monthly data suggests that asset stocks achieve equilibrium in 2 months, we would expect quarterly data to suggest equilibrium in one quarter. The likelihood ratio test of the zero parameter restriction on the second lagged interest rate term for quarterly data is 0.8. Table 5.6 presents a set of quarterly results for the model; only FIML results will be reported.

These results are very similar to those of Table 5.4. The effect of interest rates on the exchange rate is correctly signed and significant. As we might expect, with quarterly data the effect of the lagged exchange rate has fallen in magnitude and it is marginally insignificant. However, the earlier conclusions seem to be born out by this quarterly model.

The final set of results, in Table 5.7, presents a quarterly version of Table 5.5, which includes the ratio of exports to imports.

The addition of trade effects to the exchange rate equation has again had a marked effect on the value of the log likelihood function. It has also produced a general rise in the *t* values associated with the exchange rate equation.

The results for the quarterly model therefore confirm the picture presented by the earlier monthly model. The open arbitrage equation is again rejected on three counts of a significant effect from trade, the lagged exchange rate and the lagged interest differential.

Table 5.7: A quarterly model with trade effects (FIML)

	The exchange rate equation	
Constant	0.0016	(0.26)
α	0.215	(3.2)
β	0.010	(4.3)
LXM	0.101	(3.3)
	$\Sigma e^2 = 0.06$	DW = 2.4
	The interest rate equation	
Constant	0.65	(0.6)
$(E_t - E_{t-1})$	41.9	(4.4)
ΔP_t	−14.6	(2.5)
ΔP_{t-1}	0.0	(−)
$(r_D - r_F)_{t-1}$	0.82	(6.6)
$(r_D - r_F)_{t-2}$	0.32	(−2.45)
	$\Sigma e^2 = 421$	DW = 1.8
	Log likelihood function = 83.84	

IMPLEMENTING SUCH AN EQUATION IN A FULL MACRO MODEL

In implementing an equation for the exchange rate such as those presented above, in a full econometric model, there are a number of ways of handling the term in the expected exchange rate. In the most general sense there are two broad alternatives; first, we could make the expected exchange rate a function of current and lagged variables, so an explicit expectations equation would be estimated and specified. The second approach would be to use the model's own forecast of the exchange rate as the expected future exchange rate; this approach will require a special model solution technique as well as a set of terminal conditions (see Hall, 1983).

The use of a special equation for the expected exchange rate has the advantage that it makes the expectations formation process explicit and model solution is much easier. One possible option would be to use the expected exchange rate equation from the Wickens estimation as an explicit model equation. Alternatively, a special equation could be specified and estimated in its own right. There are two disadvantages to this approach: first, there is no reason why the model forecast of the actual exchange rate should coincide, on average, with the expected exchange rate. So there is no requirement for expectations to be either rational or unbiased within a model forecast. Second, any explicit expectations equation is likely to be subject to the Lucas critique, that a change in regime would cause a change in the structure of expectations formation.

The use of consistent expectations in the full model has the advantage that the model is then much more robust to the Lucas critique. Also expectations within the model are, by definition, fulfilled. The disadvantages are the increased difficulty of solving the model and the need for a terminal condition.

There are a number of possibilities for a suitable terminal condition. One approach would be to estimate a simple long run relationship between such factors as oil prices and the trade balance and the exchange rate. This could be used to set the terminal value of the exchange rate. An example of such a simple equation might be

$$\mathrm{Log}(E)_t = \underset{(33.6)}{4.14} + \underset{(1.9)}{0.03} \log (VOIL)_{t-1} + \underset{(7.4)}{0.96}\, UKVB_{t-1}$$

where $VOIL$ = real dollar value of North Sea oil reserves, $UKVB$ = UK visible balance.

Such an equation would set the terminal condition at a level which the market might regard as reasonable given the prevailing trade conditions, but it would not impose any form of long run equilibrium. A second alternative would be to use a condition with the form $E_{T+1} = E_T + \alpha.\mathrm{UKVB}_{T-1}$.

If for simplicity we write the exchange rate equation as $E_t = E_{t+1} + \phi\Delta r_t$ then we see that a solution to these two equations implies $\phi\Delta r_t = -\alpha UKVB_t$. If $\Delta r_t = 0$ in the final period, then the trade balance must be in balance. Such a condition would force trade equilibrium to be reached by the final period of any model solution when interest rates were stabilized. Otherwise the effect would be to allow an imbalance in trade which would exactly offset the interest rate effect.

There are, however, obvious disadvantages to both of these approaches. The simple regression may yield a long run relationship between the exchange rate, oil prices and trade, but this is not necessarily of any relevance to the long run expected exchange rate at any point in time. The second idea of imposing long run trade balance is appealing at an intuitive level but in practical model application it would be undesirable to impose an equilibrium trade balance in a fixed time horizon forecast. The proposition that the current balance will be zero after say 2 or 5 years would be highly restrictive.

A third alternative is to derive a series for the expected long run exchange rate which is consistent with the exchange rate equation being used. This series could then be used as the dependent variable in a regression to determine the structure of long run expectations formation. We may generate such a series fairly easily by a process of successive substitution of the structural exchange rate. For example if the exchange rate equation has the following form

$$E_t = \alpha E_{t-1} + (1 + \alpha)E^e_{t+1} + \beta\Delta(r_D - r_F)_t$$

$$=> E^e_{e+1} = \frac{E_t}{1 + a} - \frac{\alpha}{1 + \alpha} E_{t-1} - \frac{\beta}{1 + \alpha} \Delta(r_D - r_F)_t$$

and so by successive substitution we may write

$$E^e_{t+N} = \phi_1 E_t + \phi_2 E_{t-1} + \sum_{j=1}^{N} \phi_{3i}\Delta(r_D - r_F)_{t+J-1}$$

If we assume that in the future expected $\Delta(r_\delta - r_F) = 0$ then eventually the series of E^e_{t+N} should converge to the long run expected future exchange rate where $E^e_{t+N} = E^e_{t+N+1}$.

The exchange rate equation in Table 5.6 was used to produce a series of expected long run exchange rates (E^L_t) by this process of successive substitution. In fact the series converged after about eight substitutions suggesting that at any point in time the exchange rate 2 years ahead is assumed to be in equilibrium by the markets. A simple equation for the equilibrium exchange was then estimated as follows:

$$E^L_t = \underset{(0.5)}{0.14} + \underset{(16.5)}{0.97}\, E_{t-1} + \underset{(5.8)}{0.65}\Delta LXM + \underset{(1.12)}{0.047}\, VOIL$$

(t statistics in parenthesis) DW = 1.92

SEE = 0.05 $R^2 = 0.89$

This could then be used to set the terminal period exchange rate conditional on data available in the first period of the model solution.

CONCLUSION

This chapter has investigated a structural exchange rate model incorporating an explicit role for exchange rate expectations. It uses both monthly and quarterly data. The main conclusion is that the simple open arbitrage equation which lies at the heart of many current exchange rate models is significantly rejected by both monthly and quarterly data on a number of counts in favour of a richer more complex model.

DATA APPENDIX

Exchange rate: UK trade-weighted effective index 1980=100.
UK prices: UK CPI source MEI OECD.
US prices: US CPI source MEI OECD.
World prices: world wholesale prices source NIESR.
UK wholesale prices: source ET.
UK Treasury Bill rate: source FS.
UK Treasury Bill rate: source FS.
UK exports: source MRETS.
UK imports: source MRETS.
Value of UK oil exports: MRETS.
UK oil reserves: Brown book.

REFERENCES

Buiter, W. H. and Miller, M. M. (1981) 'Monetary policy and international competitiveness: the problem of adjustment', *Oxford Economic Papers*.

Dornbusch, R. (1976) 'Expectations and exchange rate dynamics', *Journal of Political Economy*, **84**, 1161–1176.

Frenkel, J.A. (1979) 'On the mark: a theory of floating exchange rates based on real interest differentials', *American Economic Review*, **69**, 610–622. ·

Haache, G. and Townend, J. (1981) 'Exchange rates and monetary policy: modelling sterling's effective exchange rate', in Eltis, W. A. and Sinclair, P. J. N. (eds), *The Money Supply and the Exchange Rate*, Clarendon Press, Oxford, 1981.

Hall, S. G. (1983) 'The exchange rate', in Britton, A. J. C. (ed.) *Employment, Output and Inflation*. Heinemann Books, London.

Hall, S. G. (1985) 'On the solution of large econometric models with consistent expectation', *Bulletin of Economic Research*, **37**(2), 157–161.

Wickens, M. R. (1982) 'The efficient estimation of econometric models with rational expectation', *Review of Economic Studies*, **49**, 55–68.

6 Dominant Factors in Dollar–Sterling Exchange Rates Movements, 1965–1981

G. W. McKenzie and S. H. Thomas

Although there have been many attempts in recent years to model exchange rate behaviour, it is fair to say that there has been relatively little success. In particular, no single model can be claimed to be satisfactory both in its ability to capture the process generating exchange rate movements and in non-nested comparisons with competing explanations (e.g. see Backus, 1984). In other words, no *congruent* models have been found.[1] There are two possible causes for this failure. First, the various models based on purchasing power parity theory, the 'monetary' approach, the 'asset' approach, *et al.* may simply be incorrect. Second, the processes characterized by the popular models may influence the data but possibly over a longer time horizon than is allowed by the estimation sample period. Other factors may dominate medium and short term adjustments.

Whatever the reason, it is clear that departures from contemporary thinking need to be considered. In this chapter, we offer one possible approach, a new empirical model of exchange rate determination which is based upon the influence of dominant factors rather than purely theoretical considerations. We introduce a variant of the portfolio approach which we believe includes key financial items that have been omitted from conventional models focusing upon domestic and foreign money and bond holdings. We take as our point of departure the now well-established fact that over $300 billion per day of foreign exchange transactions involve the US dollar; some 95 per cent of these are not directly related to either trade or investment, and over 90 per cent do not involve US residents. In other words, the use of the dollar as a vehicle currency must call into question explanations of the exchange value of the dollar which rely on transactions in money and bonds by US and, say, UK residents, (in the case of the dollar–sterling rate). In a similar vein we may think of financial items denominated in sterling and held by 'offshore' residents which will not enter conventional asset models but which play an important role in explaining exchange rate movements. Consequently we suggest that the range of assets and type of holder usually included in portfolio models may exclude key classes of financial products which are particularly relevant to foreign exchange markets.

1. MODELLING STRATEGY

We believe that a complete model of exchange rates should be capable of simultaneously explaining the following variables:

(i) the spot foreign exchange rate;
(ii) the forward exchange rate;
(iii) the 'forward' exchange rate implied by uncovered interest parity;
(iv) the spot exchange rate expected to hold at some future date given currently available information;
(v) the interest rate in the home country.

Our interest in modelling this particular set of open-economy price signals derives from our broader research programme examining the linkages between the real and financial sectors of the UK economy. The focal point of this work is the role of financial intermediation within the monetary transmission process in the UK during the period 1965–1981. This involves the explanation of sterling and foreign currency assets and liabilities of the UK monetary sector and hence an understanding of relevant yields is essential. As such this research programme represents a reexamination of important issues raised by the Radcliffe Commission (1959), Gurley and Shaw (1955, 1960) and others some 25 years ago.

As Johnson (1962) emphasized in his classic survey paper, the crucial concern of that analysis is the degree of substitution between various financial liabilities: primary securities (i.e. bonds), the deposits of monetary financial intermediaries (i.e. banks) and the liabilities of non-monetary financial intermediaries (e.g. building societies, the Eurocurrency system). If a wide range of 'near-monies' exists and if these are to some degree substitutable for transactions balances then there exists the potential for significant offset effects to the operation of monetary policy. In an important financial entrepôt such as the United Kingdom such effects are likely to be particularly significant. Both domestic and foreign residents respond to changes in covered interest rate differentials and in exchange rate expectations in such a way as to affect the credit and liquidity available to the UK economy. In turn, these portfolio adjustments involving substitution of assets and liabilities denominated in one currency for financial items denominated in another will influence movements in the spot exchange rate. Since these portfolio and relative price effects will cause variations in real output and expenditure, a complete analysis of the foreign exchange market is crucial to an understanding of the macroeconomics of financial intermediation.

In general, theories of foreign exchange market behaviour assume that economic agents are highly efficient in the processing of economic information. Intuitively, this would appear to be a very reasonable assumption. Bankers are highly educated individuals with access to a wide range of information and sophisticated data-processing equipment. In many instances they are advised by professional economists. Under such circumstances it does not seem possible either that systematic errors could be made or that unexploited profit opportunities could exist for very long.

With respect to the five variables listed at the beginning of this paper on the basis of much current thinking we would expect the following to hold:

(1) There should exist a general consensus as to the process generating the current spot exchange rate.
(2) The forward exchange rate should reflect expectations as to the future exchange rate.
(3) The actual forward exchange rate and the rate implied by the uncovered interest parity condition should be equal.
(4) As a result international interest rate differentials should reflect expected changes in exchange rates.
(5) The expected exchange rate formed by the above process should be an unbiased forecast of the actual future exchange rate.

Unfortunately, if we take the recent survey paper by Levich (1985) as our benchmark, we are led to conclude that none of these situations actually holds in practice. There exists no consensus amongst economists as to the actual processes generating exchange rate movements, with purchasing power parity, monetary and portfolio balance theories all apparently providing competing explanations. Further not only are the actual forward and parity forward rates-biased predictors, they also frequently differ significantly and systematically from each other. This state of the art as surveyed by Levich together with several preliminary experiments which we undertook suggested that a rethink of methods utilized to model exchange rates was in order. The conclusion that we reached was that a less rigid, more eclectic attitude toward the role of economic theory in applied econometric research is called for. Two related points are of relevance:

(A) Basically, the method of *economic theory* is one of comparative statics. It enables us to understand the interrelationship between variables as they exist in a stationary state. However, economic theory rarely provides us with an insight into the processes which characterize movement between states. Thus theories based upon market efficiency and requiring that the expected exchange rate, the actual forward rate and the forward parity rate all be equal may best be viewed as theories of long run behaviour. As Levich (1978) has suggested:

it may be helpful to view market efficiency as a process rather than as a hypothesis to accept or reject. Given that traders have diverse information, speculative markets will approach full efficiency in the long run but can never reflect all information in the short run.

The immediate question concerns the approach to be utilized in modelling short run behaviour. Here the methodology advocated by Hendry, Mizon and others in a series of papers (e.g. 1978, 1985) appears appropriate. It seems reasonable to suggest that a major objective of empirical research should involve the search for models which adequately capture the process generating the economic variables of interest within a plausible theoretic framework. Economic theory plays an important role in suggesting potentially important variables or functional forms. For Hendry and Mizon, as for Levich, this is most likely to be the case with respect to long run equilibrium relationships. However, economic theory provides little guidance as to the dynamic processes characterizing the data. One possible approach is then to take a general distributed lag as our maintained model and then successively simplify to eliminate terms which appear to be unimportant. This is the procedure which we adopt here. A wide range of criteria is considered in selecting a final model, involving both data and theory consistency. Where our model is not satisfactory we state this explicitly.

(B) *Econometric analysis* is a sophisticated form of historical research aimed at characterizing the data generation process over the particular sample period. Economic theory may play a very important role in calling attention to certain key relationships. However, the 'testing' of theory cannot be the ultimate objective of applied work. There are three reasons why this should be so.

(1) Theoretical analysis typically develops as a result of some real world problem which is only poorly understood and hence requires systematic treatment. However, a theory may only become sufficiently developed after a particular problem has long since passed and other factors have come to *dominate*. For

this reason it is important to look beyond theory to identify the many one-off events and institutional and structural developments which influence interest rates, exchange rates, etc., but for which there currently exists no adequate theory.

(2) In any case, most theory, including that relevant to exchange rate movements, is designed for the pedagogic task of logically analysing the interrelationship between two or possibly a very limited number of variables, *ceteris paribus*. They are not designed to be tested, since the variables being held constant for the purpose of the theoretical investigation are usually considered to be quite important in practice.

(3) It is for this reason that statistical tests must be interpreted with great care. No theory can be accepted or rejected *per se* since all tests necessarily incorporate maintained hypotheses concerning unimportant variables, functional form and the stochastic process generating the data. Thus tests purporting to accept or reject market efficiency *vis-à-vis* the exchange markets, or the Fisher hypothesis are ambiguous, a point emphasized by Levich (1978, 1985). At best one can only accept or reject joint hypotheses. It is impossible to determine whether any success or failure arises from the relationship of interest or because of the role played by the maintained hypotheses.

2. AN ALTERNATIVE MODEL

A distinctive feature of our project is the desire to model not just the spot exchange rate but a set of related variables as well. As noted above, this purpose derives from our wider interest in modelling the linkages between the real and financial sectors of the UK economy as they occur through portfolio adjustments. The model consists of four equations (three behavioural and one identity) describing: the spot exchange rate, the actual forward rate, the parity forward rate and a domestic rate of interest (here the eurosterling rate). If we neglect dynamic considerations, we are able to write the long run or static specification of the model as follows:

$$Le^s = s(e^s_p, LOIL, LSL, LSA) \qquad (6.1)$$

$$L\hat{e}^f = Le^s \qquad (6.2)$$

$$Le^f = Le^s \qquad (6.3)$$

$$Lr_2 = Lr_1 + 4(Le^s - L\hat{e}^f) \qquad (6.4)$$

where, e^s = spot exchange rate ($ per £); e^f = 3-month forward exchange rate; $\hat{e}^f$ = 3-month forward exchange rate implied by the uncovered interest parity conditions; r_2 = 3-month Eurosterling interest rate; r_1 = 3-month Eurodollar interest rate; SA = Sterling assets of the UK banking sector *vis-à-vis* non-residents; SL = Sterling liabilities of the UK banking sector *vis-à-vis* non-residents; OIL = UK oil production; e^s_p = official par value ($ per £) under Bretton Woods exchange rate system until the end of 1972(2).

The above variables, when prefixed by L, refer to natural logs of the respective variables. A 0 subscript on the exchange rate variable indicates that it refers to the period until 1972(2), whereas a 1 subscript refers to the following period.

Let us consider these equations in turn:

(a) The Spot Exchange Rate, e^s

Contrary to most studies, we wish to examine the behaviour of e^s during fixed and floating exchange rate eras. This seems a legitimate exercise given the specification of the rest of our model: it would be quite unsatisfactory to throw away information from this earlier period, particularly if it can be captured satisfactorily by our model. To that end we have isolated three dominant factors which we believe explain dollar–sterling rate movements over our period of interest; 1964(3) to 1981(4).

(i) Prior to the collapse of the Bretton Woods exchange rate system in the early 1970s, movements in spot exchange rates were confined to a narrow band around an officially set parity exchange rate, e_p^s. This variable will obviously be the dominant factor until 1972(2).

(ii) Oil has been an influence on the behaviour of sterling since the mid 1970s, both in terms of simple current account arithmetic and in terms of a positive effect on the psychology underlying investors' expectations about the future value of the currency. Obviously, some of the variables such as real income in Tables 6.2 and 6.3 should go some way towards capturing the influence on exchange rates, but it is clear from the equations' diagnostics that this is not sufficient. Haache and Townend (1981) report little success with oil-related variables, such as the present discounted value of North Sea production. We found no role for energy or oil prices, but a considerable one for the quantity of oil produced. It may be that the jumps in the oil price were not useful in explaining e^s, but that the more gradual quantity changes represented the underlying views on the role of oil output at that time. Hence we include the production of oil as a variable representing the arrival of sterling as a sort of petrocurrency in the late 1970s.

(iii) The first two influences may be thought to represent special features of the period under discussion, and certainly have not been derived in the context of an economic model which assumes optimizing behaviour by market participants. The third influence we wish to emphasize does have its roots, however, in the portfolio approach to exchange rate determination. The UK financial sector has acted as a major financial intermediary between international borrowers and lenders, and the role of London as a centre of Eurocurrency transactions has provided non-residents with the facility to switch between sterling and non-sterling with relative ease. As we noted earlier it is now widely accepted that foreign currency transactions worldwide amount to $300bn per day, only 5 per cent of which is directly related to trade or physical investment activities. The great majority of the transactions are between banks in the form of buying and selling bank deposits. It is our contention that transactions in such financial products can have an important influence on exchange rates, and is a natural extension of portfolio models which include money and bonds, (e.g. see Obstfeld, 1983). Of course, we once again have a problem in obtaining suitable data, but we have found that variations in commercial bank sterling assets and liabilities *vis-à-vis* non-residents have important explanatory power in the dollar–sterling exchange rate equation. We may conjecture that at a very crude level such funds represent 'smart' money: transactions in the assets and liabilities of financial intermediaries lead to exchange rate changes in exactly the same way as do transactions in money and bonds, and we may conjecture quantitatively dominate the latter. The variables we find important are readily available from official statistics, though we recognize that other elements of a portfolio could also be important. Note that Haache and Townend (1981) recognized the importance of overseas holdings of sterling, though they were more interested in their relation to oil and oil exporters' investment behaviour (see also Golub, 1983).

As a result of these considerations we choose to work with equation (6.1) to explain the spot dollar–sterling exchange rate. One would obviously like to think of a longer list of variables, including those within the usual asset approach, from which agents can choose in selecting their portfolio of financial items. Satisfactory data on bond holdings are not available, and data on offshore sterling assets and liabilities from other centres are also not available for our time period. Hence we once again are only examining an incomplete set of the financial items, transactions in which will affect the dollar–sterling rate: but our analysis is, in the very least, a step in the right direction and captures the data generation process better than conventional portfolio models. It does serve to emphasize the practical importance both of the assets and liabilities of financial intermediaries in general (see McKenzie and Thomas, 1983), and the Eurocurrency markets in particular for the determination of exchange rates and, indeed, interest rates. Conventional macro models which involve only money and primary securities ignore this important aspect of modern economies. The existence of the oil variable further emphasizes the incomplete nature of the data we have on financial assets, since the effect of oil would largely be captured by the changes in holding of relevant financial assets. The lags on all variables indicates partly the need to consider the gradual adjustment of portfolios over time, and their effect on exchange rates, and also the need to proxy omitted influences by related variables.

Two points should be explained. First, we are assuming that a stable exchange rate equation exists over the *entire* period, 1964(3) to 1981(4) despite the fact that this period covers both the adjustable peg and (dirty) float regimes. We feel that it is desirable to have models which perform well over both subperiods; certainly there must be useful information in the data which can be utilized effectively. *Ex post* dynamic simulations provide support for this approach.

Secondly, we treat the variables *LSL* and *LSA* as predetermined. Although this is the standard procedure in empirical models based on portfolio balance theories (e.g. see Branson *et al.*, 1977), it is not in general satisfactory since these variables will depend upon both home and foreign rates of interest. In practice another strand of our research seeks to explain these quantities within a portfolio framework. If we believe the authorities always provide sufficient funds to maintain a given interest rate target, and financial intermediaries price their product on a 'mark-up' basis, then a set of interest rate supply functions and portfolio demand equations will complete the model. However, for the analysis thus far we conform to accepted practice by considering the said quantities to be 'exogenous'.

(b) The Forward Exchange Rates

We define a forward parity rate, $\hat{e}^f$, to be that generated by the differential between the 3-month Eurosterling and Eurodollar interest rates (see equation (6.4)). In a long run steady state the actual forward rate, e^f, and $\hat{e}^f$ will be equal to each other and to the spot rate e^s, provided that markets are efficient. Over the short run, however, there are compelling reasons why the two parity rates may diverge. Kesselman (1917) and Kindleberger (1980) offer some insight into possible reasons for this. They call attention to the fact that hedgers, arbitrageurs and speculators will all react differently to profitable opportunities that may arise in foreign exchange markets. In particular, divergences between e^f and $\hat{e}^f$ may emerge periodically because arbitrageurs neither have the time nor sufficient financial resources to close the gap. Banks lending to arbitrageurs and the arbitrageurs themselves may simply be unwilling to devote a large proportion of their portfolios of investments to a single activity. They may be (i) risk averse, (ii) guided by arbitrary rules of thumb only infrequently revised by management, or (iii) constrained by legally binding prudential regulations. If this is the case then we would expect the dynamic specification of the equations for $\hat{e}^f$ and e^f to be different even though both have the same long run solution. Further, it will be an indication that both of these rates may be useful in modelling portfolio choice between assets in different currencies. The actual specification chosen is described in Section 5.

(c) The Domestic Interest Rate

We believe that a sensible view of UK interest rates is to tie them substantially to overseas rates, in particular US rates. The latter are truly exogenous. Haache and Townend (1981, p. 229) offer a substantial list of quotations from the Bank of England to this effect. So the nominal interest differential between similar sterling and dollar denominated assets inherent in our definition of the forward parity rate, $L\hat{e}^f$, together with knowledge of the US interest rate, will drive the domestic interest rate. This seems appropriate for a small open economy, though note the switch of attention to domestic monetary conditions after 1977. In practice, of course, there will be several parity forward exchange rates depending upon which similar assets are being compared and some authors do introduce term-structure effects (see Davidson, 1985). However, for the purposes of this paper we define $L\hat{e}^f$ on the basis of the difference between the 3-month Eurodollar and 3-month Eurosterling interest rates (see equation (6.4)). Obstfeld (1983) makes a similar appeal to Eurocurrency differentials, but in this case he actually generates 'expectations' with them. In this paper we adopt the view that it is difficult to separate expectational relationships from the welter of dynamic adjustment processes which affect the economy. Hence we concentrate on unrestricted lag processes.

3. THE RESULTS

Our model selection procedure involves estimating the most general formulation by ordinary least squares (OLS). As a partial test of the Lucas critique that structural changes need to be modelled explicitly, we have estimated coefficients on the lagged dependent variable separately for (a) the period prior to 1972(2), and (b) the period following. Other variables were not subjected to this procedure since their influence is felt only in one of the two subperiods (e.g. oil production in the UK was negligible in the period prior to 1972(2)). The model is then simplified by eliminating all variables with *t*-statistics less than one in value. Particular attention is paid to the residual correlograms. The resulting specification is then estimated by the full information maximum likelihood method.

For the equation describing the spot exchange rate (see Table 6.1), we begin with a general dynamic specification containing fourth-order lags. Our prior belief is that portfolio adjustments do take time in the real world and that the influence of oil production on sterling leads to gradual changes in market perception and current account reality. From column 1 it is seen that several simplifications are in order. In particular, all lagged dependent variables except one for the pre-1972(ii) period were insignificant and hence eliminated. In addition, the variable *SL*, sterling bank liabilities to foreigners, only generates a first-order transitory effect on the spot rate. The resulting equation shown in column 2 possesses a reasonably flat residual correlogram (Table 6.3, column 1). This is confirmed by the $\chi^2(8)$ statistic whose value is considerably less than the 1 per cent value of 20.09. This equation was then re-estimated by FIML in conjunction with the three other equations of this submodel. In the process two other variables were eliminated with the result that there is no role for any lag effects on the spot exchange rate for the period prior to 1972(ii). These results are shown in column 3. Not surprisingly the parity exchange rate e_p^s has a large and positive effect on the actual spot exchange rate. So does the volume of oil production although it is distributed over three-quarters, a plausible result given invoicing and delivery procedures. As already noted, changes in sterling bank liabilities to foreigners only has a first-order transitory effect. However, sterling bank lending to foreigners does possess a negative long run effect as well as a four-quarter lag process. This reflects in large measure the important role of the UK banking sector as a financial entrepôt. The provision of sterling credits to foreigners is bound to be subject to leading and lagging activities of foreign traders as well as outright speculation. A future project in our research programme is to model this behaviour explicitly.

As Leamer (1985, p. 308) quips: 'There are two things you are better off not seeing in the making: sausages and econometric estimates'. We have some sympathy with this point of view, particularly since a complete exposé of the actual steps taken in model selection would be considerably longer than article length. However, we do feel that the applied worker should reveal any issues of particular importance which arise in the search process. It is particularly interesting to note that interest rate differentials play no role at all. Changes in UK foreign exchange reserves are also insignificant as was domestic real GDP and domestic $M1$.

The forward parity and forward rate equations are shown in Table 6.2a and b respectively. As previously indicated long run market efficiency suggests that these two rates should both equal the spot rate. However, in the short run we would expect some dynamic process involving e^s, $\hat{e}^f$ and e^f. To begin with we have assumed that these processes involve the same specification; as shown in column 1 if the two foreign exchange markets were fully efficient in the short run as well as the long run the two equations should be identical. The immediate impression is that they are quite different, however. As a double check, we re-estimated the two together as seemingly unrelated equations in unrestricted form and then with the parameters of the two

Table 6.1: Estimates for spot exchange rate equation: 1964(3)–1981(4)

Variable	(1)		(2)		(3)	
Constant	1.601	(3.88)	1.397	(4.03)	0.954	(3.35)
Oil	0.222	(3.12)	0.200	(4.03)	0.146	(3.66)
SA	−0.213	(−3.25)	−0.140	(−3.47)	−0.104	(−3.00)
SL	0.044	(0.725)				
e_p^s	0.825	(4.32)	0.713	(14.6)	0.803	(14.99)
$e_o^s(-1)$	−0.202	(−0.995)				
$\Delta e_o^s(-1)$	−0.141	(0.659)				
$\Delta e_o^s(-2)$	0.015	(0.069)				
$\Delta e_o^s(-3)$	0.295	(1.40)	0.286	(1.45)		
$e_1^s(-1)$	0.678	(8.89)	0.759	(16.8)	0.831	(16.64)
$\Delta e_1^s(-1)$	0.333	(2.62)	0.348	(3.28)	0.484	(5.50)
$\Delta e_1^s(-2)$	−0.192	(−1.39)	−0.228	(−1.99)	−0.217	(−1.76)
$\Delta e_1^s(-3)$	0.316	(2.05)	0.314	(2.46)	0.226	(2.03)
ΔOIL	−0.131	(−0.935)				

$\Delta OIL(-1)$	−0.476	(−3.30)	−0.415	(−3.53)	−0.330	(−2.49)
$\Delta OIL(-2)$	−0.759	(−4.96)	−0.698	(−5.17)	−0.437	(−3.86)
$\Delta OIL(-3)$	−0.416	(−2.66)	−0.335	(−2.41)		
ΔSL	0.225	(2.75)	0.270	(4.28)	0.273	(5.13)
$\Delta SL(-1)$	0.016	(0.185)				
$\Delta SL(-2)$	0.022	(0.287)				
$\Delta SL(-3)$	−0.001	(−0.001)				
ΔSA	−0.284	(−2.64)	−0.310	(−3.29)	−0.295	(−3.39)
$\Delta SA\ (-1)$	0.125	(1.11)	−0.141	(1.34)	0.224	(2.62)
$\Delta SA(-2)$	−0.131	(−0.131)	−0.166	(−1.83)	−0.132	(−2.04)
$\Delta SA(-3)$	0.156	(1.47)	0.112	(1.17)	0.182	(2.21)
SSR	0.03433		0.03733		0.04767	
SE	0.02762		0.02654		0.02610	
$\overline{R}^2$	0.9639		0.9666		0.9429	
dw(1)	1.90		2.03		2.33	
$\chi^2(8)$	9.5341		5.4257		8.33	
LLF	167.384		164.453		—*	

All variables are expressed in logarithmic form; *t*-statistics are given in parentheses.
* The LLF for the system is reported in the text.

Table 6.2

Variable	(1)		(2)		(3)		(4)	
(a) Estimates for forward parity exchange rate equation: 1964(3)–1981(4)								
Constant	−0.006	(−0.993)	−0.004	(−0.810)	−0.006	(−1.45)	−0.008	(−1.10)
e^s	0.497	(3.18)	0.407	(4.08)	0.392	(3.98)	0.391	(6.77)
$\hat{e}^f_o(-1)$	0.623	(1.50)	0.596	(6.05)				
$e^f_o(-1)$	−0.116	(−0.264)						
Δe^s_o	0.545	(3.44)	0.635	(6.05)				
$\hat{e}^f_1(-1)$	−0.385	(−0.298)	0.594	(6.02)				
$e^f_1(-1)$	0.892	(0.758)						
Δe^s_1	0.500	(3.22)	0.598	(5.75)				
$\hat{e}^f(-1)$					0.613	(6.30)	0.616	(11.34)
Δe^s					0.614	(6.14)	0.668	(11.23)
SSR	0.00193		0.00195		0.00201		0.00236	
SE	0.00586		0.00552		0.00552		0.00580	
$\overline{R}^2$	0.9986		0.9986		0.9986		0.9971	
dw(1)	1.94		1.92		1.94		2.09	
$\chi^2(8)$	2.3578		3.2629		9.509		1.60	
LLF	268.044		267.718		266.742		—*	

(b) Estimates for forward exchange rate equation: 1964(3)–1981(4)

Constant	−0.007	(−1.11)	−0.005	(−0.936)	−0.007	(−1.49)	−0.009	(−1.06)
e^s	0.519	(3.04)	0.423	(4.17)	0.413	(4.10)	0.414	(6.15)
$\hat{e}^f_o(-1)$	0.037	(0.083)						
$e^f_0(-1)$	0.449	(0.937)	0.581	(5.80)				
Δe^s_o	0.526	(3.04)	0.621	(5.76)				
$\hat{e}^f_1(-1)$	−0.993	(−0.703)						
$e^f_1(-1)$	1.479	(1.15)	0.580	(5.77)				
Δe^s_1	0.477	(2.81)	0.579	(5.45)				
$e^f(-1)$					0.592	(5.96)	0.593	(9.15)
Δe^s					0.591	(5.76)	0.645	(9.26)
SSR	0.00230		0.00232		0.00238		0.00276	
SE	0.00609		0.00602		0.00600		0.00627	
$\bar{R}^2$	0.9983		0.9983		0.9983		0.9967	
dw(1)	1.96		1.93		1.93		2.10	
$\chi^2(8)$	2.9505		3.6941		10.5086		1.56	
LLF	261.967		261.684		260.831		—*	

All variables are expressed in logarithmic form; *t*-statistics are given in parentheses.
* The LLF for the system is reported in the text.

equations restricted to be identical. The resulting log likelihood function values were 625.128 and 601.220 respectively. Twice the difference of these two values is considerably greater than the one percent $\chi^2(6)$ value of 16.8, thereby indicating overwhelming rejection of dynamic market efficiency.

Simplifications were then introduced as shown in column 2 since it did not appear that e^f affected $\hat{e}^f$ and vice versa. It then appeared that the dynamic processes were unchanged over the entire sample period. This restriction was then introduced with the results shown in column 3 of Tables 6.2a and b. On the basis of the $\chi^2(8)$ statistics we would accept the hypothesis of no residual correlation for these two equations and this is confirmed by an examination of the correlograms themselves in columns 2 and 3 of Table 6.3. The only possible sources of concern are the seventh-order lags which appear relatively large. Attempts to reduce this coefficient were fruitless, however, and a decision was taken to neglect this problem. The system estimates by FIML are shown in column 4 of Tables 6.2a and b. As a final check on our work we estimated the unconstrained model by FIML and compared it with the simplified version shown in the preceding tables. The log of the likelihood function was 846.412 for the unconstrained version, whereas it was 843.863 for the constrained. Twice the difference of these two values, 5.098, is less than the 1 per cent $\chi^2(3)$ statistic whose value is 11.3.

4. DYNAMIC SIMULATIONS

Although we appreciate the shortcomings of simulations as a method of model evaluation (Hendry and Richard, 1982), such exercises do provide descriptive statistics of the performance of the model and may offer hints as to missing variables. Specifically, *static* simulations may be helpful in identifying structural characteristics of the model which have been incorrectly specified, whereas *dynamic* simulations may help identify misspecifications of the lag process. Summary statistics for static and dynamic simulations over the period 1965(1)–1981(4) are presented in Table 6.4a and b, respect-

Table 6.3: Residual correlograms

Lag period	(1) e^s		(2) $\hat{e}^f$		(3) e^f	
1	−0.0251	(−0.2080)	0.0266	(0.2190)	0.0365	(0.3010)
2	−0.0946	(−0.7990)	0.0071	(0.579)	0.0020	(0.0162)
3	−0.0849	(−0.7030)	−0.0117	(−0.0922)	−0.0174	(−0.1360)
4	0.1760	(1.4400)	−0.0632	(−0.4950)	−0.0558	(−0.4340)
5	−0.0616	(−0.4930)	0.0818	(0.6140)	0.0549	(0.4060)
6	0.0035	(0.0276)	−0.0161	(−0.1180)	−0.0147	(−0.1060)
7	−0.1100	(−0.8380)	0.2020	(1.3700)	0.2360	(1.5800)
8	0.0370	(0.2610)	−0.0341	(−0.2210)	−0.0258	(−0.1630)

The above residual correlograms are associated with the final OLS estimation of the model: e^s, Table 6.1 column 2; $\hat{e}^f$, Table 6.2a column 3; e^f, Table 6.2b column 3.
The figures in brackets are the t-statistics associated with the coefficients.

Table 6.4

Variable	RMSE	Mean % abs. error	RMSE*/Std. dev.	Inequality coeff.	Theil statistics: Error due to bias	Error due to diff. variation	Error due to diff. covar.
(a) Static simulations 1965(1)–1981(4)							
e^s	0.06	1.94	0.18	0.00	0.00	0.01	0.99
e^f	0.05	1.86	0.17	0.00	0.00	0.01	0.99
$\hat{e}^f$	0.05	1.89	0.17	0.00	0.00	0.00	0.99
r_2	2.24	15.83	0.56	0.03	0.00	0.00	0.99
(b) Dynamic simulations 1965(1)–1981(4)							
e^s	0.09	3.07	0.29	0.00	0.00	0.04	0.96
e^f	0.09	2.99	0.28	0.00	0.00	0.04	0.96
$\hat{e}^f$	0.09	3.01	0.28	0.00	0.00	0.03	0.96
r_2	2.85	19.25	0.71	0.06	0.00	0.00	1.00

* RMSE/(Std. dev.) is defined as $\sqrt{\Sigma(X_i - \hat{X}_i)^2 / \Sigma(X_i - \overline{X})^2}$ where X_i is the actual value, $\hat{X}_i$ is the simulated value and $\overline{X}$ is the mean of X.

ively. On the basis of the four Theil statistics, it would appear that little improvement in model performance is possible. More revealing are the descriptive indicators (shown in the first three columns) which tend to indicate that the Eurosterling interest rate is relatively poorly tracked in comparison to the three exchange rate equations.

Figures 6.1 and 6.2 depict the track of the dynamic simulations for the spot exchange rate and for the Eurosterling rate. Both pick up fundamental turning points reasonably well and provide small final period errors. It would thus seem reasonable to conjecture that the relatively poor performance of the Eurosterling interest rate equation is due to noise in the underlying data rather than some fundamental misspecification of the model.

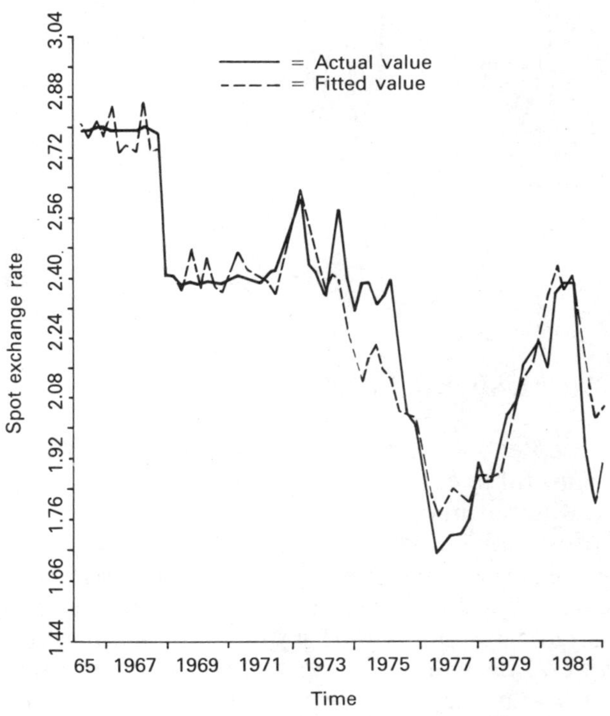

Figure 6.1: Dynamic simulation for the spot exchange rate

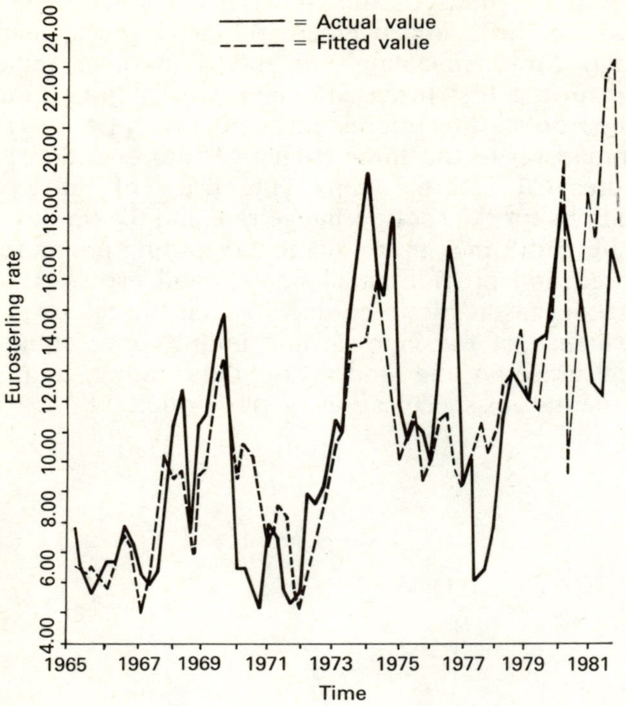

Figure 6.2

5. CONCLUSIONS

In this chapter we have sought to emphasize two things: first, it is useful to extend the conventional range of financial items considered in bilateral portfolio models to reflect the reality of a sophisticated modern financial world. Second, the emphasis on 'efficiency' and rational expectations has led researchers to focus on essentially static empirical models of exchange rates. It may be more sensible to start from a more general distributed lag model and explicitly recognize the adjustment lags and market imperfections which do exist in practice. At least these first two points have led us to a data-consistent model for e^s which we can understand theoretically and which dominates some competing explanations. We also emphasized the role of both $\hat{e}^f$ and e^f in providing information as to the dynamic efficiency of the dollar/sterling foreign exchange markets and conjecture that both jointly will influence exchange rate expectations.

Exchange rate modelling will always be a particularly difficult area of applied econometrics due to the numerous changes in policy, the presence of non-quantifiable 'news', and the difficulty of obtaining suitable data on financial stocks. However, we feel that our own model succeeds reasonably well in capturing the essentials of the process generating the dollar–sterling rate over the period 1965–1981, and perhaps suggests some new avenues for empirical research along the way.

NOTES

1. Hendry and Mizon (1985) consider a model to be *congruent* if it is both data and theory consistent and can account for the results obtained by alternative explanations.

REFERENCES

Backus, D. (1984) 'Empirical models of the exchange rate: separating the wheat from the chaff', *Canadian Journal of Economics*, **16**(4), 824–845.

Branson, W. H., Haltunnen, H. and Masson, P. (1977) 'Exchange rates in the short-run: the dollar Deutschmark rate', *European Economic Review*, **10**, 303–304.

Cornell, B. (1977) 'Spot rates, forward rates and exchange market efficiency', *Journal of Financial Economics*, **5**, 55–65.

Cumby, R. E. and Obstfeld, M. (1981) 'A note on exchange-rate expectations and nominal interest differentials: a test of the Fisher hypothesis', *Journal of Finance*, **36**, 697–703.

Davidson, J. (1985) 'Econometric modelling of the sterling effective exchange rate', *Review of Economic Studies*, **169**, 231–250.

Golub, S. S. (1983) 'Oil prices and exchange rates', *The Economic Journal*, **93**, 576–593.

Gurley, J. G. and Shaw, E. S. (1955) 'Financial aspects of economic development', *American Economic Review*, **XIV**, 515–538.

Gurley, J. G. and Shaw, E. S. (1960) *Money In a Theory of Finance*. Brookings, Washington DC.

Haache, G. and Townend, J. (1981) 'Exchange rates and monetary policy: modelling sterling's effective exchange rate', in Eltis, W. A. and Sinclair, P. J. N. (eds), *The Money Supply and The Exchange Rate*, Clarendon Press, Oxford.

Hendry, D. F. and Mizon, G. E. (1978) 'Serial correlation as a convenient simplification, not a nuisance: a comment on a study of the demand for money by the bank of England', *Economic Journal*, **88**, 549–563.

Hendry, D. F. and Mizon, G. E. (1985), 'Procrustean econometrics, or stretching and squeezing data', Mimeo, Southampton University.

Hendry, D. F. and Richard, J.-F. (1982), 'On the formulation of empirical models in dynamic econometrics', Journal of Econometrics, **20**, 3–33.

Johnson, H. G. (1962) 'Monetary theory and policy', *American Economic Review*, **52**, 335–84.

Kesselman, J. (1971) 'The role of speculation in forward-rate determination: the Canadian dollar, 1953–60', *Canadian Journal of Economics*, **4**(3), 279–298.

Kindelberger, C. P. (1980) 'Myths and realities of forward exchange markets', in Kindelberger, C. P. and Chipman, J. S. (eds) *Flexible Exchange Rates and the Balance of Payments*. North-Holland, Amsterdam.

Leamer, E. E. (1985) 'Sensitivity analyses would help', *American Economic Review*, **75**(3), 308–313.

Levich, R. M. (1978) 'The efficiency of markets for foreign exchange: a review and extension', in Lessard, D. R. (ed.) *International Financial Management*. Warren, Gorham and Lamont, New York.

Levich, R. M. (1985), 'Empirical studies of exchange rates: price behaviour, rate determination and market efficiency', in Jones, R. W. and Kenen, P. B. (eds) *Handbook of International Economics, Vol. 2*. North-Holland, Amsterdam.

McAleer, M., Pagan, A. R. and Volker, P. A. (1985) 'What will take the con out of econometrics?', *American Economic Review*, **75**(3), 293–307.

McKenzie, G. W. and Thomas, S. H. (1983) 'Liquidity, credit creation, and international banking: an econometric investigation', *Journal of Banking and Finance*, **7**(4), 467–480.

Obstfeld, M. (1983) 'Exchange rates, inflation and the sterilization problem', *European Economic Review*, **23**, 161–189.

Radcliffe Report (1959) Committee on the Working of the Monetary System, Cmnd. 827 (HMSO, London).

7 Testing the Monetary Approach to Balance of Payments in Developing Countries

H. Leon and H. Molana

1. INTRODUCTION

Over the past two decades the International Monetary Fund's staff have researched balance of payments problems in developing countries, and have emphasized the role of money in the income formation process and as an explanation of balance of payments deficits. One line of research has focused on the formulation and estimation of models using data from a broad range of developing countries. Such models were designed to provide a framework for quantitative analysis that could be used as a guide when discussing monetary management with member countries requesting financial help. In general, comparative studies, utilizing the same model for a number of countries, and pooled sample analyses have featured prominently in the literature (for example, see Aghevli and Khan, 1977, 1978; Khan, 1977).

Given the broad spectrum of IMF operations and the paucity of economic data in most developing countries, the attempt to formulate models capable of achieving sufficient generalization so as to be representative of a broad class of developing countries is easily understood; in particular, such models may—due to data and/or manpower limitations—be the only available means of providing useful quantitative information with regard to the practical questions of policy analysis. Thus, an essential aspect of empirical research should be the utilization of a modelling procedure that minimizes the probability of making a wrong decision, in view of the fact that the results of such models may have potential implications for both the formulation of an appropriate financial policy aimed at improving the balance of payments and the performance criteria set as a condition for maintaining access to the fund's resources. In particular, great care should be exercised in choosing the sample with respect to both countries included and time period studied as well as the imposition of restrictions (i.e. in addition to the *a priori* restrictions which are believed to represent the underlying theoretical structure) which relate to the adjustment and/or expectational mechanisms of the economies under study.

This chapter attempts to demonstrate the above issues within the context of a macroeconomic model that has been developed by Khan and Knight (1981) (hereafter KK) in the research department of the IMF. The model is 'a particular interpretation of the basic theoretical paradigm underlying the financial programming exercises of the fund' (KK, 1981), and supposedly representative of a broad class of developing countries. KK estimate the model for the period 1968–1975 on a pooled sample of twenty-nine developing countries[1] in an attempt to quantify relationships that feature prominently in IMF stabilization programs. As KK state:

> The implementation of stabilisation program will have simultaneous effects on output, inflation, and the balance of payments. While practitioners generally attempt to make allowances for these effects in qualitative terms, relatively little is known about the precise quantitative nature of the relationships among these major economic aggregates in the context of developing countries. This lack of knowledge, of course, creates considerable problems when one wishes to assess the effects of a particular policy initiative—say, for example, a change in monetary policy—on important macroeconomic variables, and conversely, *to derive the appropriate policy to achieve stabilisation objectives*.

Further, the main focus of the KK exercise was the derivation of meaningful policy conclusions, for they argue that:

> perhaps the most important part of the paper, a set of simulation experiments is conducted using the estimated version of the model ... to investigate the general path that might be followed by major economic aggregates in different circumstances.

This paper contends that whilst the objective of the KK study is indeed commendable, their research methodology used in implementing it is not wholly adequate, and can be subject to the above mentioned criticisms. We have chosen to demonstrate these issues through formal statistical analysis on a sample of seven developing countries[2] for the period 1953–1981. Because we use a much smaller number of countries and a much longer sample period, it will be evident that *our aim is not to provide a rerun of KK*. Rather, it is firstly to highlight estimation pitfalls within a pooled sample, and secondly, with regard to applicability, to demonstrate that if the 'pooled model' of seven countries does not represent the individual countries, then, *a fortiori*, the same result will hold for twenty-nine countries. In addition, the failure of this study to support restrictions imposed by KK in both the pooled sample and its individual components indicates the need to test those restrictions at both the disaggregated (individual) and aggregated (pooled) levels.

The remainder of the chapter contains three sections. In Section 2, the structure of the model and the imposed restrictions are explained. Section 3 details the results, whilst Section 4 provides a compact view of the broad conclusions of the study.

2. STRUCTURE OF MODEL AND PARAMETER RESTRICTIONS

2.1 Structural Equations

The model, intended to represent the macroeconomic structure of a typical developing country, assumes that the economy is small relative to the rest of the world, maintains a pegged exchange rate, is open to international trade in goods and services and financial flows, and the domestic financial sector is relatively underdeveloped.

The structural equations embody a disequilibrium system in the tradition of the monetary approach to the balance of payments consistent with the philosophy underlying the Fund's financial programming approach. The model is essentially demand oriented, highly aggregated, and assigns a central linking role to the demand for money and monetary disequilibrium in the behaviour of domestic prices, output and the balance of payments. Whilst long run output growth is exogenously determined an attempt is made to capture the effects of short term deviations of real income from its long run trend. Further, the small open economy–fixed exchange rate assumption recognizes the authorities' lack of control over the money stock, and the underdeveloped financial sector assumption, with its implicit government deficit–domestic credit growth nexus, alludes to the interdependence of monetary and fiscal policy. The nine-equation system (see Table 7.1) describes the domestic rate of inflation (1), the overall balance of payments (2), government expenditure (3a), and revenues (3b), the rate of growth of real output (4), the demand for real money balances (5), and the anticipated rate of inflation (6). The government deficit is related to domestic credit expansion in (7), whilst (8) is the consolidated balance sheet for the banking system; (9) defines real money balances.

2.2 Parameter Restrictions

Parameter restrictions can, in general, originate either as part of an economic theory or from the estimation process itself. In the former, they take the form of assumed priors whereas in the latter they constitute assumed properties of the data. Although both types of restrictions are testable, our study concentrates mainly on the latter set of restrictions as imposed by KK. Hence, our tests are conditional on the validity of the *a priori* restrictions which are embodied in the KK model. In fact, we do not wish to dispute their theoretical framework as such, but aim to improve the empirical methodology that they employ.

2.2.1 Restrictions concerning adjustment processes

KK restrict both γ_3 and γ_{14} to unity; $\gamma_3 = 1$ implies that domestic prices are unit elastic with respect to foreign prices, whilst $\gamma_{14} = 1$ states that economic agents' expectations of the rate of domestic inflation are simply determined as being equal to last period's inflation rate. These restrictions are imposed at the outset and do not belong to the class of

Table 7.1: Model specification

Inflation

$$\begin{aligned}\Delta\log P_t = {} & \gamma_2\beta_0 + \gamma_1(\log m_{t-1} - \log m_t^d) \\ & - \gamma_2\{(\log P_{t-1} - \log(\epsilon_{t-1}{}^*P_{f,t-1})\} \\ & + \gamma_3\Delta\log(\epsilon_t{}^*P_{f,t}) + \lambda_1 \end{aligned} \tag{1}$$

Balance of payments

$$\begin{aligned}\Delta\log R_t = {} & \gamma_6(\log m_t^d - \log M_{t-1} + \log P_t) - \gamma_7\{\log P_{t-1} \\ & - \log(\epsilon_{t-1}{}^*\mathrm{P}_{f,t-1}) - \beta_0\} + \Delta\log\epsilon_t \end{aligned} \tag{2}$$

Government sector

(a) Expenditures:

$$\log G_t = \gamma_8\beta_2 + \gamma_8\gamma_9(\log y_t + \log P_t) + (1 - \gamma_8)\log G_{t-1} \tag{3a}$$

(b) Revenues:

$$\log T_t = \gamma_{10}\beta_3 + \gamma_{10}\gamma_{11}(\log y_t + \log P_t) + (1 - \gamma_{10})\log T_{t-1} \tag{3b}$$

Real output

$$\Delta \log y_t = \gamma_{12}(\log m_{t-1} - \log m_t^d) + \gamma_{13}(\log y_t^* - \log y_{t-1}) + \lambda_2 \tag{4}$$

Money Demand

$$\log m_t^d = \beta_1 + \gamma_4 \log y_t - \gamma_5\Pi_t \tag{5}$$

Expected inflation

$$\Delta\Pi_t = \gamma_{14}(\Delta\log P_{t-1} - \Pi_{t-1}) \tag{6}$$

Domestic credit

$$DC_t = DC_{t-1} + (G_t - T_t) + \Delta CP_t \tag{7}$$

Money supply

$$M_t = DC_t + R_t \tag{8}$$

Real money balances

$$m_t = M_t/P_t \tag{9}$$

Definition of variables:
Endogenous—$\Delta\log P_t$ = rate of inflation; $\Delta\log R_t$ = growth rate of international reserves; G_t = nominal government expenditures; T_t = nominal government revenues; y_t = real output; Π_t = expected rate of inflation; DC_t = domestic credit of the consolidated banking system; M_t = nominal money stock; m_t = real money balances. Exogenous—ϵ_t = exchange rate, index of units of domestic currency per unit of foreign currency; $P_{f,t}$ = foreign price index; y^* = trend value of real income; ΔCP_t = change in net claims of the banking system on the domestic private sector and other items (net) in the consolidated balance sheet; λ_1,λ_2 = constants reflecting steady state properties of the system.

a priori economic restrictions which determine the structure of the economy, although required for the simple steady state. Therefore, their validity can be tested both jointly and separately.

It is worth noting that while $\gamma_3 = 1$ is one of the main features of the monetary approach to the balance of payments, $\gamma_{14} = 1$ was assumed by KK on the grounds of simplicity, and computational ease; estimating the simultaneous model on the relatively large sample of 232 observations with a grid of values of γ_{14} would have been costly in computing time. However, the latter assumption is also 'justified' by KK on the grounds that 'ordinary least squares tests on the pooled sample using the money demand equation in [their] Appendix V revealed that the value of γ_{14} that maximized the log-likelihood function was indeed unity' (KK, 1981). This two-step approach of first finding an optimal γ_{14} and then using the corresponding π series (see equation (6) of Table 7.1) in estimating the model can be justified only if the money demand function is properly specified and estimated. (KK's OLS estimates could be biased.) Even then, if the $\gamma_{14} = 1$ restriction is invalid the consequent misspecification would filter through the model via the expectations generating mechanism.

In addition, KK restrict the coefficient of $\Delta \log \epsilon_t$ in equation (2) of Table 7.1 to unity. They state that the changes in the domestic currency value of foreign exchange reserves that are due solely to exchange rate movements ought to be eliminated in the balance of payments equation since such valuation changes do not affect the domestic money stock or the excess demand for money. However, expectations of future changes in the exchange rate will influence the decisions of domestic agents unless foreign exchanges reserves in the economy are predominantly held as assets of the banking system. If one were analysing a time period for the greater part of which the dollar exchange rates of the sample countries had remained fixed, as in the KK 1968–1975 sample, such an influence would probably not be discernible. On the other hand, the investigation of a period during which the exchange rate was altered frequently such as the more recent period included in this paper, may uncover a significant effect. In order to capture any additional effect of movements in the exchange rate, an additional term $\phi_0\ \Delta\log\epsilon_t$ was added to the right-hand side of the balance of payments equation *after having eliminated* the in-sample valuation changes from the domestic currency value of foreign exchange reserves. With this redefinition, the relevant hypothesis of interest is now whether the coefficient, ϕ_0, on $\phi\Delta\log\epsilon_t$ is significantly different from zero. We note that, strictly speaking, a test of $\phi_0 \neq 0$ is *not a test of a restriction imposed by KK during estimation* for it is in the nature of an omitted variable and hence, a possible specification error. Further, in the absence of explicit modelling of the expectations mechanism, $\Delta\log\epsilon_t$ can be thought of as a proxy for the difference between the spot rate and the expected future rate of exchange. We include the test because of our longer time period (1953–1981) for completeness. In fact, the inclusion of an additional $\Delta\log\epsilon_t$ would not alter KK's results as the variable was generally zero over their estimation period. Since $\phi_0 = 0$ is equivalent to the KK specification we have consequently, for pedantic reasons, characterized the three restrictions of the KK specification that we wish to examine as

$$\begin{bmatrix} \gamma_3 \\ \gamma_{14} \\ \phi_0 \end{bmatrix} = \begin{bmatrix} 1 \\ 1 \\ 0 \end{bmatrix}$$

Thus, ϕ_0 measures the 'excess' sensitivity of the balance of payments to changes in the exchange rate. Since misspecification of the above type can yield non-constant parameters outside the estimation period, evidence in favour of including $\Delta\log\epsilon_t$ would serve the purpose of highlighting the limitations of a simulation based on the original model.

2.2.2 Restrictions concerning the constancy of parameters

KK assume that the countries exhibit in their sample identical behavioural parameters (they allow variations in the intercepts) and that these parameters remain constant over time. In view of the fact that the representative cross-section model has potential applicability to individual countries, parameter constancy tests should accompany the estimation of the model. Since KK had only eight observations for each of the twenty-nine countries in their sample, they were not able to test for country and time constancy of their estimated parameters. To highlight this issue, therefore, we have chosen a sample that contains a much smaller number of countries than KK (seven as opposed to twenty-nine) and a much longer time period (27 as opposed to 8 years). With this sample, we can consider three sets of tests.

(1) First, we can test for constant parameters across countries. The null hypothesis, in that case, is

$$H_0 : \boldsymbol{\beta}_i = \boldsymbol{\beta} \tag{7.1}$$

where $\boldsymbol{\beta}_i$ denotes the vector of structural parameters for the *i*th country in the sample, and the test is performed by estimating the model with $\boldsymbol{\beta}_i$ unconstrained, and constrained to equal $\boldsymbol{\beta}$.

(2) Second, we can delete a country's observations and test the null hypothesis

$$H_0 : \boldsymbol{\beta}^* = \boldsymbol{\beta} \tag{7.2}$$

where $\boldsymbol{\beta}^*$ is the parameter vector of the 'shortened' sample. The two tests, however, are not equivalent in the sense that they will have different power against the alternative.

If the excluded observations are from the same population as the retained observations, then the sampling distributions would not differ significantly so as to reject the null hypothesis. In this context, it may be practicable to test whether the countries of one geographical grouping are similar to those of another. We can think of this test as measuring an 'index of structure similarity' of one country or group of countries to another country or group of countries.

(3) Third, and even more vital for policy purposes, we can test for parameter constancy over time. Two

concepts are important here: structural change and predictive accuracy. On the one hand, we can estimate the model for different sample periods and test for structural change. On the other, we can test for post-sample predictive accuracy of the estimated model. Various likelihood ratio tests (and their Wald and Lagrange multiplier versions) can be constructed depending on which null is of interest and against what alternative power is required (see Anderson and Mizon, 1984). Whilst the first two tests can be an aid in determining the degree of aggregation possible, the third test has profound implications of policy.

3. RESULTS

This section reports the results of testing the restrictions specified in the previous section. We present results for both the pooled sample and the individual countries. First we test two of KK's hypotheses in the context of the simple partial adjustment money stock equation that KK used as a benchmark against which to test the dynamic properties of their simultaneous model. KK's imposition of $\gamma_{14} = 1$ is based on simplicity, but also because it is consistent with the estimates of this standard money demand equation using their sample. However, if γ_{14} is jointly estimated within the simultaneous system then money demand results are superfluous. Otherwise, we would contend that a two-step approach of first finding an 'optimal' γ_{14}, by an appropriate estimation technique, is to be preferred to an arbitrarily imposed value. The question then will be whether the adjustment parameters are approximately equal for the pooled sample and the individual countries; conversely, whether the individual adjustment parameters are likely to be distributed about the pooled value with small variance. Thus, the money demand results in this section are more of an implicit rather than a direct test of KK as, in their model, changes in the real money stock are determined by the overall dynamic structure. The point though is that

KK's results are conditional, at least in part, on the assumption that expectations are predetermined at time t. Therefore, the money demand results are, in a sense, *instructive rather than destructive*, since we go on to 'endogenize' expectations. All tests reported are based on the likelihood ratio statistic, and the critical value is at the 5 per cent level of significance.

3.1 Test of Restrictions in 2.2.1

The parameter restrictions tested relate to the money demand equation on the one hand, and the structural model on the other.

3.1.1 Money Demand

Consider the dynamic money demand equation

$$\Delta \log m_t = \theta(\log m_t^d - \log m_{t-1}) \tag{7.3}$$

where $0 \leqslant \Theta \leqslant 1$ is the coefficient of adjustment.

Substituting for log m_t^d from (5) in Table 7.1 implies

$$\log m_t = \theta(\beta_1 + \gamma_4 \log y_t - \gamma_5 \pi_t) + (1 - \theta)\log m_{t-1} \tag{7.4}$$

Since π_t is unobservable, and defined by

$$\pi_t = \gamma_{14}\Delta \log P_{t-1} + (1 - \gamma_{14})\pi_{t-1} \tag{7.5}$$

it is possible to perform a grid search on γ_{14} by generating alternative π series, conditional on different values of γ_{14}, for some given initial value π_0, and observe which value of γ_{14} maximizes the log-likelihood function of (7.4). In this approach π_t is exogenously determined and so ordinary least squares is applicable to (7.4). An alternative more efficient approach is to solve (7.5) for π_t and substitute into (7.4). The resulting equation is thereby specified only on observable variables

$$\begin{aligned}\log m_t = {} & \theta\beta_1\gamma_{14} + [(1 - \gamma_{14}) \\ & + (1 - \theta)]\log m_{t-1} - (1 - \theta)(1 - \gamma_{14})\log \\ & \mathrm{m}_{t-2} + \theta\gamma_4 \log y_t - \theta y_4 (1 - \gamma_{14})\log y_{t-1} \\ & - \theta\gamma_5\gamma_{14}\Delta \log P_{t-1}\end{aligned} \tag{7.6}$$

We must note that since (7.6) is a transformation of (7.4) the error structures are not equal. If the stochastic version of (7.4) had an error term μ_t with white noise properties, then the error term in (7.6) would be given by

$$\omega_t = \mu_t - (1 - \gamma_{14})\mu_{t-1} \tag{7.7}$$

which is a first-order moving average process. As is well known, models with moving average error structures pose enormous computational problems and require iterative methods to minimize the residual sum of squares.[3] On the other hand, if we assume that ω_t is a white noise process, then the implicit inference is that (7.4) is probably misspecified and that μ_t is a first-order autoregressive process. Ordinary least squares would therefore provide an unbiased estimator of the coefficients but the sampling variances are likely to be seriously understated.[4] Of course, if $\gamma_{14} = 1$ then ω_t is equal to μ_t. In the estimation we assume ω_t is a white noise error and test this assumption using a Lagrange multiplier test statistic.[5]

Equation (7.6) can be thought of as an indicator of how much information is lost in using the grid search method as opposed to *the joint estimation* of θ and γ_{14}. Further, the general specification (7.6) nests three restricted cases. The null hypothesis

$$\mathrm{H}_0: \theta = 1 \tag{7.8}$$

questions whether a disequilibrium framework is justified,

$$H_0: \gamma_{14} = 1 \tag{7.9}$$

tests KK's assumption directly and

$$H_0: \theta = \gamma_{14} = 1 \tag{7.10}$$

poses the question, 'Does a simple transactions-type equilibrium model capture the main features of the data generation process?'

In addition, the above framework can be used to examine the appropriateness of the expectations-generating mechanism, and the implications of *a priori* assumptions. For example, we can ask whether the model would accent the restriction $\theta = 1$, given that $\gamma_{14} = 1$ is a valid prior. Formally, we can test

$$H_0: \theta = 1 | \gamma_{14} = 1 \quad (7.11)$$

and

$$H_0: \gamma_{14} = 1|_{\theta=1} \quad (7.12)$$

In the event that we reject either of the prior assumptions, the money demand equation will be misspecified. Further, in view of its central importance in the structural system, the model itself will be poorly specified, and the systems estimator will exacerbate rather than attenuate the unfortunate circumstance.

Table 7.2 presents the results of the tests for the pooled sample and the individual countries using both ordinary least squares (parameters unconstrained) and non-linear least squares (parameters constrained).

Pooled Sample

The null hypothesis $\theta = 1$ is not rejected in the single equation estimation. This implies that there is a tendency for the supply of and demand for real money balances to equilibrate. If any disequilibrium tendencies exist, their effects are negated within a year and are therefore unobservable. This result is conditional on the assumptions that the money demand function is correctly specified and that the determining variables are exogenous. Otherwise, a simultaneous structure would be more appropriate. This possibility of simultaneous equation bias has been referred to in connection with the appropriateness of the two-step approach.

Both hypotheses $\gamma_{14} = 1$ and $\theta = \gamma_{14} = 1$ are strongly rejected at the 5 per cent level of significance. The implication of this is that if a sequential nesting procedure is employed and we accept $\theta = 1$ as a 'primary' hypothesis that is analysed earlier in the sequence then, given the fact that $\theta = 1$ has not been rejected by the data, the relevant null would now be the conditional hypothesis:

$$H_0: \gamma_{14} = 1|_{\theta=1} \quad (7.13)$$

Table 7.2: Likelihood ratio tests for money demand functions

Countries	Pooled	Thailand	India	Sri Lanka	Panama	Peru	Honduras	Jamaica
Test for non-linearity when unrestricted	R	√	√	√	√	R	√	√
Test for $\delta_2 = 0$ implied by $\theta = 1$	√	√	√	√	√	R	√	√
Test for non-linearity when $\theta = 1$	R	√	√	R	√	√	√	√
Non-linear least squares test for $\theta = 1$	√	√	√	R	√	√	√	√
Test for $\delta_2 = \delta_4 = 0$ implies by $\gamma_{14} =$	R	√	R	√	√	R	√	√
Non-linear least squares test for $\gamma_{14} = 1$	R	√	R	√	√	R	√	√
Test for $\delta_1 = \delta_2 = \delta_4 = 0$ implied by $\theta = \gamma_{14} = 1$	R	R	R	R	R	R	R	R
Test for $\gamma_{14} = 1\|_{\theta=1}$	R	R	R	R	R	R	R	R
Test for $\theta = 1\|_{\gamma_{14}=1}$	R	R	R	R	R	R	R	R

Notes:
1. *Unrestricted OLS equation:* $\log m_t = \delta + \delta_1 \log m_{t-1} + \delta_2 \log m_{t-2} + \delta_3 \log y_t + \delta_4 \log y_{t-1} + \delta_5 + \log P_{t-1} + \mu_t$.
2. *Unrestricted NLLS equation:* $\log m_t = \alpha^1 + [(1 - \gamma_{14}) + (1 - \theta)]\log m_{t-1} - (1 - \theta)(1 - \gamma_{14})\log m_{t-2} + \theta\gamma_4 \log y_t - \theta\gamma_4(1 - \gamma_{14})\log y_{t-1} - \theta\gamma_5\gamma_{14}\, \Delta\log P_{t-1} + \omega t$.
3. 'R' & '√' denote 'reject' & 'do not reject' respectively, at 5 per cent level.

That test is also rejected. We can think of this, more simply, as asking whether the restriction $\gamma_{14} = 1$ would be data admissible if we had started off with the assumption that $\theta = 1$ and *we were correct in doing so* (i.e. $\theta = 1$ is a valid prior). In addition, the non-linear restrictions for the unrestricted (general) and $\theta = 1$ cases are both rejected at the 5 per cent level.

With regard to the parameter values, all OLS estimates have expected signs and plausible magnitudes. The lagged inflation term is significant only in the KK($\gamma_{14} = 1$) formulation. The omission of the lagged-income term in that formulation seems to impart an upward bias as well on the income elasticity ($\gamma_{14} = 1.56$). Further, although significant for the unrestricted non-linear case, γ_{14} turns out to be fairly small (0.1). The pooled results therefore seem to indicate that within the single-equation framework estimated, a disequilibrium framework may not be justified, and that the expectations-generating mechanism is not as naive as assumed. Further, the implausibly low value of γ_{14}, if relevant to the model at all, ought to be jointly estimated.

Individual Countries

How do the individual country estimates compare? Table 7.2 presents the test results for the seven countries and the pooled sample.

With the exception of the hypotheses $\theta = \gamma_{14} = 1$, $\gamma_{14} = 1|_{\theta=1}$ and $\theta = 1|_{\gamma_{14}=1}$, which are rejected by all countries and the pooled sample, the hypotheses are specific to countries. If we regard rows 2 and 4 of Table 7.2 as the composite set of results for the hypothesis $\theta = 1$, then we find that Peru and Sri Lanka are the only two countries that do not reject a disequilibrium framework. Further, although Peru is the only country to reject the non-linearity assumption for the unrestricted case the pooled sample also rejects the test for non-linearity. In addition, although the pooled sample rejects the naive expectations-generating mechanism ($\gamma_{14} = 1$) five of the countries actually accept the restriction. It is therefore clear that the pooled result can be dominated by the result of one country or a small proportion of countries in the sample, thereby emphasizing that the results of the pooled sample may be unrepresentative of those of the components of the pool.

The country results show that the omission of different variables affects countries differently. Thus the cross-section result is more than likely to be an average/netting-out result to which limited significance can be attached. It is further clear that the *a priori* imposition of restrictions on the money demand equation can lead to possibly false inference about the magnitude and even sign of the parameters. In addition, the residuals are generally well behaved across countries, except for the equation with $\theta = \gamma_{14} = 1$ for which all countries exhibit first-order serial correlation.

3.1.2 The Model

Having examined several restrictions in the context of a standard single-equation framework, we now consider some aspects of estimation in the context of KK's simultaneous model. In contrast to KK's two-step approach, we pursue the alternative method of allowing γ_{14} to be determined within the model structure jointly with all other structural parameters. This approach avoids the potential simultaneous equation bias that could result from the two-step approach, provides direct information on the size and significance of γ_{14}, and is likely to produce more efficient estimates. In addition, we do not impose the three restrictions of KK described on p. 143, but instead allow these parameters to be freely determined by the data for our seven-country sample. As in the money demand equation above, we solve (6) of Table 7.1 for π_t and substitute into the relevant equations to yield the generalized model specification (See Table A1 in appendix). The above modifications simply provide a more general (unrestricted) version of the KK specification, but maintain their original simultaneous structure.

We can indicate the difference between the two versions of the model by characterizing the KK formulation as being equivalent to a set of restrictions on the more general unrestricted version, namely

$$\begin{bmatrix} \gamma_3 \\ \gamma_{14} \\ \phi_0 \end{bmatrix} = \begin{bmatrix} 1 \\ 1 \\ 0 \end{bmatrix}$$

These restrictions can be tested using an ordered nesting procedure in which a single (or joint) hypothesis is followed by a conditional hypothesis. Whilst each single (or joint) hypothesis is tested against the unrestricted model, the subsequent conditional hypothesis is concerned with the validity of imposing a further set of restrictions, and, in principle, can only be tested if the primary hypothesis has not been rejected.

The results that follow are obtained from FIML estimates of the most unrestricted and various restricted versions of the model. We have also effected a few minor changes. In comparison with KK, who linearize identities (7) and (8) of Table 7.1 in terms of the logarithms of the variables, we use the original levels specification. In addition, the foreign rate of inflation was proxied by the rate of world inflation rather than the US rate of inflation, and the $\Delta \log \epsilon_t$ term of equation (1) in Table 7.1 is not omitted as in KK. Ideally, an exchange rate index with the same weights should also be used, rather than the US$ exchange rate. But this, we think, will complicate the analysis without altering the substance of the results. In view of the fact that we have lengthened the time series and reduced the number of countries in the pooled sample, our parameter estimates are *not directly comparable* with the KK estimates. However, that *does not alter the nature of our conclusions*.

Pooled Sample

The results for the pooled and country tests for parameter restrictions in the structural model are contained in Tables 7.3 and 7.4. In interpreting the tables the top row is the alternative (maintained) hypothesis. Thus, for example, the null hypothesis

$$H_0\colon \phi_0 = 0|_{\gamma_{14}=1} \tag{7.14}$$

of Table 7.3 corresponds to row H_4 and column H_2.

Table 7.3: Likelihood ratio tests for pooled sample

ALT NULL	General model	H_1	H_2	H_3	H_4	H_5	H_6
H_1	R	—	—	—	—	—	—
H_2	√	—	—	—	—	—	—
H_3	R	—	—	—	—	—	—
H_4	R	√	R	—	—	—	—
H_5	R	R	—	√			
H_6	R	—	R	√			
H_7	R	R	R	√	R	√	√

H_1: $\phi_0 = 0$; H_2: $\gamma_{14} = 1$: H_3: $\gamma_3 = 1$; H_4: $\phi_0 = 0, \gamma_{14} = 1$; H_5: $\phi_0 = 0, \gamma_3 = 1$; H_6: $\gamma_3 = 1, \gamma_{14} = 1$; (KK) H_7: $\gamma_3 = 1, \gamma_{14} = 1, \phi_0 = 0$.
'R' and '√' denote 'reject' and 'do not reject' respectively at 5 per cent level.

Consider firstly the pooled results. Of the seven basic hypotheses (column 1) the only hypothesis that is not rejected by the data is $\gamma_{14} = 1$. Conditional on that result, we can examine the hypotheses shown in column H_2 of Table 7.3. We find that the conditional hypotheses

$$H_0\colon \phi_0 = 0|_{\gamma_{14}=1}$$

$$H_0\colon \gamma_3 = 1|_{\gamma_{14}=1}$$

$$H_0\colon \gamma_3 = 1, \phi_0 = 0|_{\gamma_{14}=1}$$

are all rejected at the 5 per cent level of significance. If the researcher is not keen on testing all subset hypotheses and follows a sequentially ordered nesting procedure to reduce the parameter space of the most general model, then the preferred hypothesis, abstracting from other considerations, would be $\gamma_{14} = 1$. Although this outcome is consistent with the KK result (following their two-step approach), it differs from our single-equation demand for money results (the two are not comparable) which reject the hypothesis $\gamma_{14} = 1$. Thus, if we had followed a two-step approach the π series (see equation 6 of Table 7.1) would have been generated using a value of γ_{14} that was different from unity.

Table 7.4: Likelihood ratio test for individual countries

Null	Alt.	General Model	H_1	H_2	H_3
Thailand	H_1	√	—	—	—
	H_2	√	√	—	—
	H_3	R	R	—	—
	H_4	R	R	R	R
India	H_1	√	—	—	—
	H_2	R	R	—	—
	H_3	R	R	—	√
	H_4	R	R	R	√
Sri Lanka	H_1	√	—	—	—
	H_2	√	√	—	—
	H_3	R	R	—	—
	H_4	R	R	R	√
Panama	H_1	—	—	—	—
	H_2	R	—	—	—
	H_3	√	—	—	—
	H_4	R	—	√	R
Peru	H_1	√	—	—	—
	H_2	√	√	—	—
	H_3	R	R	—	—
	H_4	R	R	R	√
Honduras	H_1	—	—	—	—
	H_2	√	—	—	—
	H_4	R	—	R	R
Jamaica	H_1	√	—	—	—
	H_2	R	R	—	—
	H_3	R	R	—	—
	H_4	R	R	R	√

Notes: H_1: $\phi_0 = 0$; H_2: $\phi_0 = 0$, $\gamma_{14} = 1$; H_3: $\phi_0 = 0$, $\gamma_3 = 1$ (KK) H_4: $\phi = 0$, $\gamma_3 = 1$, $\gamma_{14} = 1$.
'R' and '√' denote 'reject' and 'do not reject' respectively at 5 per cent level.

Consider now the alternative modelling procedure which imposes additional restrictions to a primary set of maintained prior restrictions without first testing the latter. This procedure corresponds to the approach utilized by KK who consider $\phi_0 = 0$ and $\gamma_3 = 1$ to be 'maintained theoretical priors' but allow the data to determine γ_{14}. Within our framework, we can treat $\gamma_{14} = 1$ (found 'true' by KK) as a secondary hypothesis which can be tested conditional on either $H_1(\phi_0 = 0)$, $H_3(\gamma_3 = 1)$, or $H_5(\phi_0 = 0, \gamma_3 = 1)$. The results are shown in columns H_1, H_3 and H_5 of Table 7.3. We find that although H_3, H_5 and H_7 (the KK specification) are all rejected against the unrestricted model, H_7 is not rejected when either H_3 or H_5 are postulated to be maintained priors! Thus, we are led to accepting the restriction $\gamma_{14} = 1$ if we *believed* $\phi_0 = 0$ and $\gamma_3 = 1$ to be valid assumptions, even though we can demonstrate conclusively that the joint hypothesis H_7 is rejected *against the unrestricted model.*

Individual Countries

Table 7.4 reports the results for each country, using a specific nesting branch which starts from $\phi_0 = 0$.[6] Again the KK specification ($\phi_0 = 0$, $\gamma_3 = \gamma_{14} = 1$) is rejected in every case against the unrestricted model. Yet $\gamma_{14} = 1$ is not rejected by four countries conditional on the maintained priors $\phi_0 = 0$ and $\gamma_3 = 1$ (see columns 1 and 4). It is interesting to note that whilst $\gamma_{14} = 1$ is an unconditionally acceptable restriction for the pooled sample (i.e. not conditional on $\phi_0 = 0$ and $\gamma_3 = 1$) and can therefore be validly incorporated with $\phi_0 = 0$ and $\gamma_3 = 1$—assuming those restrictions are correct—the same result does not hold for the individual countries.

A comparison of the pooled model and individual-country estimates shows that whilst the pooled model produced acceptable results in terms of expected sign and magnitude of the parameters the same does not hold for all the individual countries. In fact, the model fits the individual countries with differing degrees of accuracy—a point, no doubt, in favour of a country-by-country modelling approach.

3.2 Parameter Constancy Tests for Structural Model (Pooled Sample)

With regard to parameter constancy we perform two sets of tests on the pooled sample—parameter constancy *over time* and *across countries*. For constancy across countries we delete one country from the sample space and test whether the remaining six, posited to have equal slope coefficients, different intercepts and equal covariance matrices, can predict the seventh country. The prediction test, distributed chi-square, is rejected in all cases. The over-time parameter constancy test used is the Mizon–Anderson (1984) (see their Table 2) test statistic for which equal covariance matrices are assumed. The relevant hypothesis of interest is whether the model estimated up to 1975 can predict the 1976–1981 period. It is clear that if the model rejects parameter constancy then inference based on the estimates of the model, with regard to future economic policy (say), is at least suspect. In fact, not only does the model fail the standard 5 per cent test, but a 0.5 per cent test would also fail. Other switch-points were also tried (1978/1979) but none accepted parameter constancy.

As is well known, parameter constancy may be induced by genuine structural change or by the interaction of equation misspecification with changed behaviour of some variables of the system. Therefore, the possibility that the estimation period contains three distinct periods (1955–1967, 1968–1975, and 1976–1981) must be examined carefully. If the latter conjecture is correct the model fitted over the whole period will not uniformly represent any one subperiod and may not be able to reasonably predict the latter observations in any particular subperiod. In fact, for estimation on the period 1955–1975, the model exhibits a switch-point in 1967. Pursuing this point further, we find that examination of the parameters of the model estimated over the subperiods 1955–1967, 1968–1975, 1955–1975, 1968–1981 is such that the 1955–1981 estimates are in some instances (for the more variable coefficients) average values. For example, we find that ϕ_0 is significant over the 1968–1975 period, and insignificant for both 1955–1967 and 1955–1981. Further, signs and magnitudes of coefficients are sensitive to the different estimation periods. From the above, it would seem that further research on the parameter constancy aspect of the model seems desirable.

An alternative method of testing for cross-country differences in the structural parameters is to replace the parameter to be tested by a linear combination of the basic parameter and one multiplied by a country-specific dummy. Whilst we have not yet pursued that point, it is similar in content to the first parameter constancy test proposed in Section 2.2.2 above. In fact, this method allows one to focus on all the structure parameters or on *some parameters of interest*. For example, we may want to posit that the government sector adjustment parameters are constant across countries but the other structural parameters are not. This sort of restriction should, of course, follow initial individual country estimation; basically, a data-instigated type of modelling strategy.

4. SUMMARY AND CONCLUDING REMARKS

This chapter has focused on a model developed at the IMF which was estimated on a time series cross-section sample of *twenty-nine* developing countries. After highlighting various methodological issues relating to the estimation process used by the authors, we formulate a less restricted version of their model which is then estimated on both a pooled sample of *seven* developing countries as well as the individual countries, using a much longer time period than KK. The less restricted model is used for testing a number of theoretical assumptions posited in the 'IMF model' as well as the assumption of parameter constancy both across countries and over time.

Our conclusions are twofold. First, from a modelling perspective, whilst a model can be based on a set of prior restrictions that are believed to be theoretically valid, the imposition of any further restriction or set of restrictions ought to be tested against a more general model which does not incorporate the primary restrictions unless these maintained priors have already been validated against the more general model. We have shown that, even given the *a priori* restrictions of their model, certain properties of the sample set assumed in KK should have been tested, since in our sample (which differed from the KK sample) they do not hold. It needs to be stated that, although the 'general-to-specific' nesting procedure advocated will depend on the branch of the nest followed (with different branches leading to probably different results!), the alternative method of starting with a set of maintained theoretical (and therefore untested) priors will, if incorrect, inevitably produce results which will be misleading to an unknown degree. Further, if the maintained priors are not valid, inferences based on them can at best be suboptimal.

Secondly, from a policy perspective, our results point out the potential hazard of applying the implications of a time series cross-section model, generally or as a guideline, to any specific country. Not only is the model unlikely to characterize adequately the economic process of that country, but also policy prescriptions based on it may have no hope of succeeding except by accident. Given on the one hand, the observed disparities between the results of the pooled sample and the corresponding results of the individual countries and, on the other, the strong rejection of the assumption of parameter constancy we are led to conclude that, whenever possible, a country-by-country modelling approach is to be recommended.

It is arguable that the intrinsic value of a time series cross-section model is dependent on how well it characterizes that broad class of countries of which it is representative. Representative models can be useful and necessary, especially where data and manpower limitations so dictate. We recommend, however, that various tests should be performed to check the validity of the assumptions contained, both implicit and explicit, in the representative model. Perhaps what should be encouraged is further research to investigate the question 'What is an appropriate degree of (pooling) aggregation?'

ACKNOWLEDGEMENT

The authors would like to thank George McKenzie, Jan Podivinsky, Malcolm Knight, Peter Smith, Grayham Mizon and an anonymous referee for helpful comments on previous versions of the paper. Our thanks also to participants of the International Economics Study Group Tenth Annual Conference at which the latest version was presented. We remain responsible for all errors made.

NOTES

1. The countries in the sample are Argentina, Brazil, Chile, Colombia, the Dominican Republic, Ecuador, El Salvador, Guatemala, Haiti, Honduras, Nicaragua, Panama, Paraguay, Uruguay, Jamaica, Jordan, Sri Lanka, India, Korea, Malaysia, Nepal, the Philippines, Singapore, Thailand, Burundi, Ghana, Kenya, Malawi and Zambia.
2. The seven countries are Thailand, India, Sri Lanka, Panama, Peru, Honduras and Jamaica, and were chosen primarily on the grounds that a comparable data set existed for the period 1953–1981. Of the seven, Peru is the only country not included in the KK sample.
3. For an authoritative exposition on time series analysis, *see* Box and Jenkins (1976).
4. See Johnston (1972).
5. *See* Godfrey and Wickens (1982), also Breusch and Godfrey (1981).
6. $\phi_0 = 0$ is not a testable restriction for Panama and Honduras as their exchange rates were unchanged throughout the period.

APPENDIX 1

Data

The data used are annual observations for the period 1953–1981. The series were obtained from the IMF's *International Financial Statistics 1982 Yearbook*. For Jamaica, the government expenditure and revenue series were augmented for the periods 1953–1959 and 1980–1981 from the *United Nations National Accounts Yearbook* and the *Bank of Jamaica Statistical Digest* respectively. All prices are period averages and stocks are end of period values.

Definitions

P = consumer price index, 1975 = 100; line 64.
R = domestic value of net international reserves (line

Table A1: Generalized model specification

Inflation

$$\begin{aligned}\Delta\log P_t = {} & \alpha_0 + \gamma_1\{\log m_{t-1} - (1-\gamma_{14})\log m_{t-2} - \gamma_4 \log y_t + \gamma_4(1-\gamma_{14})\log y_{t-1}\} \\ & + \{1 + \gamma_{14}(\gamma_1\gamma_5 - 1) - \gamma_2\}\Delta\log P_{t-1} \\ & + \gamma_3\Delta\log(P_{f,t}{}^{*}\,\epsilon_t) + \{\gamma_2 - \gamma_3(1-\gamma_{14})\} \\ & \Delta\log(P_{f,t-1}{}^{*}\,\epsilon_{t-1}) - \gamma_2\gamma_{14}LPR_{t-2} + \lambda_1\end{aligned} \tag{1}$$

Balance of payments

$$\begin{aligned}\Delta log\, R_t^{*} = {} & \delta_0 + (1-\gamma_{14})\Delta\log R_{t-1}^{*} + \gamma_6\{\gamma_4\log y_t - \gamma_4(1-\gamma_{14})\log y_{t-1} \\ & - \log m_{t-1} + (1-\gamma_{14})\log m_{t-2} + \Delta\log P_t \\ & - (1-\gamma_{14}(1-\gamma_5))\Delta\log P_{t-1}\} - \gamma_7 LPR_{t-1} \\ & + \gamma_7(1-\gamma_{14})LPR_{t-2} + \phi_0\Delta\log\epsilon_t\end{aligned} \tag{2}$$

Government sector

(a) Expenditures:

$$\log G_t = \gamma_8\beta_2 + \gamma_8\gamma_9(\log y_t + \log P_t) + (1-\gamma_8)\log G_{t-1} \tag{3a}$$

(b) Revenues:

$$\log T_t = \gamma_{10}\beta_3 + \gamma_{10}\gamma_{11}(\log y_t + \log P_t) + (1 - \gamma_{10})\log T_{t-1} \tag{3b}$$

Real output

$$(1 + \gamma_4\gamma_{12})\Delta\log y_t = \mu_0 + (1 - \gamma_{14})\Delta\log y_{t-1} + \gamma_{12}[\log m_{t-1} - (1 - \gamma_{14})\log m_{t-2} - \gamma_4\gamma_{14}\log y_{t-1} + \gamma_5\gamma_{14}\,\Delta\log P_{t-1}\} + \gamma_{13}(\log y_t^* - \log y_{t-1}) - \gamma_{13}(1 - \gamma_{14})(\log y_{t-1}^* - \log y_{t-2}) + \lambda_2 \tag{4}$$

Domestic credit

$$DC_t = DC_{t-1} + (G_t - T_t) + \Delta CP_t \tag{5}$$

Money supply

$$M_t = R_t^* + DC_t + RES_t \tag{6}$$

Definitions:

1. The approximation $R_t^* = F_t{}^*\epsilon_{t-1}$ where F_t is the stock of reserves valued in foreign currency (US$) is used to adjust the domestic value of international reserves for the effects of in-sample exchange rate changes.
2. RES is the residual term implied by the data-admissible identity $M_t = R_t^* + DC_t + RES_t$.
3. $LPR_t = \log P_t - \log(\epsilon_t{}^*P_{f,t})$

	$1d$ multiplied by line *ae*).
G	= government expenditure; line 82.
T	= government revenue; line 81.
y	= real income; line 99b divided by line 64.
DC	= net domestic credit to the consolidated banking system; line 32.
M	= money broadly defined; line 34 plus line 35.
m	= real money balances, M/P.
y^*	= trend level of real income derived from $y^* = y_o^* e^{gt}$ where g is trend growth rate during estimation period; y_o^* is the value of real income in the base year.
P_f	= world consumer price index.
ϵ	= exchange rate; line *ae*.
ΔCP_t	= residual from domestic credit identity: $\Delta CP_t = \Delta DC_t - G_t + T_t$.

Software

The computer program employed was TSP, version 3.5 (Hall and Hall, 1980). The model was estimated using Full Information Maximum Likelihood.

REFERENCES

Aghevli, B. B. and Khan, M. S. (1977) 'The monetary approach to balance of payments determination: an empirical test', in IMF (1977) (below).

Aghevli, B. B. and Khan, M. S. (1978) 'Government deficits and the inflationary process in developing countries', *IMF Staff Papers*, **25**, 383–416.

Anderson, G. and Mizon, G. (1984) 'Parameter constancy tests: old and new'. Discussion Paper, University of Southampton, No. 8325.

Box, G. and Jenkins, J. M. (1976) *Time Series Analysis: Forecasting and Control*. Holden-Day, San Francisco.

Breusch, T. S. and Godfrey, L. G. (1981) 'A Review of recent work on testing for auto-correlation in dynamic economic models', in Currie, D., Nobay, R. and Peel, D. (eds) *Macroeconomic Analysis: Essays in Macroeconomics and Econometrics*. Croom Helm.

Godfrey, L. G. and Wickens, M. (1982) 'Tests of misspecification using locally equivalent alternative models', in Chow, G. C. and Corsi, P. (eds) *Evaluating the Reliability of Macroeconomic Models*, John Wiley & Sons, Chichester, New York.

Hall, B. H. and Hall, R. E. (1980) 'Time series processor, version 3.5, user guide', Unpublished.
IMF (1977) *The Monetary Approach to the Balance of Payments*. Washington, DC.
Johnston, J. (1972) *Econometric Methods*. McGraw Hill, New York.
Khan, M. S. (1977) 'The determination of the balance of payments and income in developing countries', in IMF (1977) (above).
Khan, M. S. and Knight, M. D. (1981) 'Stabilisation programs in developing countries: a formal framework', *IMF Staff Papers*, **28**, 1–53.

8 Exchange Rate Dynamics and the Labour Market

Elias Karakitsos

1. INTRODUCTION

Early theories of flexible exchange rates emphasized the current account as the most important determinant of the exchange rate (see e.g. Robinson, 1937;: Machlup, 1940). The capital account was considered as independent of the exchange rate with capital movements being treated as transfer payments. Since the seminal papers by Mundell and Fleming in the 1960s, however, the importance of the capital account in exchange rate determination grew continuously, whereas that of the current account declined. The so-called asset market view of the exchange rate became the order of the day in the 1970s.

Recently, however, several authors have attempted to integrate the current account with the asset market view within a general equilibrium macro framework (see e.g. Frenkel and Rodriguez, 1975; Branson, 1976; Kouri, 1976; Kouri and de Macedo, 1978: Dornbusch and Fischer, 1980; Branson and Buiter, 1983). In these models, however, the analysis concentrates on essentials with many aspects of modern macro theory and many sources of dynamics being ignored or suppressed. Usually, one or more of the following simplifying assumptions are made: perfect asset substitutability; output is assumed to be exogenously fixed at its full employment level and the analysis concentrates on the price level or, alternatively, output is endogenous and the price level is fixed; even when output is endogenous, no attention is paid to the supply side, with the labour market and the capital accumulation process being ignored; the government budget constraint and, consequently, some aspects of the wealth accumulation process are usually omitted from the analysis; no attention is paid to the effects of interest payments on the current account or the government budget constraint. Although all these studies concentrate on the dynamic adjustment of the system, they choose to ignore all but one or two sources of dynamics, so that the evolution of the model can be described by a low order system of differential equations.

The reason why these studies abstract from all these aspects of modern macro theory and dynamics is analytical tractability and concentration on essentials. But it might be useful to investigate the effects of these simplifying assumptions so as to determine whether the main conclusions would be altered. Indeed, as it will be shown in this paper, this is the case.

The aim of this paper is to relax all these assumptions and to study in that broadened context the behaviour of the exchange rate when both the current and the capital accounts interact for its determination. The emphasis is on the dynamic behaviour of the exchange rate following a fiscal or monetary policy change. Further insight into the determinants of the exchange rate is gained by considering the role of the current account and capital account separately within a general equilibrium framework. In this comparison, attention is also paid to the consequences for reserves of assuming that the exchange rate adjusts to clear only one of the accounts.

The model developed in this paper is basically an extended *IS–LM* for an open economy, with the assets markets clearing faster than the goods/labour markets. The model allows for trade as well as capital flows under perfect capital mobility, but imperfect asset substitutability. Capital flows consist of both bonds and money which are issued at home and abroad and are held by both domestic and foreign residents. The role of the government budget constraint in affecting the asset accumulation process and its effects on expenditure and portfolio decisions are recognized with strong wealth effects built into the *IS* and *LM* curves.

Furthermore, interest payments are also included. On the supply side, it is recognized that investment leads to capital accumulation, which affects the supply of output, along with a Phillips curve. Expectations in the foreign exchange market are assumed to be rational, whereas in the labour/goods market they are formed adaptively.

The additional realism that is built into the model, and the incorporated richer dynamics, add significantly to the complexity of the model and make it impossible to study it analytically. Instead, the model is solved numerically by assigning plausible numerical values to the coefficients of the behavioural equations. This approach makes it possible to build up a more realistic model and to concentrate on its dynamic behaviour, which is of importance in real life problems. In contrast, analytical models concentrate on comparative statics of an instantaneous equilibrium, which is too short a time, and in comparative statics of the steady state, which is too long a time for all practical purposes. When attention is paid to the dynamics, analytical models sacrifice reality with a low order system of differential equations. The disadvantage of a numerical approach, on the other hand, is that the results are coefficient specific. The solution to this problem is to submit the system to extensive sensitivity analysis in order to examine the robustness of the results within a critical parameter range.

The rest of the chapter is organized as follows. The next section discusses the model. The effects of fiscal and monetary policy are analysed in Section 3, with the sensitivity of the results to parameter variation dealt with in Section 4. A comparison of the results with those from other studies is discussed in Section 5, while some conclusions are offered in Section 6.

2. THE MODEL

The model (Table 8.1) consists of six parts. Equations 1 deal with aggregate demand; equation 1.1 defines equilibrium in the product market. Consumer expenditure, equation 1.2, is influenced by real disposable income, *YD*, the real interest rate, $R - \pi$, changes in real consumer credit, $\Delta BLH/CPI$, and real wealth, V. Disposable income is deflated by the consumer price index, CPI, reflecting that foreign prices and thus the exchange rate, are important in consumers' decisions. Real disposable income, equation 1.3, is defined to include expected capital gains or losses on private sector holdings of nominal financial assets, due to inflation and on holdings of foreign financial assets due to exchange rate fluctuations. Interest income, equation 1.4, arises from holdings of domestic government bonds, BD, foreign government bonds, BW, time deposits with domestic banks in domestic currency, TD, time deposits with foreign banks in foreign currency, TDW, less interest payments on bank lending to households and companies. Revaluation effects of interest income from abroad due to exchange rate fluctuations are incorporated. Interest receipts are allowed to be taxed differently from labour income and the marginal propensity to consume out of these two sources of income are also allowed to differ.

Real investment is specified in equation 1.5 as a lagged adjustment of the actual to the desired stock of physical capital. The desired stock depends on output, Y, the real interest rate, $R - \pi$, and changes in real bank lending to companies, $\Delta BLC/PGDP$.

Equations 2 deal with the foreign sector. Competitiveness, or the real exchange rate, $COMP$, is defined in equation 2.1 as the ratio of domestic to foreign prices, expressed in domestic currency. The volume of exports, X, depends on world trade, WT, and competitiveness. The volume of imports is influenced by output, Y, and competitiveness. The import price, equation 2.4, is a weighted average of the price of imported final goods, PW, and imported raw materials, PIW. The weight, a_{28}, reflects the extent to which the country depends on imported raw materials in the production of its output. The distributed lag function of weights, $a_{29}(L)$, measures the lags, if any, in the adjustment of import prices. The balance of payments identity consists of trade flows, capital flows, which comprise both currency and bonds, and interest payments on capital flows. Capital flows induce revaluation of the stock of assets due to

Table 8.1: The model

Aggregate Demand

1.1 $$Y = C + I + G + X - Q$$

1.2 $$C = a_1 a_2(L)\, YD + a_3 a_4(L)\,(1 - HRT)\frac{OPI}{CPI} + a_5 a_6(L)\,(R - \pi) + a_7 a_8(L)\frac{\Delta BLH}{CPI} + a_9 V_{t-1} + a_{10} C_{t-1}$$

where $0 < a_1, a_3, a_9, a_{10} < 1,\ a_7 > 0,\ a_5 < 0$

1.3 $$YD = (1 - SRT)\frac{PGDP\ Y}{CPI} - \pi(V_{t-1} - K_{t-1}) - EGER\ \frac{BW_{t-1} + TDW_{t-1}}{CPI\ ER}$$

1.4 $$\mathrm{OPI} = [(1 + \mathrm{R}_{t-1})^{1/4} - 1]\mathrm{BD}_{t-1} + [(1 + \mathrm{RW}_{t-1})^{1/4} - 1]\frac{\mathrm{BW}_{t-1}}{\mathrm{ER}} + [(1 + \mathrm{RW}_{t-1} - \mathrm{K}_2)^{1/4} - 1]\frac{\mathrm{TDW}_{t-1}}{\mathrm{ER}} + [(1 + \mathrm{R}_{t-1} - \mathrm{K}_1)^{1/4} - 1]\mathrm{TD}_{t-1} - [(1 + \mathrm{R}_{t-1} + \mathrm{K}_3)^{1/4} - 1]\,(\mathrm{BLH}_{t-1} + \mathrm{BLC}_{t-1})$$

1.5 $$\mathrm{I} = \mathrm{a}_{11}\mathrm{a}_{12}(\mathrm{L})\ \mathrm{Y} + \mathrm{a}_{13}\mathrm{a}_{14}(\mathrm{L})\,(\mathrm{R} - \pi) + \mathrm{a}_{15}\mathrm{a}_1(\mathrm{L})\frac{\Delta \mathrm{BLC}}{\mathrm{PGDP}} + \mathrm{a}_{17}\mathrm{K}_{t-1}$$

$a_{11}, a_{15} > 0 \qquad a_{13}, a_{17} < 0$

The Foreign Sector

2.1 $$COMP = \frac{PGDP\ ER}{PW}$$

2.2 $$X = a_{18}a_{19}(L)\ COMP + a_{20}a_{21}(L)\ WT + a_{22}X_{t-1}$$

$a_{18} < 0, \qquad a_{20} > 0, \qquad 0 < a_{22} < 1$

2.3 $$Q = a_{23}a_{24}(L)\ COMP + a_{25}a_{26}(L)\ Y + a_{27}Q_{t-1}$$

$a_{23} > 0, \qquad 0 < a_{25}, a_{27} < 1$

2.4 $$PM = \frac{a_{28}\ PIW + (1 - a_{28})\ PW}{a_{29}(L)\ ER}$$

2.5 $$\Delta RES = PGDP\,X - PM\,Q + \Delta BF - \left[\frac{BW}{ER} - \frac{BW_{t-1}}{ER_{t-1}}\right] - \left[\frac{TDW}{ER} - \frac{TDW_{t-1}}{ER_{t-1}}\right] + \Delta TDF + [(1 + RW_{t-1})^{1/4} - 1] \frac{BW_{t-1}}{ER} + [(1 + RW_{t-1} - K_2)^{1/4} - 1] \frac{TDW_{t-1}}{ER} - [(1 + R_{t-1})^{1/4} - 1]BF_{t-1} - [(1 + R_{t-1} - K_1)^{1/4} - 1]TDF_{t-1}$$

2.6 $GER = a_{29}\,\Delta RES$

Production and Wage-Price Sector

3.1 $YCAP = a_{30}K_{t-1} + a_{31} \qquad a_{30} > 0$

3.2 $GW = a_{32}a_{33}(L)\,(Y - YCAP) + \pi \qquad a_{32} > 0$

3.3 $$\ell nPGDP = a_{34}a_{35}(L)\,\ell nW + (1 - a_{34})\,a_{36}(L)\,\ell n \frac{PIW}{ER} + a_{37}a_{38}(L)\,(Y - YCAP)$$

$$0 < a_{34} < 1 \qquad a_{37} > 0$$

3.4 $$\ell nCPI = a_{39}a_{40}(L)\,\ell nPGDP + (1 - a_{39})\,a_{40}(L)\,\ell nPM$$

$$0 < a_{39} < 1$$

Financial Markets

4.1 $URD = R - RW + EGER$

4.2 $$\frac{M}{CPI} = a_{41}a_{42}(L)\,Y + a_{43}a_{44}(L)\,R + a_{45}V_{t-1}$$

$$a_{41} > 0 \qquad a_{43} < 0 \qquad 0 < a_{45} < 1$$

4.3 $$\frac{BD}{CPI} = a_{46}a_{47}(L)\,Y + a_{48}a_{49}(L)\,URD + a_{50}V_{t-1}$$

$$a_{46} \leq 0 \qquad a_{48} > 0 \qquad 0 < a_{50} < 1$$

4.4 $$\frac{BF\,ER}{PW} = a_{51}\,URD + a_{52} \qquad a_{51} > 0$$

4.5 $B = BD + BF$

4.6 $$\frac{BW}{ER\ CPI} = a_{53}Y + a_{54}a_{55}(L)\ URD + a_{56}V_{t-1}$$

$$a_{53} \leq 0 \qquad a_{54} < 0 \qquad 0 < a_{56} < 1$$

4.7 $$\frac{TDW}{ER\ CPI} = a_{57}a_{58}(L)\ Y + a_{59}a_{60}(L)\ URD + a_{61}V_{t-1}$$

$$a_{57} > 0 \qquad a_{59} < 0 \qquad 0 < a_{61} < 1$$

4.8 $$\frac{BLH}{CPI} = a_{62}a_{63}(L)\ Y + a_{64}a_{65}(L)\ (R + K_3) + a_{66}\ V_{t-1}$$

$$a_{62} > 0 \qquad a_{64} < 0$$

4.9 $$\frac{BLC}{PGDP} = a_{67}a_{68}(L)\ Y + a_{69}a_{70}(L)\ (R + K_3)$$

$$a_{67} > 0 \qquad a_{69} < 0$$

4.10 $$TD = BLG + BLH + BLC - TDF$$

4.11 $$\frac{TDE\ ER}{PW} = a_{71}\ URD + a_{72} \qquad a_{71} < 0$$

4.12 $$V = \frac{M + BD + \dfrac{BW + TDW}{ER} + TD - BLH - BLC}{CPI} + K$$

Asset Accumulations

5.1 $$\Delta BLG = PSBR - \Delta B - \Delta M + \Delta RES$$

5.2 $$PSBR = PGDP\ G + [(1 + R_{t-1})^{1/4} - 1]B_{t-1} - SRT\ PGDP\ Y - HRT\ OPI$$

5.3 $$K = I + (1 - a_{73})K_{t-1} \qquad 0 < a_{73} < 1$$

Expectations Formation

6.1 $$\pi = \pi_{t-1} + a_{74}[GCPI - \pi_{t-1}] \qquad 0 < a_{74} < 1$$

6.2 $$EGER = GER_{t+1}$$

where $a_{ij}(L)$ = a distributed lag function of weights
L = the lag operator
Δ = the first difference operator

Variable	*Definition*
B	= total nominal stock of government bonds
BLC	= nominal stock of bank lending to companies
BLG	= nominal stock of bank lending to government
BLH	= nominal stock of bank lending to households
BD	= nominal stock of government bonds held by the private sector
BF	= nominal stock of government bonds held by foreigners
BW	= foreign government bonds held by the domestic private sector
C	= real consumption
COMP	= competitiveness index
CPI	= consumer price index
ER	= exchange rate, units of foreign currency per unit of domestic currency
EGER	= expected appreciation of the exchange rate
G	= real government expenditure
GCPI	= actual inflation in CPI
GER	= actual appreciation of the exchange rate
GW	= actual wage inflation
HRT	= higher rate of income tax on other personal income
I	= real gross investment
K	= capital stock
M	= nominal stock of outside money
OPI	= other personal income − interest income
PGDP	= price of output
PIW	= price of imported materials, in foreign currency
PM	= import price, in domestic currency
PW	= price of imported final goods, in foreign currency
Q	= volume of imports
R	= interest rate on government bonds
RES	= foreign reserves
RW	= interest rate on foreign government bonds
SRT	= standard rate of income tax
TD	= time deposits of non-bank private sector in domestic currency
TDF	= time deposits in domestic currency with domestic banks by foreigners
TDW	= private sector deposits in foreign currency with foreign banks
URD	= uncovered interest differential
V	= real stock of private wealth
W	= nominal wage
WT	= world trade
X	= volume of exports
Y	= real output
YCAP	= capacity output
YD	= real disposable income
π	= expected inflation in CPI

exchange rate fluctuations. The exchange rate adjusts to clear the foreign exchange market. The demand for, and supply of, foreign exchange, arise from transactions in the balance of payments, equation 2.6.

The next set of equations deal with the supply side of the economy. Capital accumulation increases the capacity level of output, *YCAP*, equation 3.1. The rate of money wage inflation, *GW*, is assumed to be determined by an expectations-augmented Phillips curve, with the coefficient on expected price inflation being unity, reflecting the 'accelerationist' view, equation 3.2.

The price of domestic output, *PGDP*, is determined via a variable mark-up on wage cost, *W*, and the cost of imported materials, expressed in domestic currency, *PIW/ER*. The mark-up varies with demand conditions, pushing prices further up with excess demand, and vice versa. The weight $(1-a_{34})$ reflects the extent to which the country depends on imported materials, and it is one aspect of the openness of the economy.

The consumer price index, *CPI*, is a geometric average of the price of domestic output, *PGDP*, and import prices. The imported inflation comes via two routes: imported raw materials and final products. An increase in *PIW* pushes the price of domestic output up, but it also raises the *CPI* directly because certain raw materials, like oil, are also used by the consumers. An increase in *PIW*, if other foreign prices are constant, leads, therefore, to a loss in competitiveness. An increase in *PW*, on the other hand, leads to an initial gain in competitiveness and substitution of domestic output for foreign output. The weight, $1-a_{39}$, reflects the share of the price of imported goods in the consumer price index, and it is therefore another aspect of the openness of the economy.

Equations 4 deal with the financial markets. There are six financial assets in the model: money, *M*, and bonds, *B*, which are the liabilities of the government; time deposits of the non-bank private sector, *TD*, which are the liabilities of the banking sector; equities which are issued by firms to finance their investment; foreign government bonds, *BW*; and domestic residents' deposits with foreign banks in foreign currency, *TDW*. Money does not bear any interest, while government bonds offer interest, *R*. Money is held mainly for transactions purposes and it is a substitute for government bonds. The opportunity cost of holding money is therefore *R*.

The interest rate offered on time deposits is lower than that on bonds by a risk premium, K_1, which is assumed to be constant. Thus time deposits give interest $R - K_1$. Foreign bonds, *BW*, are denominated in foreign currency and are a gross substitute for domestic bonds. Their return is *RW-EGER*, where *EGER* is the expected appreciation in the exchange rate. Time deposits in foreign currency, *TDW*, offer an interest rate which is lower than that of foreign bonds by another risk premium, K_2, which is also taken to be constant; hence the return on *TDW* is RW-K_2-*EGER*.

These assumptions allow us to define a simple measure for the relative return between domestic and foreign bonds, the uncovered interest differential, or risk premium, $URD = R - RW + EGER$, given in Equation 4.1. Similarly, the relative return between domestic and foreign time deposits is $R - K_1 - RW + K + EGER$ which, on the assumption that the risk premia K_1 and K_2, are constant, is reduced to the uncovered interest differential plus a constant $K_1 - K_2$.

The non-bank private sector can allocate its portfolio amongst four assets: domestic government bonds, *BD*, foreign government bonds, *BW*, time deposits in domestic currency with domestic banks, *TD*, and time deposits in foreign currency with foreign banks, *TDW*. The portfolio allocation decision determines capital flows which, in turn, influence the exchange rate, while investors form expectations about the future exchange rate which affects their portfolio decision.

Government bonds are held by the domestic and foreign non-bank private sector, equations 4.3 and 4.4. The banking sector is assumed not to hold any government bonds. The instrument of monetary policy is assumed, here, in line with the actual behaviour of many central banks of the industrialized countries, to be the interest rate, rather than money or bonds which is usually assumed in analytical models. This means that the government has an infinitely elastic supply of bonds or cash at the level which decides to fix the interest rate. Thus the stock of government bonds is demand determined and the equilibrium condition in the bond market is given by equation 4.5.

All other domestic interest rates are linked with the interest rate on government bonds through simple mark-up relationships. Thus commercial banks offer $R - K_1$ interest on time deposits, and loan money to households, *BLH*, and companies, *BLC*, at $R + K_3$ interest rate. Bank lending to the private sector is therefore demand determined at the given interest rate, equations 4.8 and 4.9.

The government issues bonds and money to finance its public sector borrowing requirement (*PSBR*). Since both are demand determined, any residual borrowing is met by commercial banks. Bank lending to the government, *BLG*, is thus determined from the government budget constraint, equation 5.1. The commercial banks then balance their books by issuing certificates of deposits. We aggregate retail and wholesale time deposits into a single instrument called time deposits, *TD*, which are determined from the banks' balance sheet, equation 4.10. Time deposits by foreigners, *TDF*, are demand-determined, equation 4.11.

Real money balances, *M/CPI* (equation 4.2), depend on income, the interest rate and wealth. The demand for the stock of real domestic bonds, equation 4.3, and real foreign bonds expressed in domestic currency, equation 4.6, depend on income, the uncovered interest differential and wealth. Since bonds are not held for transactions purposes but as a store of value, an increase in income reduces their demand. In other words, an increase in the demand for money for transactions purposes is met, in the short run, by reducing holdings of bonds. Time deposits in foreign currency are held as a store of value, but also for transaction purposes and thus an increase in income increases their demand.

The demand by foreigners for government bonds, *BF*, depends on the uncovered interest differential, foreign income and foreign wealth. The last two variables can be suppressed into a constant. Finally, equation 4.12 defines private sector real wealth.

The fifth set of equations describe the asset accumulation process. Equation 5.1 is the familiar government budget constraint. It asserts that the *PSBR*, plus any changes in foreign reserves, must be financed by printing more money, issue of bonds and borrowing from commercial banks. The *PSBR* is defined in equation 5.2 as the excess of government expenditure on goods and services, along with interest payments on government debt over tax receipts from income at factor cost and interest payments. Equation 5.3 describes the identity linking the rate of investment and rate of capital accumulation, assuming depreciation is proportional to the stock of capital.

The last set of equations determines the expectational variables. There are two of these in the model: (i) the expected rate of inflation, π, (ii) the expected appreciation in the exchange rate, *EGER*. The former is assumed to be generated by a conventional adaptive expectations hypothesis and the latter via rational expectations. The adaptive expectations hypothesis in the labour market reflects the existence of long term wage contracts (see e.g. Taylor, 1979). In this model inflationary expectations, based on past inflation rates, matter for today's choices of employment production, etc. The rational expectations hypothesis is imposed here within an optimization framework.[1] The expectational variable is defined as a control which is used to minimize the difference between the actual and expected appreciation over the horizon 1, ... , T. The optimization determines $T - 1$ values for the expectational variable and there remains a terminal (or transversality) condition to be imposed from outside. This takes the form of a stationarity condition (for more details, see Karakitsos, 1985).

There are five forces that determine the dynamics of the system: the adjustment of expectational variables; the asset accumulation process; the adjustment of the exchange rate; a partial adjustment hypothesis covering the real sector of the economy, but not the monetary sector; and, finally, the explanatory variables are assumed to affect the system via distributed lag functions. In the exercises reported below, this last channel of dynamics is absent and $a_{ij}(L) = 1$. In addition, the availability of credit does not affect investment and consumption.

There are four instruments in the model: the interest rate on government bonds, R; the standard rate of income tax, SRT; the higher rate of income tax applicable to interest income, HRT, and government expenditure, G. There are only four exogenous variables in the model and these relate to the rest of the world: world trade WT, world prices of raw materials, PIW, and final goods, PW, and the world interest rate, RW. All other variables are endogenous.

The choice of values in the basic parameter set is subject to the restrictions imposed by the private sector budget constraint.

3. MONETARY AND FISCAL POLICY IN THE FULL MODEL

In this section we consider the effects of fiscal and monetary policy. The former is defined in terms of one unit step increase in government expenditure, G. This is equivalent to 1 per cent of GNP. We now wish to investigate: (a) whether the system would again approach steady-state equilibrium after the change in policy variable; (b) the steady-state effects of the policy change; (c) the adjustment path of the system between the two steady states.

We consider two variants of the model, depending on the assumption about the speed of adjustment in the labour market, captured by the coefficient a_{32}. The first variant assumes sluggish adjustment, and we shall refer to it as model-K. The other assumes that the labour market clears ten times faster, and we shall refer to it as model-C.

The model is assumed to be quarterly and is run for eighty quarters. The results appear in Figures 8.1–8.3 for a few key variables. It is immediately clear how important the assumption about the speed with which the labour market clears is for the policy implications of the model. In model-C the government expenditure multiplier on

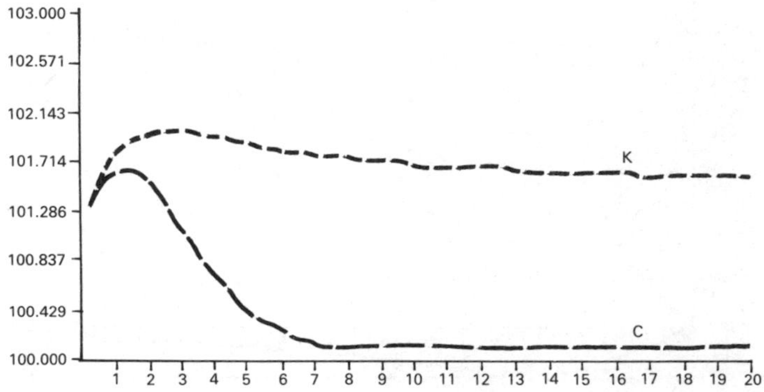

Figure 8.1: The effects of 1 unit step increase in G on output in model-K and model-C

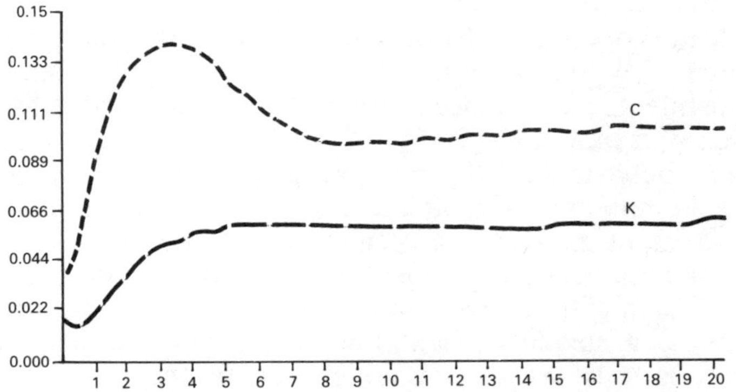

Figure 8.2: The effects of 1 unit step increase in G on inflation in model-K and model-C

output becomes less than unity after 3 years and reaches zero within 7 years, full crowding out.[2] In model-K, on the other hand, the output multiplier remains above unity for 20 years.

The increase in government expenditure leads to a positive inflation rate in the long run in both models, although it is slightly higher in model-C (see Figure 8.2). The adjustment

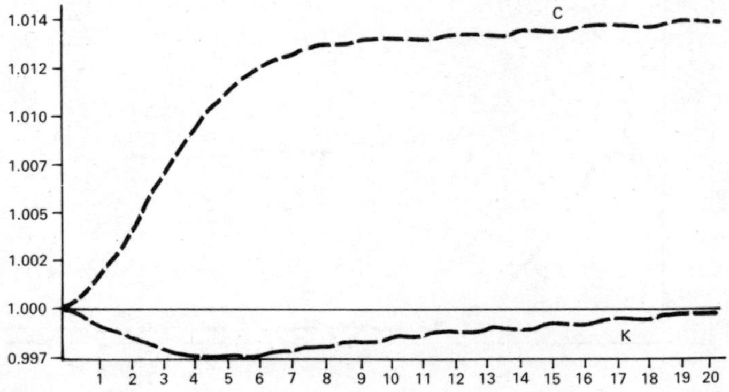

Figure 8.3: The effects of 1 unit step increase in G on real exchange rate in model-K and model-C

path in model-K is characterized by undershooting and in model-C by overshooting of the long run equilibrium. Full adjustment takes place within 4 years in model-K and 7 years in model-C.

The behaviour of the real exchange rate or competitiveness is very different in the two models. An increase in government expenditure results in a temporary small gain in competitiveness that lasts for 20 years in model-K and to a loss in competitiveness in model-C. In the former, this leads to a small transient boost in exports which, at its peak, is only 0.4 per cent higher than the initial steady state. The income effect is much stronger than the price effect, and imports rise by 2.3 per cent on average. This forces the current account into deficit, which depreciates the nominal exchange rate by 4.1 per cent in model-K.

In model-C, competitiveness is harmed both during the adjustment and in the new steady state. This makes exports less by 1.9 per cent and imports more by 3.5 per cent in the new steady state. This produces a deficit in the current account that depreciates the nominal exchange rate by 7.0 per cent.

The behaviour of the real exchange rate is thus largely responsible for the crowding out in model-C. It should be noted that this result follows even though the exchange rate adjusts ten times faster than wages and prices. In spite of this difference in the speed of adjustment, it is the fact that prices respond immediately to exchange rate that is instrumental to the loss in competitiveness in model-C. In model-K, on the other hand, the response of wages is so sluggish that it leads to a gain in competitiveness. But the degree of the openness of the economy is also important here. As this is increased, the gain in competitiveness is reduced in model-K.

Thus, whether there is a loss or gain in competitiveness following a fiscal stimulus depends on the combination of four factors: the response of the exchange rate to clear the balance of payments, the response of wages to excess demand, the degree to which domestic prices depend on import prices, and the response of the latter to the exchange rate.

The transmission mechanism of fiscal policy is as follows. An increase in government expenditure leads to an expected depreciation in the exchange rate. This implies a substitution of foreign bonds for domestic bonds, in real terms, in the portfolios of both the domestic and foreign private sector. Similarly, there is a currency substitution with domestic residents increasing their real holdings of foreign time deposits. The rise in income necessitates an increased demand for money, in real terms, for transactions purposes, and a higher stock of physical capital. The net effect of this portfolio adjustment results in an outflow of capital but, nevertheless, an increase in real wealth, because of increased government borrowing. The outflow of capital strengthens the depreciation of the nominal exchange rate. But the fiscal stimulus is only temporary because prices start to rise, because of both excess demand in the labour and output markets and higher import prices due to actual exchange depreciation.

This part of the transmission mechanism is common in both models. The difference until now is one of degree. Wages rise by only 4.5 per cent in model-K, whereas they rise by 9.3 per cent in model-C in 20 years. The qualitative difference between the two models, as has already been indicated, lies in the behaviour of the real exchange rate which leads to full crowding out in model-C. And this depends, as has already been indicated, on the assumption about the speed of adjustment in the labour market. Sluggish wage adjustment is the backbone assumption in any Keynesian model and it is sufficient for an effective fiscal policy even in the long run, a period over 20 years. A rapidly clearing labour market is, on the other hand, consistent with models of classical, monetarist and new classical persuasion and is sufficient to generate fiscal policy ineffectiveness. For this reason, we have named our variant-K of the model as Keynesian and our variant-C as classical.

The effects of monetary policy are considered through a sustained increase of 1 per cent point in the interest rate, which brings it up from 10 to 11 per cent. The results are presented in Figures 8.4–8.6. The rise in the interest rate creates a recession that reaches its trough in 9 months in both models. Although output falls to a maximum of about 1.7 per cent in both models, it is restored to its preshock level within 3 years in model-C, whereas it takes 4½ years in model-K. Inflation falls much faster and to a larger extent in model-C. The price level falls by 1 per cent within 4 years in model-C, whereas it falls only by 0.4 of 1 per cent in model-K.

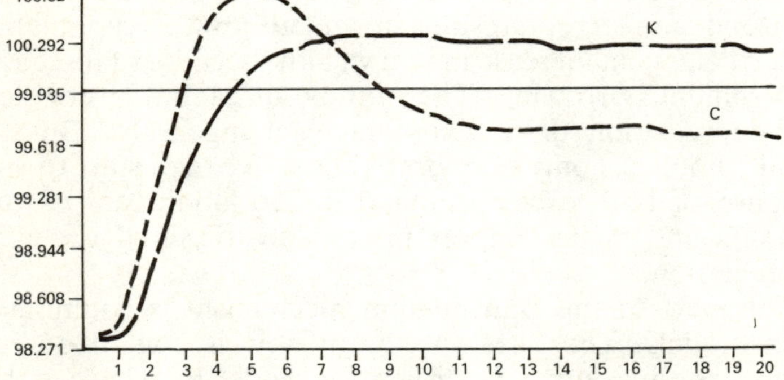

Figure 8.4: The effects of 1 per cent step increase in R on output in model K and model-C

The increase in the interest rate raises, initially, the real exchange rate in both models. But the loss in competitiveness is wiped out in 9 months in model-C, whereas it lasts for as long as 5 years in model-K. In the latter, the real exchange rate is finally restored to its original steady state value, whereas in the former, after a long period of increased competitiveness, the real exchange rate finally appreciates.

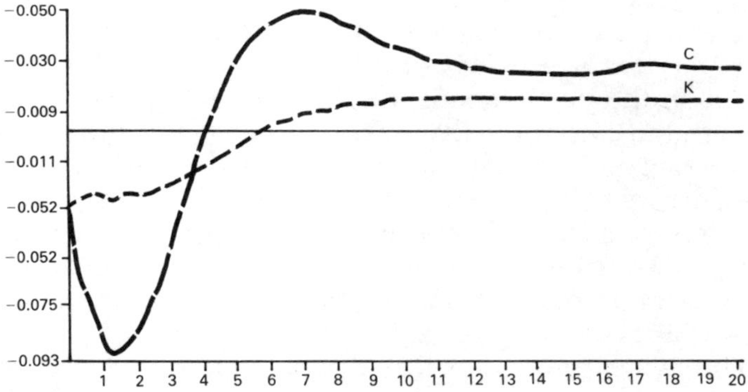

Figure 8.5: The effects of 1 per cent point step increase in R inflation in model-K and model-C

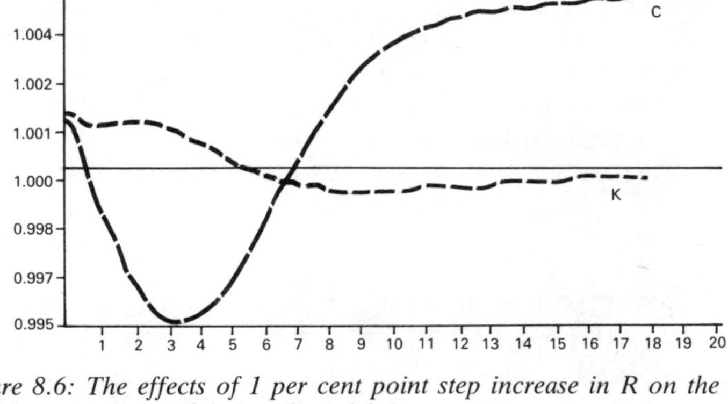

Figure 8.6: The effects of 1 per cent point step increase in R on the real exchange rate in model-K and model-C

The loss in competitiveness reduces exports for 5 years in model-K. Imports are reduced for the same period, but to a much larger extent, because of the income effect which reinforces the relative price effect. This produces a surplus in the current account that results in an appreciating nominal exchange rate in model-K.

The appreciation in the exchange rate is strengthened, initially by a surplus in the capital account. The capital inflow comes about as follows. The increase in the interest rate generates an expectation of appreciation in the exchange rate that makes the uncovered interest differential positive. This induces a substitution of domestic bonds for foreign bonds in the portfolios of the domestic and foreign private sector. Furthermore, there is a currency substitution with domestic residents decreasing their real holdings of foreign time deposits. The biggest expected appreciation, however, occurs within the first year, in fact, the only year of a capital inflow. Afterwards, the rate of expected appreciation is reduced and, indeed, after $3\frac{1}{2}$ years it turns into an expected depreciation which gradually accelerates.

The switch from an expected appreciation to depreciation comes a year earlier than the end of the recession, which is, of course, what one would have expected under rational expectations. When the recession is over, the current balance turns into a deficit and that, coupled with a continuous capital outflow, produces thereafter an actual rate of depreciation.

The direction of capital flows in model-C is the same with that in model-K. Although the adjustment path of the real exchange rate is different in the two models, the relative price effect is weak and therefore imports are falling faster than exports rise, producing a surplus in the current account. In fact, a surplus is the result also in model-K, although it is arrived at from a different route.

4. SENSITIVITY OF FISCAL AND MONETARY POLICY MULTIPLIERS TO PARAMETER VARIATION

Since the model is used with a specific set of parameters, it is natural to ask how robust are the results to parameter variation. There are two possible approaches to this problem. First, one can specify a range for each parameter, drawing from empirical evidence and then consider each parameter to be an independently distributed normal variate, with its mean being the value used in the basic set, and its standard deviation (SD) chosen so that ± 2 SD will cover the specified range. In this approach, one can combine parameters through a normal number generator to arrive at different possible sets of parameters and then choose among them those sets which satisfy *a priori* restrictions (see e.g. Nguyen and Turnovsky, 1983). This approach treats the economic system as stochastic to its parameters and it is thus at variance with that adopted usually in econometric estimation. The fact that there is uncertainty as to the true value of a parameter does not imply that it is stochastic. The alternative approach, used in this paper, is to consider the economic system as deterministic to its parameters and examine the sensitivity of the results as these parameters change within the specified range. The advantage of this approach is that given the initial choice of parameters, one can examine which parameters are important with respect to specific results.

The sensitivity analysis carried out takes the form of: (i) doubling, (ii) halving the coefficients of the system, one at a time, and calculating the change in the government expenditure and interest rate multipliers. In addition, multipliers are calculated also for extreme values of certain coefficients. If the model were linear, the resulting change in the multiplier can be attributed to the perturbation in the parameter. In other words, the multipliers in a linear model are independent of the initial state. But this is not true for a non-linear system like ours. To be able to claim, therefore, that the resulting change in a multiplier is due to a given parameter change, we have to calculate the new multiplier at the same initial state. This can be implemented by simultaneously adjusting the constant in the equation in which the parameter is perturbed.

A parameter perturbation might drive the system into an unstable region. Given the complexity of the model analysed, it is impossible to derive stability conditions. In the exercises reported below, stability is tested by examining whether the new system with the parameter change converges to its steady state after the policy change. In none of the cases considered did the system fail to converge.

Tables 8.2 and 8.3 provide the output multipliers for fiscal and monetary policy obtained from the basic set of coefficients, and for each perturbed parameter, with all other coefficients remaining unchanged. The perturbed coefficient is indicated also by the partial derivate (e.g. C_r = the partial derivative of C with respect to R). The marginal propensity to consume is the only exception where the increase is not 100 per cent but 14.2 per cent. In addition, we also perturb groups of parameters by 100 per cent. Two such groups are considered: (i) those relating to the interest rate effect; and (ii) those relating to the wealth effect. When groups of coefficients are perturbed, the restrictions imposed on them by the private sector budget constraint are still satisfied.

The values of the multipliers given are for the first year, which is the average of the first four quarters, the 20th year, which is the final year, and the overall average over the 20-year horizon. In addition, the Tables also provide the elasticity of the first year multiplier with respect to the perturbed parameter. This elasticity is a measure of the sensitivity of fiscal and monetary multipliers and allows a comparison of parameters with respect to their contribution in the multiplier change. A value near to zero indicates that this parameter does not contribute to a multiplier change.

By inspection of Table 8.2, it can be established that the fiscal policy multipliers on output are completely insensitive to all but three parameters, a_1, a_{25} and a_9. These relate to the marginal propensity to consume, a_1, the marginal propensity to import, a_{25}, and the wealth effect in the consumption function, a_9. This is true for both models. Although the output multiplier to an increase in government expenditure is higher in model-K relative to model-C, the percentage change in the multiplier to a 100 per cent change in a parameter is remarkably the same between the two models for all parameters. Thus the elasticity of the fiscal multiplier with respect to the marginal propensity to consume is 0.58 and model-K and 0.56 in model-C. The elasticity with respect to the marginal propensity to import is 0.19 in both models, and the elasticity with respect to the wealth effect in the consumption function is 0.08 in both models.

In considering a 100 per cent perturbation in both groups of coefficients, the elasticities of the fiscal multiplier with respect to all wealth effects and all interest rate effects are 0.10 and 0.01 respectively.

A 50 per cent decrease in all parameters, one at a time, reveals exactly the same picture. The same coefficients are important for any multiplier change and in the same order: a_1, a_{25} and a_9.

When the wealth effect is excluded from the consumption function, the fiscal multiplier falls from 1.56 to 1.44 in model-K.

Table 8.3 provides the sensitivity of monetary policy multipliers on output under the same conditions. These are also insensitive to all coefficients but five, and in the following order or importance: the interest rate effect in the consumption function, a_5; the marginal propensity to consume, a_1; the interest rate effect on investment, a_{13}; the marginal propensity to import, a_{25}; and the interest rate effect on time deposits in foreign currency, a_{59}. This is again true for both models. The elasticities are remarkably similar between the two models. A 50 per cent decrease in all parameters, one at a time, indicates the same degree of insensitivity of interest rate multipliers. In addition, it implies the same coefficients and in the same order with those of 100 per cent increase as being responsible for any multiplier change.

We also consider the sensitivity of monetary policy multipliers to extreme values in certain coefficients. It is assumed that there is no effect from the interest rate on: (i) consumption, (ii) investment, (iii) time deposits in foreign currency, and (iv) the wealth effect in the consumption function. When the interest rate effect on consumption is zero, the interest rate multiplier on output falls from -1.54 to only -0.49. This is not surprising since this is the most important factor of the sensitivity of the monetary policy multipliers. What is, perhaps, even more important, is that the profile of the interest rate multiplier changes if

Table 8.2: Sensitivity of government expenditure multipliers on output to parameter variation—fiscal policy multipliers

Case (i): 100% increase in all parameters, one at a time, except for C_y, which increases by 14.2%

Year	Basic coeff.	a_5 C_r	a_{13} r_r	a_{48} BD_r	a_{54} BW_r	a_{43} M_r	a_{59} TDW_r	a_9 C_v	a_{45} M_v	a_{61} TD W_v	a_{50} BD_v	a_{56} BW_v	a_{18} X_e	a_{23} Q_e	a_{25} Q_y	a_1 C_y	a_{41} M_y	a_{57} TD W_y	*All interest rate parameters*	*All wealth parameters*
Keynesian model																				
1	1.56	1.57	1.57	1.56	1.56	1.56	1.57	1.68	1.56	1.57	1.56	1.57	1.57	1.57	1.26	1.69	1.56	1.57	1.58	1.71
20	1.57	1.55	1.56	1.56	1.56	1.56	1.56	1.55	1.56	1.56	1.56	1.56	1.55	1.55	1.09	1.54	1.56	1.56	1.55	1.55
Aver.	1.71	1.71	1.71	1.71	1.71	1.71	1.71	1.71	1.71	1.71	1.71	1.71	1.75	1.78	1.17	1.71	1.71	1.71	1.71	1.71
Elast.	—	0.01	0.01	0.00	0.00	0.00	0.01	0.08	0.00	0.01	0.00	0.01	0.01	0.01	0.19	0.58	0.00	0.01	0.01	0.10
Classical model																				
1	1.50	1.53	1.51	1.50	1.50	1.50	1.51	1.62	1.50	1.51	1.50	1.50	1.48	1.48	1.22	1.62	1.50	1.51	—	—
20	0.07	0.05	0.09	0.06	0.06	0.06	0.06	0.06	0.06	0.06	0.06	0.06	0.05	0.04	0.08	0.06	0.06	0.06	—	—
Aver.	0.36	0.35	0.38	0.35	0.35	0.36	0.36	0.36	0.36	0.36	0.36	0.36	0.28	0.25	0.35	0.35	0.36	0.36	—	—
Elast.	—	0.02	0.01	0.00	0.00	0.00	0.01	0.08	0.00	0.01	0.00	0.00	0.01	0.01	0.19	0.56	0.00	0.01	—	—

Case (ii): 50% decrease in all parameters, one at a time, except for C_y, which decreases by 14.2%—Keynesian model

1	1.56	1.56	1.56	—	—	—	1.57	1.50	—	—	—	—	—	—	1.77	1.45	—	—	—	—
20	1.57	1.56	1.56	—	—	—	1.56	1.58	—	—	—	—	—	—	1.97	1.58	—	—	—	—
Aver.	1.71	1.71	1.71	—	—	—	1.71	1.69	—	—	—	—	—	—	2.22	1.70	—	—	—	—
Elast.	—	0.00	0.00	—	—	—	0.00	0.08	—	—	—	—	—	—	0.27	0.49	—	—	—	—

Case (iii): Extreme values $C_y = 0$, Keynesian model

1	1.56	—	—	—	—	—		1.44	—	—	—	—	—	—		—				
20	1.57	—	—	—	—	—		1.45	—	—	—	—	—	—		—				
Aver.	1.71	—	—	—	—	—		1.48	—	—	—	—	—	—		—				

Notes: Years 1 and 20 are the averages of four quarters. Aver. is the overall average over 20 years. Elast. is the elasticity of the first year multiplier to the variation of the parameter in question.

Table 8.3: Sensitivity of interest rate multipliers on output to parameter variation—monetary policy multipliers

Case (i): 100% in all parameters, one at a time, except for C_y which increases by 14.2%

Keynesian model

Year	Basic coeff.	a_5 C_r	a_{13} r_r	a_{48} BD_r	a_{54} BW_r	a_{43} M_r	a_{59} TDW_r	a_9 C_v	a_{45} M_v	a_{61} TDW_v	a_{50} BD_v	a_{56} BW_v	a_{18} X_e	a_{23} Q_e	a_{25} Q_y	a_1 C_y	a_{41} M_y	a_{57} TDW_y	All interest rate parameters	All wealth parameters
1	−1.54	−2.60	−1.91	−1.54	−1.57	−1.54	−1.66	−1.59	−1.54	−1.55	−1.54	−1.54	−1.59	−1.59	−1.24	−1.67	−1.54	−1.55	−3.17	−1.60
20	0.24	0.37	0.24	0.24	0.24	0.24	0.25	0.16	0.23	0.23	0.24	0.23	0.24	0.24	0.16	0.23	0.24	0.24	0.40	0.15
Aver.	0.01	−0.01	−0.03	0.01	0.01	0.02	0.02	0.04	0.01	0.01	0.01	0.01	0.01	0.02	0.01	0.02	0.01	0.01	−0.04	0.03
Elast.	—	0.69	0.24	0.00	0.02	0.00	0.08	0.03	0.00	0.01	0.00	0.00	0.03	0.03	0.19	0.59	0.00	0.01	1.06	0.04

Classical model

Year	Basic coeff.	a_5 C_r	a_{13} r_r	a_{48} BD_r	a_{54} BW_r	a_{43} M_r	a_{59} TDW_r	a_9 C_v	a_{45} M_v	a_{61} TDW_v	a_{50} BD_v	a_{56} BW_v	a_{18} X_e	a_{23} Q_e	a_{25} Q_y	a_1 C_y	a_{41} M_y	a_{57} TDW_y	All interest rate parameters	All wealth parameters
1	−1.48	−2.53	−1.85	−1.48	−1.51	−1.48	−1.60	−1.53	−1.48	−1.49	−1.48	−1.49	−1.49	−1.50	−1.20	−1.60	−1.48	−1.49	—	—
20	−0.31	−0.30	−0.63	−0.31	−0.31	−0.31	−0.31	−0.32	−0.31	−0.32	−0.31	−0.32	−0.33	−0.33	−0.29	−0.32	−0.31	−0.31	—	—
Aver.	−0.19	−0.17	−0.42	−0.18	−0.19	−0.19	−0.19	−0.20	−0.19	−0.19	−0.19	−0.19	−0.21	−0.22	−0.17	−0.19	−0.19	−0.19	—	—
Elast.	—	0.71	0.25	0.00	0.02	0.08	0.08	0.03	0.00	0.00	0.00	0.00	0.01	0.02	0.19	0.57	0.00	0.01	—	—

Case (ii): 50% in all parameters, one at a time, except for C_y which decreases by 14.2%—Keynesian model

1	−1.54	−1.01	−1.36	—	—	—	−1.48	−1.52	—	—	—	—	—	—	−1.74	−1.43	—	—
20	0.24	0.17	0.23	—	—	—	0.23	0.40	—	—	—	—	—	—	0.32	0.24	—	—
Aver.	0.01	0.03	0.04	—	—	—	0.01	−0.07	—	—	—	—	—	—	0.02	0.01	—	—
Elast.	—	0.69	0.23	—	—	—	0.08	0.03	—	—	—	—	—	—	0.26	0.50	—	—

Case (iii): Extreme values $C_r = I_r = C_v = TDW_r = 0$, one at a time—Keynesian model

1	−1.54	−0.49	−1.18	—	—	—	−1.42	−1.49	—	—	—	—
20	0.24	0.10	0.23	—	—	—	0.22	−0.33	—	—	—	—
Aver.	0.01	0.04	0.06	—	—	—	0.00	−0.93	—	—	—	—

the wealth effect in consumption is assumed to be zero. In this case, the first year effect is −1.49, and then gradually declines *monotonically*. After 20 years, it is still −0.33, with an overall average of −0.93. The multiplier in the basic set of coefficients is −1.54 for the first year, but then soon becomes positive and the overall 20-year average is almost zero.

The difference in the dynamic profile of the multiplier is due to the fact that a contractionary monetary policy is associated with a wealth increase that stimulates consumption and therefore turns the multiplier from negative to positive after 4 years. In the absence of a wealth effect in consumption, the interest rate multiplier remains negative throughout, and it is reduced in value as prices start to rise.

There are four points worth mentioning as far as the efficacy of fiscal and monetary policy is concerned. First, two of the three parameters upon which the sensitivity of the fiscal policy multiplier depends are also of equal importance for the sensitivity of the monetary policy multiplier. These parameters are the marginal propensity to consume and the marginal propensity to import. To the extent, then, that the debate on the relative efficacy of fiscal over monetary policy revolves around specific parameter values, it seems that, within the general model considered in this paper, the effectiveness of fiscal policy must be less controversial than monetary policy, since the latter depends on the parameters of the former, plus a few more.

Second, the consumption function is the most important relationship in the model. The marginal propensity to consume is of equal importance in determining the sensitivity of fiscal and monetary policy multipliers, 0.58 in model-K and 0.59 in model-C for fiscal policy, and 0.56 and 0.57 for monetary policy for the two models respectively. The interest rate effect in consumption is the prime factor in the sensitivity of the monetary policy multiplier, 0.69. The wealth effect in consumption is the third important factor for the sensitivity of the fiscal policy multiplier, 0.08. Its absence affects the dynamic profile of the monetary policy multiplier.

Table 8.4: The dynamic effects on the real exchange rate

	Classical model			Keynesian model		
Exchange rate clears	Balance of payments	Current balance	Capital account	Balance of payments	Current balance	Capital account
Expansionary fiscal policy						
Impact	+	−	+	+	0	+
Short run	−	−	−	+	+	+
Long run	+	+	+	0	0	0
Contractionary monetary policy						
Impact	+	+	+	+	+	+
Short run	+	+	+	−	−	+
Long run	+	+	+	0	0	+

Notes: + indicates appreciation; − depreciation. Impact effect means first 3 months; short run up to 5 years; long run over 5 years.

Third, traditional parameters, like the interest and the income elasticity of the demand for money upon which the textbook puts so much emphasis, are of little importance. The reason for this is that money forms a small proportion of total private wealth, and interest rate is the policy instrument. It is worth remembering that the money considered here, as well as in the analytical models in the literature, it 'outside money'. This is the liability of the government and it is a small percentage relative to demand and time deposits, and even smaller relative to total wealth. The importance of time deposits in the sensitivity of the monetary policy multiplier is not a paradox in this context. This is treated as money, in the sense that it is also held for transactions purposes, it enters the wealth of the private sector and forms a much larger proportion of wealth than money. Bonds, on the other hand, are held solely as a store of value.

Fourth, in a truly non-linear model, the relative magnitudes of the variables are of importance too. In the context it is not surprising that the consumption function is the most important relationship in the model, whereas the demand for money is not. This makes any policy analysis much more complicated than analytical models led us to believe.

Finally, it should be noted that the parameter variation considered of 100 per cent increase and 50 per cent decrease is very wide, and includes even extreme values known from empirical evidence. In this sense, the results on fiscal and monetary policy appear to be robust to a wide parameter variation.

5. COMPARISON OF RESULTS WITH OTHER STUDIES

It is sensible at this stage to compare the results of the general model with those from other studies which employ less general models. There are three points worth mentioning. The first relates to the ineffectiveness of fiscal policy. In the Mundell–Dornbusch model (Mundell, 1963; Dornbusch, 1976), with perfect capital mobility and a freely floating exchange rate, fiscal policy is completely ineffective, a result that was also obtained as a long run proposition in model-C. However, the conditions under which this result is obtained are different in model-C and in the Mundell–Dornbusch framework. In the Mundell model, with the price level fixed and output endogenous, the real exchange rate appreciates, producing an exactly offsetting change in net exports, thus leaving output unchanged. Hence the fiscal stimulus is transmitted abroad. In this model, output is determined in the money market and the exchange rate in the goods market. In the Dornbusch model, with output exogenously fixed and the price level endogenous, money market equilibrium determines the price level in the long run, independently of fiscal policy. A decrease in government expenditure causes an offsetting depreciation in the nominal exchange rate, with no effect on prices.

By now it is well known (see, e.g. Tobin and de Macedo, 1980; Branson and Buiter, 1983) that the complete ineffectiveness of fiscal policy in the Mundell–Dornbusch model depends on three special assumptions: (i) perfect asset substitutability, (ii) the domestic price level does not depend on the exchange rate, and (iii) omission of the exchange rate from the asset demand functions. The relaxation of any one of these assumptions destroys the extreme ineffectiveness result in the Mundell framework, but it does not in the context of the general model specified here. With high, but not perfect, asset substitutability, an increase in government expenditure, in the Mundell–Dornbusch model, will raise the interest rate, and this will cause appreciation which will reduce net exports. The reduction in the latter only partially offsets the fiscal stimulus because, with a given money supply, the reduction in the demand for money caused by the higher interest rate is more than offset by an increase in income.

If the price level is made a function of the exchange rate in the Mundell–Dornbusch model, then the resulting appreciation reduces the price level, which makes higher the real money stock, thus allowing for an increase in output. The model retains, however, the uncomfortable property that a government expenditure increase results in a decline in the price level. This is a direct consequence of a partial equilibrium analysis in which the labour market is ignored.

Omission of the exchange rate from the asset demand functions in the Mundell model implies that the adjustment to a fiscal stimulus occurs only within the *IS*-curve between the components of aggregate demand and the exchange rate, making fiscal policy impotent. If, however, the *LM*-curve is made a function also of the exchange rate, then movements in the latter feed through financial markets and interest rates into aggregate demand and fiscal policy is no longer impotent.

The general model of Section 2 allows for the relaxation of all these special assumptions. Imperfect asset substitutability is hypothesized and both the consumer price index and the price of domestic output depend on the exchange rate. Furthermore, the exchange rate affects the asset demand functions through the relative rate of return and the valuation of wealth. Yet even with the relaxation of these assumptions, it does not necessarily follow that full crowding out does not occur. Depending on the assumption about the speed of adjustment in the labour market, either full crowding out occurs or fiscal policy is very effective, with the multiplier being above unity for 20 years. Therefore this assumption is the crucial one and not the other three.

The second point relates to the effect of a fiscal expansion on wealth and the consequent adjustment of the real exchange rate. Recently there has been a move to reintroduce traditional aspects of exchange rate determination, the current account and relative prices (e.g. Branson, 1976; Kouri, 1976; Kouri and de Macedo, 1978; Dornbusch and Fischer, 1980; and Branson and Buiter, 1983). In this approach, the exchange rate is determined in the assets market at a point in time, whereas its evolution through time is governed by developments in the current account. The rate at which foreign assets are accumulated or decumulated represents imbalances in the current account. In the Dornbusch and Fischer and the Branson and Buiter model, for example, which incorporates this approach to exchange rate determination, an expansionary fiscal policy is associated with an appreciating nominal and real exchange rate, in the short run. The increase in the demand for money results in a higher interest rate, which leads to an expectation of depreciation if equilibrium in the international financial markets is to be preserved. The expectation of depreciation can come about from an initial real and nominal appreciation. The resulting current account deficit implies a decumulation of foreign assets and thus a decrease in wealth over time, which dampens the excess demand in the goods market, and in the money market which is ignored in these models, thus reversing the pressure on the real exchange rate. In the adjustment process, the real exchange rate depreciates relative to its short run equilibrium until it reaches its original steady-state value with a reduced value of wealth.

In the general model of Section 2, such an interaction between the current and capital account is incorporated. However, it does not necessarily follow that the decumulation of foreign assets leads to a decrease in wealth, following a fiscal stimulus. In the Dornbusch–Fischer model, this is always the case because there is no government budget constraint and thus the implications of financing the increased government expenditure are ignored. When the finance implications are considered, the final outcome on wealth is uncertain. In our framework, the increase in government expenditure leads to a rise in the domestic part of wealth which outweighs the decrease in foreign assets and thus wealth rises. This is true in both the Keynesian and classical models. In spite of this small increase in wealth, however, the final outcome for the real exchange rate and the overall effectiveness of fiscal policy remains with the behaviour of the labour market, as we have seen.[3]

The final point is that the effectiveness of monetary policy is overstated in these models. This is partly because of the way in which monetary policy is conceived in analytical models, as a sustained increase/decrease in the rate of money creation. If, however, a change in monetary policy is viewed as a sustained change in the interest rate, coming about from changes in the stock of government bonds, then the efficacy of policy depends also on the consequent changes in interest payments. There are two channels through which, for example, an increase in interest payments affect the system: first, through interest income which will increase consumption; second, increased interest payments will necessitate further issue of government bonds which, in turn, increase private sector wealth. In our framework, a contractionary monetary policy implies selling bonds to commercial banks which increases the wealth of the private sector and thus consumption. The effects of monetary policy, therefore, through these two channels tend to partially offset the initial contractionary effect on output. The adjustment towards the preshock level of output takes 3 years in the classical model and $4\frac{1}{2}$ in the Keynesian model.

CONCLUSIONS

Imperfect asset substitutability, the dependence of domestic prices on the exchange rate and the inclusion of the exchange rate in the asset demand functions are not sufficient conditions for the non-occurrence of full crowding out, contrary to received wisdom. Rather, it is the speed at which the labour market clears that is of crucial importance. Assuming that the exchange rate adjust very rapidly to clear the balance of payments and that the contribution of import prices to domestic prices is not insignificant, a relatively fast-clearing labour market leads to a permanent loss in competitiveness and to crowding out of a fiscal expansion. This result is robust to the asset market, current account and balance of payments theories of exchange rate determination.

An expansionary fiscal policy creates a deficit in the current account, which implies a decumulation of foreign assets in the adjustment process to a new steady state. This always results in a decrease in real wealth in the absence of a government budget constraint. When the finance implications of increased government expenditure are taken into account, however, the final outcome on wealth is uncertain. The implication is that the dynamic adjustment path of the real exchange rate might be one of appreciation or depreciation, depending on specific parameter values. Certainly, the most important factor in this respect is the speed at which the labour market clears.

The government budget constraint is also important for the effectiveness of monetary policy and therefore for the dynamics of the real exchange rate. A contractionary monetary policy results in an increase in interest income and a rise in real wealth. Both increase consumption and offset, within 3 to 5 years, the initial contractionary effect on output.

NOTES

1. This approach has been adopted by Holly and Zarrop (1979) and Karakitsos *et al.* (1982).
2. It should be noted that if the response of wages is made even twice as fast as that of model-C, then the output multiplier falls below unity after six quarters, and full crowding out occurs within 3 years.
3. Branson and Buiter (1983) incorporate the government budget constraint in their analysis, but then they consider only balanced budget multipliers to examine the efficacy of fiscal policy and therefore the only changes in wealth come via current account imbalances.

REFERENCES

Branson, W. H. (1976) 'The dual roles of the government budget and the balance of payments in the movements from short to long-run equilibrium', *Quarterly Journal of Economics*, **90**(3), 345–367.

Branson, W. H. and Buiter, W. H. (1983) 'Monetary and fiscal policy with flexible exchange rates' in Bhandari, J. S. and Putnam, B. H. (eds) *Economic Interdependence and Flexible Exchange Rates*. MIT Press, Cambridge, Mass.

Dornbusch, R. (1976) 'Expectations and exchange rate dynamics', *Journal of Political Economy*, **84**(6), 1161–1176.

Dornbusch, R. and Fischer, S. (1980) 'Exchange rates and the current account', *American Economic Review*, **70**(5), 906–971.

Frenkel, J. A. and Rodriguez, C. A. (1975) 'Portfolio equilibrium and the balance of payments: a monetary approach', *American Economic Review*, **66**, 674–88.

Holly, S. and Zarrop, M. B. (1979) 'Calculating optimal economic policies when expectations are rational', *PROPE Discussion Paper*, No. 38.

Karakitsos, E. (1985) 'Bond and money finance of government expenditure under perfect foresight and adaptive expectations in a small open economy', *PROPE Discussion Paper*, No. 80.

Karakitsos, E., Rusem, B. and Zarrop, M. B. (1982) 'Robust economic policy formulation under uncertainty', *PROPE Discussion Paper*, No. 38.

Kouri, P. J. K. (1976) 'The exchange rate and the balance of payments in the short run and in the long run: a monetary approach', *Scandinavian Journal of Economics*, **78**(2), 280–304.

Kouri, P. J. K. and de Macedo, J. B. (1978) 'Exchange rates and the International adjustment process', *Brookings Papers on Economic Activity*, No. 1, 111–150.

Machlup, F. (1940) 'The theory of foreign exchanges', *Economica*, 23–49.

Mundell, R. (1963) 'Capital mobility and stabilization policy under fixed and flexible exchange rates', *Canadian Journal of Economics*, **29**(4) 475–485.

Nguyen Duc-Tho and Turnovsky, S. (1983) 'The dynamic effects of fiscal and monetary policy under bond financing', *Journal of Monetary Economics*, **11**, 45–71.

Robinson, J. (1937) 'The foreign exchanges'. *Essays in the Theory of Employment*. Basil Blackwell, Oxford.

Taylor, J. B. (1979) 'Staggered Wage Setting in a Macro Model', *American Economic Review, Papers and Proceedings*, **69**(4), Nashville, Tennessee, 108–113.

Tobin, J. and de Macedo, J. B. (1980) 'The short run macroeconomics of floating exchange rates: an exposition', in Chipman, J. S. and Kindleberger, C. P. (eds.) *Flexible Exchange Rates and the Balance of Payments*. North-Holland, Amsterdam.

9 Currency Substitution, Flexible Exchange Rates and the International Transmission of Disturbances

Athina Zervoyianni

In the standard macroeconomic analysis of open economies it is typically assumed that the only monetary asset available to domestic residents is domestic money. Recently however, it has been pointed out that in today's integrated world residents of most countries appear to hold monetary assets denominated in foreign currencies as well as in domestic currency. The literature addressing this phenomenon—itself being usually referred to as 'currency substitution' (CS), emphasizes the implications of the latter for the functioning of floating exchange rates. Contributions to this literature, such as Miles (1978) and McKinnon (1982) for example, note that CS may substantially reduce the insulative properties of a freely flexible exchange rate system suggesting in particular, that floating exchange rates may no longer insure national monetary autonomy to a country—that is, control over its own currency price level and inflation rate, under CS. McKinnon for instance, stresses the connection between CS on the one hand and the poor correlation between national inflation rates and the stance of national monetary policy on the other, proposing an average of world money supply rather than national money supplies for explaining variations in inflation rates. Moreover, Calvo and Rodriguez (1977), Girton and Roper (1981) and Daniel (1985) argue that CS may cause excessive exchange rate volatility and can be a source of exchange rate overshooting following disturbances to either the level or the rate of growth of national money stocks.

This chapter continues our earlier analysis[1] of how CS might affect the behaviour of an open economy with a flexible exchange rate addressing, in particular, the issue of the international transmission of disturbances under CS. Existing papers on CS typically abstract from the specification of complete financial equilibrium by either treating domestic interest rates as exogenously given or by assuming that domestic and foreign money are the only assets available to domestic residents. However, with the possibility of other financial assets—in particular interest-bearing assets, being ruled out, it is not always clear which of their findings reflect the consequences of CS—that is, the effects of substitution between national monetary assets, and which arise from the more common phenomenon of substitution between assets in general. Moreover, in much of the prevailing literature on CS the assumption of continuous purchasing power parity and 'full employment' output is often made. This latter assumption however, seems to preclude any likely role for real exchange rate changes and short run output movements in the behaviour of an open economy under CS.

The purpose of this chapter is to extend earlier work on the subject by integrating the CS possibility into an explicit open economy, macroeconomic framework. This is done by introducing CS into a simple dynamic model which is in the spirit of Dornbusch (1976), Buiter and Miller (1981), Branson and Buiter (1983) and Miller (1982). Thus the model, on the one hand, permits domestic residents to hold interest-bearing assets as well as domestic and foreign money and, on the other, allows for the possibility of deviations from PPP and short run departures of actual output from 'full capacity' output. While we assume that only the national currency is used in domestic transactions—as is indeed the case in most of the mature industrial countries, we follow the CS literature in postulating international transaction motives and speculative motives for CS.

The chapter is organized as follows: in Section 2 we focus on the response of a small open economy to unexpected disturbances of foreign origin under CS. The analysis demonstrates that CS limits the size of the initial real exchange rate jump following previously unanticipated disturbances to foreign interest rates but increases the latter following disturbances to foreign output. What is of considerable interest, however, is that for both of the above disturbances the degree of the resulting domestic output variation is smaller with CS than without CS. In Section 3 the CS possibility is introduced into an explicit two-country model. It is shown that the real exchange rate overshoots following unexpected changes in either the level or the rate of growth of any of the two national money supplies independently of the CS possibility. The overshooting is transmitted to the other country's output. Under CS, the significance of the transmission effect may, in fact, be mitigated via a 'terms of trade' effect and a 'foreign inflation' effect. A 'foreign income' effect associated with the presence of CS however, is found to be a source of real exchange rate overshooting. The analysis is concluded in Section 4.

2.

We consider an economy which is small in relation to the 'rest of the world' so that it is confronted with aggregate 'foreign' variables that are exogenous to its macroeconomic equilibrium. We shall allow the residents of this economy to hold as assets, domestic (outside) money M, domestic and foreign bonds—taken to be perfect substitutes for simplicity,[2] and a foreign monetary asset M^*, assumed to pay no interest as is conventional in the CS literature.[3] While only the domestic currency is used domestically, we shall postulate that the residents of this economy may wish to hold M^* to facilitate transactions with the rest of the world—as M^* holdings for example may reduce transaction costs associated with acquiring imports, earning at the same time the rate of depreciation of the domestic currency *vis-à-vis* the 'foreign currency'. For the purposes of this section we shall further assume that foreign residents do not hold assets denominated in the currency of this small economy. Thus, defining the exchange rate E as the domestic currency price of foreign currency and using asterisks to indicate foreign macroeconomic variables, we may describe the behaviour of this economy by equations (9.1a)–(9.6c) below

$$M = P_c L(Y, r, \dot{e}^e, \dot{p}_c^e) \qquad L_1 > 0, L_2, L_3, L_4 < 0 \qquad (9.1a)$$

$$EMd^* = P_c J(Y, r, \dot{e}^e, \dot{p}_c^e) \qquad J_1, J_3 > 0, J_2, J_4 < 0 \qquad (9.2a)$$

$$\dot{e}^e = r - r^* \qquad (9.3a)$$

$$Y = A(Y, r^R) + T(EP^*/P, Y, Y^*) + G$$
$$A_1, T_1, T_3 > 0, A_2, T_2 < 0 \qquad (9.4a)$$

$$\dot{P} = V(Y, \overline{Y}) + \dot{m} \qquad (9.5a)$$

$$P_c \equiv P^\alpha EP^{*(1-\alpha)}, \qquad 0 < \alpha < 1 \qquad (9.6a)$$

$$r^R \equiv r - \dot{p}_c \qquad (9.6b)$$

$$\dot{e}^e = \dot{e}, \dot{p}_c^e = \dot{p}_c \qquad (9.6c)$$

where, $\dot{e} = dE/dt\, 1/E, \dot{p}_c = dp_c/d_t 1/pc, \dot{m} = dM/dt\, 1/M$

(9.1a) expresses equilibrium in the domestic money market with the total stock of M being equal to domestic residents' demand on the right-hand side. The (real) demand for M is taken to be a positive function of a transaction variable—proxied by the volume of domestic output Y, and a negative function of the opportunity cost of holding M, that is, (a) the nominal return on bonds (i.e. the domestic interest rate r), (b) the rate of return on M^* relative to that on M (i.e. the expected rate of depreciation of the domestic currency $\dot{e}^e$) and (c) retail price index inflation $\dot{p}_c$ itself reflecting the possibility of substitution between domestic money and commodities as well as between domestic money and other financial assets. The retail price index appearing in (9.1a) is defined in (9.6a) where α reflects the share of the domestic good in total domestic consumption; P denotes the price of Y while P^* is the price of the output Y^*, produced overseas. (9.2a) specifies in a similar way domestic residents' demand for M^*. Bonds market equilibrium is given in (9.3a) with the assumption of perfect substitutability between domestic and foreign bonds implying that r equals the foreign interest rate r^* plus the expected rate of (nominal) exchange rate depreciation. (9.4a) expresses goods market equilibrium where A, is domestic private absorption, T the real trade balance surplus and G real government spending, r^R and EP^*/P denote the domestic real interest rate and real exchange rate (i.e. the terms of trade, respectively). In (9.5a) it is assumed that due to fixed nominal contracts in domestic factor and product markets, P cannot jump instantaneously. Thus (9.5a) is an augmented Phillips curve—with $\overline{Y}$ being the given 'full capacity' output, where the augmenting term has been set equal to steady state, national inflation (i.e. to the (exogenously) chosen rate of growth of domestic money $\dot{m}$).[4] Finally, (9.6c) states the rational expectations assumption which, in this deterministic model, is equivalent to perfect foresight.

Noting that $\dot{p}$ *and* $\dot{e}$ is the proportional rate of change of P and E respectively, equations (9.1a)–(9.6c) determine instantaneous solutions for Y,r,E and M^*d as functions of (a) the predetermined endogenous variable P whose behaviour is governed by (9.5a), (b) the domestic policy instruments m, M and G, and (c) the exogenous foreign variable r^*, Y^* and P^*. For the purposes of this section we assume that the rate of inflation in the rest of the world is zero. Hence r^* may be interpreted here as being both the nominal and the real foreign interest rate.

As may be seen, the specification of the model is fairly orthodox except that it takes account of the CS possibility. In terms of the macroeconomic equilibrium of this small open economy, this latter possibility is simply reflected in the fact that the demand for domestic money may be a negative function of the expected rate of nominal depreciation via a 'rate of return' effect of CS that is, through a likely speculative motive for holding foreign currency denominated, monetary assets.

We shall focus on the behaviour of this economy following a previously unanticipated fall in (a) the foreign interest rate r^* and, (b) foreign output Y^*. For the analysis that follows we use, for convenience, a log-linear specification of the model. Thus log-linearizing the system at steady state where, for convenience $\overline{E}=\overline{P}=\overline{P}^*=1$, $\overline{r}=\overline{r}^*=0$, $\dot{\overline{m}}=\dot{\overline{p}}=\dot{\overline{e}}=0$ and $\overline{Y}^*=\overline{Y}=1$, allows us to describe domestic macroeconomic equilibrium by,

$$l = (1 - \alpha)c + \phi_1 y - \lambda_1 r - k_1 \dot{p}_c - \beta_1 \dot{e} \qquad (9.1)$$

$$\dot{e} = r - r^* \qquad (9.3)$$

$$y = \sigma c - \delta(r - \dot{p}_c) + xy^* + q \qquad (9.4)$$

$$\dot{p} = vy + \dot{m} \qquad (9.5)$$

$$\dot{p} \equiv \dot{p} + (1 - \alpha)\dot{c} \qquad (9.6)$$

$$c \equiv e - p + p^* \qquad (9.7)$$

$$l \equiv m - p \qquad (9.8)$$

where lower-case letters indicate the logs of the upper-case variables in (9.1a)–(9.6b) so that for every x (except for the interest rates), $x = \log(X/\overline{X})$ with $\overline{X}$ being the steady-state value of X. c denotes the real exchange rate, while l denotes liquidity that is, the real stock of domestic money in terms of the price of the domestic output. Thus, as p is sluggish to adjust, l is a predetermined variable (except of course for the case in which m changes discontinuously as a result of an open market operation by the domestic government). The real exchange rate however, is susceptible to discrete jumps as it is dependent on e which itself is a free variable.

It may be noted that in the context of (9.1), (9.3)–(9.8) the CS possibility is identified with the presence of a non-zero β_1 in (9.1). It is worth remarking that given the interdependence between the domestic money market and the bonds markets in this model, the consequence of the latter is to enhance the (domestic) interest rate sensitivity of the demand for domestic money, see (9.1) and (9.3).

Using the definition of c and l and (9.1) and (9.4) to eliminate r and y from the rest of the model, one can reduce the system to a pair of differential equations in l and c as in (9.9) below.

$$\begin{bmatrix} \dot{l} \\ \dot{c} \end{bmatrix} = \frac{1}{\Delta} \begin{bmatrix} a_1 & a_2 \\ b_1 & b_2 \end{bmatrix} \begin{bmatrix} l \\ c \end{bmatrix} + \frac{1}{\Delta} \begin{bmatrix} a_3 & a_4 \\ b_3 & b_4 \end{bmatrix} \begin{bmatrix} r^* \\ y^* \end{bmatrix} \qquad (9.9)$$

where,

$a_1 = v\delta\alpha < 0, a_2 = -v\{\sigma\theta - \sigma\alpha(1 - \alpha)\}$ (<0),

$$a_3 = v\delta(\theta - \lambda_1\alpha) > 0, a_4 = -xv\theta < 0$$

$$b_1 = -l < 0, b_2 = (1 - \alpha) + \sigma(\phi_1 - vk_1\alpha) - v\sigma\theta \gtrless 0$$

$$b_3 = a_3 - \lambda_1 - \delta(\phi_1 - vk_1\alpha)\ (<0)$$

$$b_4 = x(\phi_1 - vk_1\alpha) + a_4\ (<0)$$

$$\Delta = \delta\alpha(\phi_1 - vk_1\alpha) + \eta\theta > 0$$

$$\theta = \lambda_1 + k_1(1 - \alpha) + \beta_1 > 0, \eta = 1 - v\delta\alpha(>0). \qquad (9.9a)$$

Note that in (9.9a), η reflects the short run income multiplier at a given level of c, which we assume to be positive. The ambiguity regarding the sign of b_2 has the following interpretation: First, $(\phi_1 - vk_1a)$ must be positive, if an exogenous increase in domestic output is to raise the desired level of liquidity at the initial level of c, an assumption we make here. Given that, a real exchange rate depreciation by stimulating output and through its positive impact on p_c, tends to raise r and hence $\dot{e}$ and $\dot{c}$ via (9.3) and (9.7); simultaneously however, the resulting increase in the domestic inflation rate tends to reduce the expost real interest rate thus exerting downwards pressures on the rate of real exchange rate depreciation. Figure 9.1 gives the phase-plane representation of (9.9). As a_2 in (9.9a) can be assumed negative without any loss of generality, the $l = 0$ locus is taken to be downwards sloping in both panels of the figure. With the sign of b_2 being unclear however, the slope of the $\dot{c} = 0$ locus itself becomes ambiguous as to sign. It may be verified though that as long as η, $(\phi_1 - vk_1\alpha) > 0$, if the $\dot{c} = 0$ locus is downwards sloping as in the case of panel (b), its slope will be larger in absolute value than that of the $\dot{l} = 0$ locus, so that (9.9) will have saddle point properties. In such circumstances, it is common in the literature to assume that upon any unanticipated disturbance, the forward looking real exchange rate will undergo a discrete jump to place the system on the unique stable path. The latter—labelled *SS*, is upwards sloping in both panels of the figure independently of the CS possibility.

It is useful to determine first the steady-state response of the endogenous variables to the above disturbances before examining the dynamics of adjustment. The steady state of

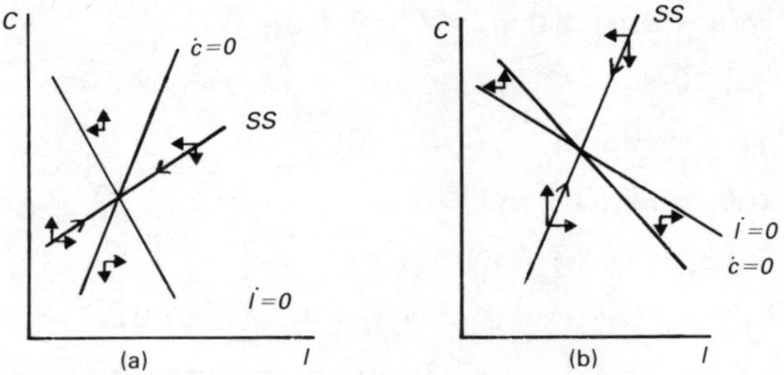

Figure 9.1

models yields (9.10a) and (9.10b) after imposing the condition that all real variables are constant, assuming that domestic policy variables remain unchanged.

$$d\bar{l} = -\{\lambda_1 - (1-\alpha)\frac{\delta}{\sigma}\}\, dr^*, \; d\bar{c} = \frac{\delta}{\sigma}\, dr^*,$$

$$d\bar{r} = dr^* \qquad (9.10a)$$

$$d\bar{l} = -\frac{X}{\sigma}(1-\alpha)d\bar{y}^*, \; d\bar{c} = -\frac{X}{\sigma}\, dy^*,$$

$$d\bar{r} = 0 \qquad (9.10b)$$

In (9.10a) as r falls proportionately to the fall in r^* to maintain (9.3), the real exchange rate appreciates to balance the demand for the domestic good with the given full capacity output. In (9.10b) however, c increases as necessary to offset the reduced demand for the domestic good caused by the fall in y^* through the trade balance. As r decreases in (9.10a), real domestic money balances have to be higher at the new steady state than what they were initially. This is partly achieved via the impact of the steady state real appreciation on p_c, but it is to be expected that the real stock of M in terms of the price of the domestic good must increase as well. Further, in (9.10b) as c depreciates l must rise to maintain long run equilibrium in the domestic money market. It may be noted that both (9.10a) and (9.10b) suggest that $\dot{p}$ must temporarily fall relative to its long run value to allow the steady state p to be lower relative to m. As the steady state values of c and l are independent of the CS possibility what the above implies is that disturbances will still be transmitted across countries even without CS. Obviously though, as $\dot{e}$ may change between steady states, the presence of CS may, in fact, influence the significance of the transmission effect. To examine this latter possibility it is necessary to see how the presence of CS might affect the slope of the unique convergent path in Figure 9.1. An algebraic formula for SS can be easily obtained by noting that the homogeneous part of the solution to (9.9) is of the following form

$$c = D_1 e^{\rho_1 t} + D_2 e^{\rho_2 t}$$

$$l = D_1 \frac{(\rho_1 \Delta - b_2)}{b_1} e^{\rho_1 t} + D_2 \frac{(\rho_2 \Delta - b_2)}{b_1} e^{\rho_2 t},$$

$$\rho_1 < 0, \rho_2 > 0 \tag{9.9b}$$

Restricting the instantaneous response of the system to the unique convergent path by setting the coefficient of the unstable eigenvalue in (9.9b) equal to zero, we can derive an algebraic expression for SS as

$$\hat{c} = \frac{-b_1}{(b_2 - \Delta\rho_1)} \hat{l} = \frac{-b_1}{(\Delta\rho_2 - a_1)} \hat{l}, \; \Delta\rho_2 - a_1 > 0 \tag{9.9c}$$

where the circumflex over the variables denotes deviations from equilibrium and, ρ_1, ρ_2 can be obtained from the characteristic equation of (9.9) as

$$\rho_1, \rho_2 = \frac{(a_1 + b_2) \pm \sqrt{(a_1 + b_2)^2 + 4\sigma v \Delta}}{2\Delta} \tag{9.9d}$$

Thus, differentiating the denominator of (9.9c) with respect to the CS parameter β_1, we get

$$\frac{d(\cdot)}{d\beta_1} = (\eta - \Delta\rho_2)v\sigma/\Delta(\rho_2 - \rho_1), \qquad \Delta(\rho_2 - \rho_1) > 0 \tag{9.9e}$$

Moreover, using the definition of c and the assumption that p^* is exogenously fixed in (9.9) we may write (9.9c) as

$$\hat{e} = -[(\eta - \Delta\rho_2)/(\Delta\rho_2 - a_1)]\hat{p} + [1/(\Delta\rho_2 - a_1)]\hat{m}, \qquad (\Delta\rho_2 - a_1) > 0 \tag{9.9f}$$

From (9.9e) and (9.9f) it may be observed that the sign of (9.9e) is dependent upon the nature of the relationship between movements in e and p and hence that between movements in c and e, along the unique saddle path, that is, for any given $\hat{m}$. Elsewhere,[1] we have noted that as long as β_1 is finite the sign of this relationship is in general invariant to the CS possibility, furthermore, for empirically plausible, parameter values it is to be expected to be negative and hence that between c and e positive. What this suggests is that in the context of (9.1a)–(9.6c) the presence of CS will in fact cause the *SS* locus in Figure 9.1 to be flatter. Thus, figure 9.2a and b can be used to illustrate the effects of an unanticipated reduction in r^* and y^* respectively. Both figures show an initial equilibrium at point A. Final equilibrium is assumed to be at point B_1 and B_2 respectively.

In Figure 9.2a upon the unanticipated fall in r^* and with the stable locus being shifted down to the right, the real exchange rate appreciates instantaneously—overshooting the amount necessary for achieving long run equilibrium depreciating subsequently relative to the initial response point along *SS*. Compared to point C_1, CS in fact limits the size of the initial real exchange rate appreciation, see point C_1^{CS}. In Figure 9.2b the negative disturbance to foreign output is accompanied with a moderate short run depreciation with c converging gradually to the new steady state equilibrium value along *SS*. As the instantaneous

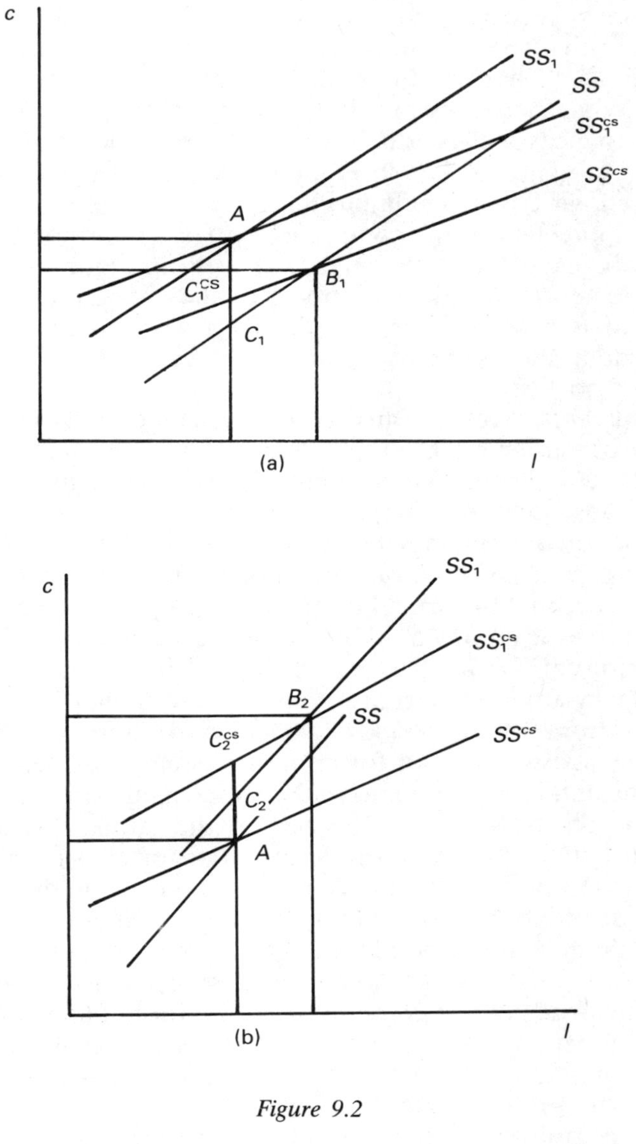
c
SS_1
SS
SS_1^{cs}
SS^{cs}
A
C_1^{cs}
B_1
C_1
(a)
I
c
SS_1
SS_1^{cs}
B_2
SS
C_2^{cs}
SS^{cs}
C_2
A
(b)
I

Figure 9.2

response of C occurs at point C_2^{CS} under CS, here CS indeed implies a relatively large initial jump in the real exchange rate so that the system moves over time from point C_2^{CS} to point B_2. What is of considerable interest though, is that the domestic recession induced by both of the above disturbances will be shallower in the presence of CS than in the absence of CS: in Figure 9.2a and with the ultimate consequence of CS being to limit the size of the immediate real appreciation, the contraction in y via the trade balance is to be expected to be smaller as well; in Figure 9.2b part of the short run adverse impact of the shock on domestic output is absorbed through the larger rise in the level of the domestic economy's competitiveness under CS than under no CS.

The above results might perhaps appear surprising in view of earlier work on CS which stresses the fact that CS tends to enhance rather than mitigate the significance of the transmission of disturbances across countries. The key factor for our findings lies in that (9.1a)–(9.6c) allows for an explicit consideration of complete financial equilibrium taking account in particular, of the interdependence between the domestic money market and the bonds markets. Specifically, note that in the case of the fall in r^*, the resulting tendency for r to decrease via (9.3) as demand is shifted away from foreign bonds, and towards domestic bonds, creates excess demand for domestic money thus leading to an instantaneous nominal and real exchange rate appreciation. The reason why the size of the latter is relatively small under CS is that the anticipation of a rising c and e along SS not only eliminates part of the existing disequilibrium in the bonds markets by increasing the attractiveness of holding foreign bonds, but it also alleviates the excess demand for domestic money by raising the incentives for holding foreign money relative to those for holding domestic money. By contrast, in Figure 9.2b the initial real exchange rate jump is larger at C_2^{CS} than at point C_2 because as the domestic private sector is aware of the real and nominal depreciation in the future, a portfolio shift towards M^* as well as towards foreign bonds takes place in the short run thus intensifying the excess supply pressures on the domestic money market that are generated by the fall in y and y^* is decreased. Table 9.1 provides a numerical illustration of the above considerations.

3.

We shall now consider two countries—hereafter called 'home economy' and 'overseas economy'—assuming that neither of them is small in relation to the other. Accordingly, we shall allow residents of both to hold as assets, the two national monetary assets M and M^*, and the two national bonds—assumed to be perfect substitutes. Using asterisks to denote variables pertaining to the overseas economy's macroeconomic aggregates and defining the exchange rate E as the price of home currency in units of overseas currency, we may specify equilibrium in the home money market as in (9.1a)–(9.1d) below.

$$M_H = P_c L_H(Y, r, \dot{e}, \dot{p}_c) \qquad L_{HL} > 0, L_{H2}, L_{H3}, L_{H4} < 0 \quad (9.1a)$$

$$M_o = EP_c^* L_o(Y^*, r^*, \dot{e}, \dot{p}_c^*) \qquad L_{01} > 0, L_{02}, L_{03}, L_{04} < 0 \quad (9.1b)$$

$$M = M_H + M_o \quad (9.1c)$$

$$P_c \equiv P^{\alpha} EP^*(1 - \alpha) \quad (9.1d_1)$$

$$P_c^* \equiv P^{*\alpha*}(E/P)^{(1-\alpha*)} \quad (9.1d_2)$$

where, for every $\dot{x}^e$, we have set $\dot{x}^e \equiv \dot{x}$ to indicate rational expectations. (9.1a) gives home residents' desired holdings of M and is similar to equation (9.1a) of the previous section. In (9.1b) overseas (real) demand for M is expressed as (a) a positive function of an overseas scale variable proxied by real overseas output Y^*, (b) a positive function of the rate of return on M relative to that on M^* from the overseas residents point of view (i.e. the expected rate of depreciation of overseas currency) and (c) a negative function of the opportunity cost of holding M, that is, the rate of return on bonds r^* and the retail price inflation overseas $\dot{p}_c^*$, where p_c^* is defined in (9.1d$_2$). Equilibrium in the market for home money is attained when the sum of home and overseas demand for M equals the existing stock of M existing stock of M as in equation (9.1c). Equilibrium in

Table 9.1

(a) Impact effects of a reduction in r^*

$\delta = 0.3$
(Assumed initial values: $y=y^*=\mu=0$, $r=r^*=0.06$, $c=0.36$, $l=0.111$
Final values: $y=y^*=\mu=r=r^*=c=l=0$)

β_1	c	y
0	−0.159	−0.095
0.5	−0.153	−0.091
0.75	−0.151	−0.089
1	−0.149	−0.088
2	−0.142	−0.083

$\delta = 0.5$
(Initial values: $y=y^*=\mu=r=r^*=c=l=0$)

β_1	c	y
0	−0.145	−0.098
0.5	−0.14	−0.093
0.75	−0.138	−0.092
1	−0.136	−0.090
2	−0.131	−0.086

(b) Impact effects of a fall in y^*
(Assumed, initial values $y=\mu=r=r^*=0$, $y^*=1$, $c=-0.5$, $1=0.125$
Final values: $y=y^*=\mu=r=r^*=c=l=0$)

$\delta = 0.3$

β_1	c	y
0	−0.179	−0.107
0.5	−0.172	−0.102
0.75	−0.170	−0.100
1	−0.168	−0.099
2	−0.160	−0.094

β_1	c	y
0	−0.172	−0.116
0.5	−0.167	−0.111
0.75	−0.164	−0.109
1	−0.162	−0.107
2	−0.156	−0.102

[a] $\mathbf{v=\sigma=0.05,\ \alpha=0.75,\ x=0.25,\ \lambda=2,\ k_1=\phi_1=1.}$

the overseas economy's monetary sector may be similarly specified in (9.2a)–(9.2c) below

$$M_o^* = P_c^* J_o(Y^*, r^*, \dot{e}, \dot{p}_c^*) \qquad J_{01}, J_{03} > 0, J_{02}, J_{04} < 0 \qquad (9.2a)$$

$$M_H^* = P_c J_H(Y, r, \dot{e}, \dot{p}_c) \qquad J_{H1}, J_{H3} > 0, J_{H2}, J_{H4} < 0 \qquad (9.2b)$$

$$M^* = M_o^* + M_H^* \qquad (9.2c)$$

where $J_0(\cdot)$ and $J_H(\cdot)$ denote overseas and home (real) demand for M^* respectively. Financial equilibrium in the world economy as a whole can therefore be expressed as in (9.1d), (9.2d)–(9.3) where (9.3) describes the behaviour of the bonds markets and in (9.1d)–(9.2d), since only the national currency is used in domestic transactions, one can expect that $L_{H1} > L_{01}$ and $J_{01} > J_{H1}$.

$$\frac{M}{P} = L_H(\cdot)\left(\frac{EP}{P}\right)^{*(1-\alpha)} + \left(\frac{EP^*}{P}\right) L_o(\cdot)\left(\frac{P}{EP^*}\right)^{(1-\alpha*)} \qquad (9.1d)$$

$$\frac{M^*}{P^*} = J_o(\cdot)\left(\frac{P}{EP^*}\right)^{(1-\alpha*)} + \left(\frac{P}{EP^*}\right) J_H(\cdot)\left(\frac{EP^*}{P}\right)^{(1-\alpha)} \qquad (9.2d)$$

$$\dot{e} = r - r^* \qquad (9.2)$$

Turning to the real sectors, equilibrium in the home economy is given by (9.4a)—which is identical to (9.4a) of Section 2 and the behaviour of the price of Y by (9.5a). Similarly, the overseas real sector may be specified as in (9.6a) and (9.7a).

$$Y = A(Y, r^R) + T(\cdot) + G \qquad (9.4a)$$

$$\dot{p} = v(Y/\overline{Y}) + \dot{m} \qquad (9.5a)$$

$$Y^* = A^*(Y^*, r^{*R}) - T(\cdot)(P/EP^*) + G^* \qquad (9.6a)$$

$$\dot{p}^* = v^*(Y/\overline{Y}) + \dot{m}^* \qquad (9.7a)$$

where $T(\cdot) \equiv T(EP^*/P, Y, Y^*)$, $r^R \equiv r - \dot{p}_c$, $r^{*R} \equiv r^* - \dot{p}_c^*$,

$$\dot{m} = dM/dt\, 1/M$$

$$\dot{m}^* = dM^*/dt\, 1/M^*$$

Equations (9.1d), (9.2d)–(9.3) and (9.4a)–(9.7a) form a complete system in seven endogenous variables (i.e. Y, Y^*, r, r^*, E and P, P^*) as functions of the policy instruments M, M^*, $\dot{m}$, $\dot{m}^*$ and G, G^*.

As may be seen from (9.1d)–(9.2d), the 'rate of return' effect of CS, once again, implies that changes in the (nominal) rate of depreciation may directly disturb the equilibrium of the national money markets. It is worth observing though that in the context of (9.1d)–(9.7a), the global demand for each individual money depends on foreign as well as on domestic interest rates, in what follows, we refer to this as the 'foreign interest rate' effect of CS. The following additional possibilities introduced by CS in this two country model may also be noted. First under CS, current movements in the real exchange rate tend to influence the global demand for M and M^* in terms of own currency price levels via a 'terms of trade effect' (i.e. via their impact on the real stocks of M and M^* held by non-residents). It is worth remarking that such an immediate impact of real exchange rate variations on the national monetary sectors, is present here even if changes in foreign prices have virtually no effect on national retail price indices in the short run (i.e. when α and α^* in (9.1d$_1$)–(9.1d$_2$) are close to unity). Second, with $L_{01} \neq 0$ $J_{H1} \neq 0$ in (9.1d) and (9.2d), fluctuations in the level of economic activity abroad may impinge directly on domestic money market equilibrium through a 'foreign income' effect. Finally, with CS a change in the rate of inflation overseas (at home) other things being equal, will change overseas residents' (home residents) real demand for all nominal assets, *including* M (M^*); this is referred to as the 'foreign inflation' effect of CS.

In what follows we shall focus on the behaviour of the system following unilateral and previously unanticipated monetary policy actions namely, an unexpected reduction in (a) the level and (b) the rate of growth of money supply overseas.

We shall proceed with this analysis by abstracting, for simplicity, from any likely, direct effect of real exchange rate movements on P_c and P_c^* thus setting α and α^* in (9.1d$_1$)–(9.1d$_2$) equal to unity. Hence by linearizing the system at long run equilibrium, where $\bar{\dot{e}}=\bar{\dot{p}}=\bar{\dot{p}}^* =\bar{\dot{m}}=\bar{\dot{m}}^*=0, \bar{T}=0$, $\overline{\mathrm{EP}}^*/\overline{\mathrm{P}}=1$, $\overline{\mathrm{M}}/\overline{\mathrm{P}}=\overline{\mathrm{M}}^*/\overline{\mathrm{P}}^*=\overline{\mathrm{Y}}=\overline{\mathrm{Y}}^* = 1$, assuming for convenience identical economies, we may have the complete model as in (9.1′)–(9.8) below

$$l_H = \phi_1 y - \lambda_1 r - k_1\dot{p} - \beta_1\dot{e} \tag{9.1′a}$$

$$l_o = \phi_2 y^* - \lambda_2 r^* - k_2\dot{p}^* - \beta_2\dot{e} + \psi c \tag{9.1′b}$$

$$l = l_h + l_o \tag{9.1′c}$$

$$l_o^* = \phi_1 y^* - \lambda_1 r^* - k_1 p^* + \beta_1\dot{e} \tag{9.2′a}$$

$$l_H^* = \phi_2 y - \lambda_2 r - k_2\dot{p} + \beta_2\dot{e} - \psi c \tag{9.2′b}$$

$$l^* = l_o^* + l_H^* \tag{9.2′c}$$

$$\dot{e} = r - r^* \tag{9.3}$$

$$y = \sigma c - \delta(r - \dot{p}) + xy^* + q \tag{9.4}$$

$$\dot{p} = vy + \dot{m} \tag{9.5}$$

$$y^* = -\sigma c - \delta(r^* - \dot{p}^*) + xy + q^* \tag{9.6}$$

$$\dot{p}^* = vy^* + \dot{m}^* \tag{9.7}$$

$$l \equiv m - p \tag{9.8a}$$

$$l^* \equiv m^* - p^* \tag{9.8b}$$

$$c \equiv e - p + p^* \tag{9.8c}$$

$$\dot{m} = \mu \tag{9.8d}$$

$$\dot{m}^* = \mu^* \tag{9.8e}$$

where in (9.1′b) and (9.2′b) the value of ψ indicates the share of foreign holdings of M and M^* in the total stock of M and M^* taken to be the same across countries. Thus, in (9.1)–(9.8), the terms of trade, foreign inflation and foreign income effect of CS are captured by a non-zero ψ, k_2 and ϕ_2 respectively, the foreign interest rate effect is reflected in that $\lambda_2 \neq 0$.

Further, using Aoki's (1981) device of expressing the system in terms of relative and global variables, we may write the model after some substitutions, as two orthogonal systems as in (9.9)–(9.10) below. As is well known, Aoki's device simplifes the dynamic analysis of models of this sort and also enables us to analyse the implications of CS for the behaviour of relative variables—such as the real exchange rate, separately from that of global variables

$$
\begin{aligned}
l^d &= 2\psi c + (\phi^* - vk^*)y^d - (\lambda_1 + \lambda)r^d - k^*\mu^d \\
\eta_1 y &= 2\sigma c - \delta(r^d - \mu^d) + g^d \\
\dot{l}^d &= -vy^d \\
\dot{c} &= r^d - vy^d - \mu^d \qquad (9.9) \\
l^w &= \{(\phi_1 - vk_1) + (\phi_2 - vk_2)\}y^w \\
&\quad - (\lambda_1 + \lambda_2)r^w - (k_1 + k_2)\mu^w \\
\eta_2 y^w &= -\delta(r^* - \mu^w) + q^w \\
\dot{l}^w &= -vy^w \qquad (9.10)
\end{aligned}
$$

where

$$\eta_1 = (1 + x - v\delta)\,(>0),\ \phi^* = \phi_1 - \phi_2 > 0,$$

$$k^* = (k_1 - k_2) \geqslant 0,\ \lambda = 2(\beta_1 + \beta_2) - \lambda_2 = 2\beta - \lambda_2 \qquad (9.9a)$$

$$\eta_2 = (1 - x - v\delta)\,(>0) \qquad (9.10a)$$

and, for every x, $x^w = x + x^*$, and $x = x = x^*$. Thus l^d for example denotes the composition of global liquidity while l^w the aggregate level of the latter. (Note that from (9.9), (9.10) one can get x and x^* as $x = 1/2(x^w + x^d)$ and $x^* = 1/2(x^w - x^d)$.) Through appropriate substitutions one can reduce (9.9)–(9.10) to the behaviour of the dynamic variables l^d, c and l^w as in (9.11), (9.12) below

$$\begin{bmatrix} \dot{l}^d \\ \dot{c} \end{bmatrix} = \frac{1}{\Delta} \begin{bmatrix} a_{11} & a_{21} \\ b_{11} & b_{21} \end{bmatrix} \begin{bmatrix} \hat{l}^d \\ \hat{c} \end{bmatrix} \qquad (9.11)$$

$$\hat{\imath}^w = \frac{a_{12}}{\Delta_2}[1^w] \qquad (9.12)$$

where the circumflex over the variables indicates deviations from equilibrium, and

$$a_{11} = -v\delta < 0, a_{21} = -2v\{\theta_1\sigma - \delta_\psi\}(<0)$$
$$b_{11} = -(1 + x) < 0, b_{21} = 2\{-b_{11}\psi + \sigma(\phi^* - vk^*) - \sigma v\theta_1\} \gtrless 0$$
$$\Delta_1 = \delta(\phi^* - vk^*) + \eta_1\theta_1 > 0, \theta_1 = \lambda_1 + \lambda \quad (9.11a)$$
$$a_{12} = -v\delta < 0$$
$$\Delta_2 = \eta_2(\lambda_1 + \lambda_2) + \delta\{(\phi_1 - vk_1) + (\phi_2 - vk_2)\} > 0 \quad (9.12a)$$

Focusing first on the 'relative' model it can be easily demonstrated that (9.11) will be saddle point stable provided that $\Delta_1 > 0$, an assumption we make here. The unique stable path labelled *SS* in Figure 9.3a can be derived as

$$\hat{c} = \frac{b_{11}}{(b_{21} - \Delta_1\rho_{11})}\hat{l}d = -\frac{b_{11}}{(\Delta\rho_{21} - a_{11})}\hat{l}^d\rho_{21} > 0, \rho_{11} < 0 \quad (9.11b)$$

where ρ_{11} and ρ_{21} denote the stable and unstable eigenvalue respectively and,

$$\rho_{11}, \rho_{21} = \frac{(a_{11} + b_{21}) \pm \sqrt{a_{11} + b_{21})^2 + 8\sigma v\Delta_1}}{2\Delta_1} \quad (9.11c)$$

Looking at (9.11b), (9.11c)–(11a) one can easily establish that CS both through the terms of trade effect and through the foreign inflation effect implies a flatter *SS* locus. This is so because with CS whenever the composition of world liquidity deviates from its steady state value, the adjustment of c required to preserve financial equilibrium along *SS* need not be too large since any given movement in c alters directly relative (real) stocks of M and M^* via its impact on foreign, real holdings of such assets; moreover, under CS any short run change in any individual inflation rate tends to have a relatively small destabilizing effect on the desired level of l^d—and hence on c itself, as it tends to alter the global demand for both M and M^* in the same direction. Furthermore, it may also be verified that the implications of the rate of return effect of CS for the stable path are analogous to those observed in Section 2. What is of considerable importance though, is that in this two-country model the influence of the rate of return effect of CS on the *SS* locus is subjected to one opposing force, namely the 'foreign interest rate' effect; see (9.9a) where the value of λ may be relatively small especially if the speculative motive for holding foreign money rather than holding domestic money as reflected in the value of β, is relatively weak. Finally the consequences of the foreign income effect of CS for (9.11b) are worth noting. Because the latter tends to reduce the sensitivity of relative money demands to changes in relative output levels, it implies that a larger adjustment of y^d must occur in the short run to maintain the balance between existing l^d with desired l^d along *SS*. Since under floating exchange rates relative outputs are considerably influenced by real exchange rate movements, a relatively large adjustment of y^d tends to necessitate in turn a relatively large adjustment of c along *SS*, hence the negative impact of a $\phi_2 \neq 0$ on the denominator of (9.11b); see (9.11a)–(9.11c).

Figure 9.3 can be used to illustrate the implications of CS following a contraction in the level of overseas money supply, achieved for example via an open market operation by the overseas government. It is easy to show that this latter disturbance will affect neither the steady state value of c nor that of l^d so that adjustments will take place along the original *SS* locus. Consequently, and in view of the above considerations, as long as the foreign income effect of CS is not unduly strong, CS must be expected to be on the whole 'stabilizing' (i.e. it must be expected to mitigate the extent of the overshooting of c following this disturbance in contrast to usual CS literature predictions); in Figure 9.3a, upon the unanticipated contraction in the level of M^* and with l^d being increased instantaneously, the real exchange rate depreciates and overshoots, independently of the CS possibility. Under CS though, the size of the overshooting is reduced as the initial response of c occurs at point C_1^{cs}.

Finally, it is interesting to note here the implications of CS for the aggregate model. Specifically, as the opposing effects of a $\lambda_2 \neq 0$, $k_2 \neq 0$ on the value of Δ_2 tend to cancel out, the net influence of CS on (9.12) is mainly via the foreign income effect. Thus, as the latter causes the $\dot{l}^w_{cs} = 0$ locus in Figure 9.3b to slope less steeply compared to that

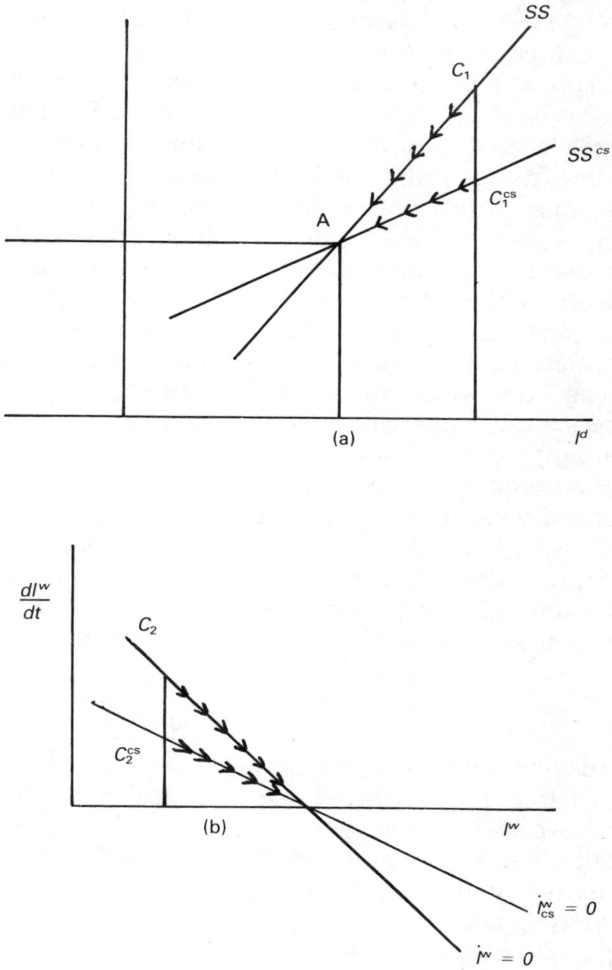

Figure 9.3

without CS, the size of the resulting global recession is, due to the foreign income effect, smaller at point C_2^{cs} than at point C_2. Given the definition of x^w and x^d, points C_1^{cs} and C_2^{cs} therefore seem to suggest that CS may not fail, under the circumstances, to limit the extent of the resulting short run fall in real output overseas, and the significance of the transmission effect to the home economy's real income.

An unexpected reduction in the rate of overseas monetary growth once again causes an immediate depreciation and overshooting of the real exchange rate independently of the CS possibility, as it raises the real interest rate differential in favour of the overseas economy in the short run. The main change from the previous analysis is that now the steady-state equilibrium itself is being altered. In particular, imposing the steady-state requirement that (a) all real variables are constant and, (b) national inflation rates equal the rate of growth of national money, it can be shown that both the nominal and the real interest rate at home remain unchanged while r^* falls proportionally to the reduction in μ^*. Thus, as r^d rises, the rate of (nominal) exchange rate depreciation increases for maintaining bond markets equilibrium. The real exchange rate though returns to its original value. The long run change in l^d can be obtained as

$$d\bar{l}^d = (\lambda_1 + \lambda + k^*)d\mu^* \qquad (9.11d)$$

As may be seen from (9.11d) and (9.11a) the steady-state value of l^d is influenced by the presence of CS in a way that is in principle ambiguous, whereas the rate of return effect of CS tends to contribute to the desired shift of global liquidity away from home money and towards overseas money as $\dot{e}$ rises both the foreign inflation and foreign interest rate effect tend to mitigate the degree to which l^d must fall. The reason for the latter is that with the values of r^* and $\dot{p}^*$ being lower at the new steady state that what they were initially, overseas demand is switched towards *both* of the two nominal, monetary assets M and M^*. It therefore follows that the net impact of CS on the long run value of l^d will effectively be dependent upon the value of β (i.e. on the relative significance of speculation on national

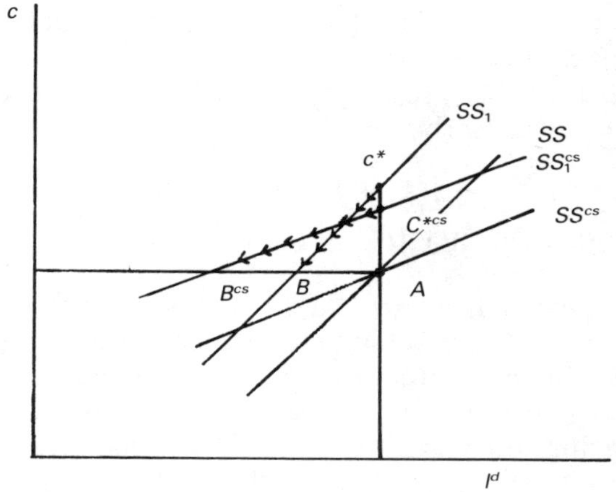

Figure 9.4

monetary assets). In a world in which other assets, in particular, interest-bearing assets as well as monetary assets, are present one would not expect the latter to be too strong.[5] It is therefore apparent that it may not be impossible for CS to weaken, on balance, the effect of the reduction in μ^* on $\bar{l}^d$. Moreover, even if $\bar{l}^d$ falls by more under CS than under no CS, the degree of this net, additional influence of CS on steady state l^d may be relatively small. In light of the above considerations, and if account is taken of the implications of the CS for the slope of the stable locus, the response of c to the reduction in the overseas economy's money growth rate may be such as that illustrated in Figure 9.4 where an initial steady state has been assumed at point A. Upon the unanticipated reduction in μ^* and with μ^d being increased instantaneously, both the SS and the SS^{cs} locus shift upwards as l^d must be lower at the new steady state than it was initially. Compared to point C^*, CS limits the extent of the initial real exchange rate overshooting it may nevertheless, imply that c stays away from equilibrium for a longer period as indicated by the fact that l^d may be required to fall by a larger amount with CS than without CS; see point B^{cs}.

As for the behaviour of the aggregate model it can be easily verified that $\bar{l}^w$ adjusts at the new steady state as in (9.12b) so that the initial response of global output to this disturbance is given by (9.12c)

$$d\bar{l}^w = -[(k_1 + k_2) + (\lambda_1 + \lambda_2)]d\mu^* \qquad (9.12b)$$

$$dy^w(0) = \delta/\Delta_2[(k_1 + k_2) + (\lambda_1 + \lambda_2)]d\mu^* \qquad (9.12c)$$

As may be seen from (9.12a), (9.12c) the net effect of a $\lambda_2 \neq 0$ in (9.12c) is most likely to be close to zero. Moreover, the foreign income effect of CS is once again stabilizing in that it tends to limit the size of the initial global recession by enhancing the sensitivity of l^w to changes in global output. It may be observed though that the foreign inflation effect of CS may have a destabilizing impact here.

A numerical illustration of the possible overall implications of CS as well as some indication of the separate contribution of the individual CS effects to the initial response of the endogenous variables to the above disturbances is provided in Table 9.2. The table shows numerical solutions for the initial adjustment of y, y^* and c for alternative values of ψ, ϕ_2 and β (and for v=0.5, δ=0.3/0.5, x=0.25, ϕ=1), and for k_1=k_2=1 and λ_1=λ_2 = 2. In Table 9.2b the assumed, initial steady-state values are: $y=y^*=c=0$, $\mu=0$, $\mu^*=0.04$, the final equilibrium is characterized by $c=\dot{m}=\dot{m}^*=\dot{p}=\dot{p}=\dot{e}=y=y^*=0$. In table 9.2a both the initial and the final equilibrium are characterized by $c=\dot{m}=\dot{m}^*=\dot{p}=\dot{p}=\dot{e}=y=y^*=0$. As is apparent from the table, CS is unambiguously stabilizing on balance, for an unanticipated contraction in the level of M^*; note, however, the 'destabilizing' influence of the foreign income effect. What is of considerable interest is that the proposition that CS *per se* is a channel for the transmission of disturbances across countries—and a source of exchange rate overshooting, may not survive even for a reduction in the rate of growth of M^* if β is not unduly large: in such circumstances CS may, in fact, mitigate the extent of variation in home output and initial real exchange rate jump—as has been indicated by Figure 9.4, the fundamental reason for which tends to be high capital mobility combined with the possibility of a less than perfectly flexible price level and not CS *per se*. Furthermore, parts (1)–(2) of the table make the obvious point that whether or not CS is on the whole 'destabilizing' following changes in the rate of growth of national money supplies becomes a matter that may depend on the values of the structural parameters of the model.

4.

In this chapter we have studied the implications that CS might have for the behaviour of an open economy with a freely flexible exchange rate. In the first part of the paper we have addressed the issue of the international transmission of disturbances under CS for the case of a small open economy. It has been found that if proper account is taken of the specification of complete financial equilibrium, the existing interdependence between the money markets and the bonds markets implies that CS may provide in fact a greater insulation of the output of a small open economy from disturbances originated abroad, namely, disturbances to foreign interest rates and foreign output. These conclusions seem to contain surprises in light of existing views that CS is a channel for the transmission of disturbances across countries.

In the second part of the chapter attention has turned to the behaviour of two large economies under CS. It has been shown that CS reduces both the size of the resulting real exchange jump and the transmission effect to the home economy's output following disturbances to the level of money supply overseas. Moreover, it has been argued that in general it cannot be asserted that CS is necessarily a source for the transmission of international disturbances even for changes in the rate of growth of national monies. In particular, it has been found that if speculation on national monetary assets is not unduly strong—as one would expect to be the case in a world in which other assets besides money are present, CS may in fact mitigate the size of the transmission effect of a change in the rate of monetary growth in one country to the other country's output—and

Table 9.2

(a) Impact effects of a contraction in m^* (Assumed, initial values: $y=y^*=\dot{p}=\dot{p}^*=\dot{m}=\dot{m}^*=c=1=1^*=0$, $p=m=0$, $p^*=m^*=1$
Final values: $y=y^*=\dot{p}=\dot{p}^*\dot{m}=\dot{m}^*=c=1=1^*=p=m=p^*=m^*=0$)

(1) $\delta = 0.3$

ψ	ϕ_2	β	y	y^*	c
0	0		0.509	−0.731	1.307
0.1	0.1	1	0.388	−0.512	0.991
0.1	0.2		0.413	−0.535	1.037
0.2	0.25		0.373	−0.495	0.960
0.25	0.25		0.349	−0.471	0.913
0.1	0.1	1.5	0.389	−0.512	0.993
0.1	0.2		0.409	−0.531	1.030
0.2	0.25		0.377	−0.498	0.967
0.25	0.25		0.357	−0.478	0.928
0.1	0.1	2	0.390	−0.513	0.994
0.1	0.2		0.407	−0.529	1.026
0.2	0.25		0.380	−0.501	0.972
0.25	0.25		0.362	−0.484	0.939
0.1	0.1	4	0.391	−0.514	0.996
0.1	0.2		0.402	−0.523	1.015
0.2	0.25		0.385	−0.506	0.983
0.25	0.25		0.374	−0.495	0.962

(2) $\delta = 0.5$

ψ	ϕ_2	β	y	y^*	c
0	0	0	0.467	−0.867	1.25
0.1	0.1	1	0.351	−0.595	0.956
0.1	0.2		0.381	−0.619	1.0
0.2	0.25		0.341	−0.576	0.933
0.25	0.25		0.316	−0.551	0.890
0.1	0.1	1.5	0.356	−0.599	0.964
0.1	0.2		0.381	−0.619	1.0
0.2	0.25		0.348	−0.584	0.945
0.25	0.25		0.327	−0.562	0.909
0.1	0.1	2	0.359	−0.603	0.969
0.1	0.2		0.381	−0.619	1.0
0.2	0.25		0.353	−0.589	0.953
0.25	0.25		0.335	−0.570	0.923
0.1	0.1	4	0.366	−0.610	0.981
0.1	0.2		0.381	−0.619	1.0
0.2	0.25		0.364	−0.600	0.971
0.25	0.25		0.353	−0.588	0.952

(b) Impact effects of a reduction in μ^*

(1) $\delta = 0.3$

ψ	ϕ_2	β	y	y^*	c
0	0	0	0.061	−0.088	0.157
0.1	0.1	1	0.21	−0.051	0.079
0.1	0.2		0.023	−0.052	0.083
0.2	0.25		0.020	−0.049	0.077
0.25	0.25		0.018	−0.047	0.073
0.1	0.1	1.5	0.039	−0.069	0.119
0.1	0.2		0.042	−0.071	0.124
0.2	0.25		0.038	−0.067	0.116
0.25	0.25		0.036	−0.065	0.111
0.1	0.1	2	0.057	−0.087	0.159
0.1	0.2		0.06	−0.089	0.164
0.2	0.25		0.056	−0.085	0.156
0.25	0.25		0.053	−0.082	0.150
0.1	0.1	4	0.13	−0.160	0.319
0.1	0.2		0.133	−0.163	0.325
0.2	0.25		0.128	−0.157	0.314
0.25	0.25		0.125	−0.154	0.308

(2) $\delta = 0.5$

ψ	ϕ_2	β	y	y^*	c
0	0	0	0.056	−0.104	0.15
0.1	0.1	1	0.009	−0.067	0.076
0.1	0.2		0.11	−0.069	0.08
0.2	0.25		0.008	−0.065	0.075
0.25	0.25		0.006	−0.063	0.71
0.1	0.1	1.5	0.028	−0.087	0.116
0.1	0.2		0.031	−0.089	0.12
0.2	0.25		0.028	−0.084	0.113
0.25	0.25		0.025	−0.082	0.109
0.1	0.1	2	0.048	−0.106	0.155
0.1	0.2		0.051	−0.109	0.16
0.2	0.25		0.047	−0.1036	0.153
0.25	0.25		0.044	−0.101	0.148
0.1	0.1	4	0.127	−0.185	0.314
0.1	0.2				
0.2	0.25		0.126	−0.182	0.311
0.25	0.25		0.122	−0.179	0.1305

the size of the initial exchange rate jump. As the above results appear to conflict in general with earlier findings about the effects of CS, it might perhaps be interesting to compare them with those of prevailing papers on CS. In a model in which the availability of assets is restricted to domestic and foreign money—as is typically the case in the existing CS literature, it is apparent that in terms of equations (9.1)–(9.8) in Section 3, $\lambda_1=\lambda_2=k_1=k_2=0$. With p and p^* being less than perfectly flexible, the real exchange rate would still overshoot in such a case following either a reduction in the level or in the rate of growth of M^*; however this overshooting as well as any required long run adjustment of the composition of global liquidity would be entirely attributed to CS (i.e. to the fact that $\beta \neq 0$ in (9.1)–(9.8)). Thus without altering the assumptions about the real sectors in the model, restricting the available menu of assets to domestic and foreign money implies that one might conclude that CS *per se* is unambiguously 'destabilizing'. Furthermore, by imposing the assumption of continuous purchasing power parity—as much of the CS literature does ψ becomes zero in (9.1)–(9.8) so that one of the stabilizing influences of CS on the exchange rate is automatically eliminated. In short, as our findings seem to suggest, a relaxation of the assumption of continuous PPP combined with an introduction of other assets besides money in the analytical framework, may destroy the presumption that CS is *per se* a channel for the transmission of disturbances across countries.

ACKNOWLEDGEMENT

Thanks are due to Marcus Miller, John Black and the participants of the IESG Conference (Sussex, September 1985) for useful comments on an earlier version of this chapter.

NOTES

1. *See* A. Zervoyianni (1985).
2. *See* A. Zervoyianni (1985) for an analysis of the effects of CS in the

context of a model with imperfect bond substitutability.

3. The assumption that M (and M^*) pays no interest can be easily modified without essentially altering the basic argument of the paper as long as the banking sector is competitive and there is a required reserve ratio; *see* Miller and Wise (1980) for a discussion of the implications of introducing interest-bearing money in a model.
4. *See* e.g. Buiter and Miller (1982) for a similar specification and economic interpretation.
5. As Cuddington (1982) indicates in a survey of the empirical literature on CS, the value of the coefficient of $\dot{e}$ in a number of estimated (aggregate) money demand functions is relatively small and in some cases less than unity.

REFERENCES

Aoki, M. (1981) *Dynamic Analysis of Open Economies* MIT Press, London and Cambridge, Mass.

Artis, M. and Gazioglou, S. (1985) 'Currency substitution, two asset two country model: a simulation approach' presented at the Franco–British Meeting, London, November.

Austin, P. and Buiter, W. (1983) 'Saddle point, a program for solving continuous time, rational expectation models'. Mimeo, University of Bristol.

Bordo, M. and Choudri, E. (1982) 'Currency substitution and the demand for money', *Journal of Money, Credit and Banking*, **14**, (1), 48–57.

Branson, W. and Buiter, W. (1983) 'Monetary and fiscal policy with flexible exchange rates', in Bhandari, J. and Putman, B. (eds) *The International transmission of Economic Disturbances*. Cambridge, MIT Press.

Buiter, W. and Miller, M. (1981) 'Monetary policy and international competitiveness', Oxford Economic Papers, **33** Supplement, 143–175.

Brillembourg, A. and Schadler, S. (1979) 'A model of currency substitution in exchange rate determination', *IMF Staff Papers*, **26**, 513–542.

Calvo, G. and Rodriguez, C. (1977) 'A model of exchange rate determination under currency substitution and rational expectations', *Journal of Political Economy*, **85**, 617–625.

Cuddington, T. (1982) 'Currency substitution, capital mobility and money demand', Institute for International Economics Disscussion Paper, University of Stockholm, July.

Daniel, B. (1985) 'Monetary, autonomy and exchange rate dynamics under currency substitution', *Journal of International Economics*, **19**, 119–139.

Dornbusch, C. (1976) 'Expectations and Exchange rate dynamics' *Journal of Political Economy*, **84**(6), 1161–1176.

Girton, L. and Roper, S. (1981) 'Theory and implications of currency substitution', *Journal of Money, Credit and Banking*, **13**(1), 12–30.

McKinnon, R. (1982) 'Currency substitution and instability in the world dollar-standard', *American Economic Review*, **72**(3), 320–337.

Miles, M. (1978) 'Currency substitution, flexible exchange rates and monetary independence', *American Economic Review*, **68**, 428–436.

Miller, M. (1982) 'A theoretical analysis of feasible policy measures under high US interest rates', Mimeo, University of Warwick.

Miller, M., and Wise, J. (1980) 'Competitive banking, money and exchange rates', Mimeo, University of Warwick.

Thomas, L. (1985) 'Portfolio theory and currency substitution', *Journal of Money, Credit and Banking*, **17**(3), 347–357.

Zervoyianni, A. (1985) 'Exchange rate overshooting, currency substitution and monetary policy', presented at the IESG Conference on Monetary Analysis of Open Economies', Sussex, September 1985. (Revised version, *Hull University Discussion Paper 142*, 1986.)

10 The Inefficiency of Uncoordinated Stabilisation Policy in Multicountry Models

Paul Turner

1. INTRODUCTION

One of the problems of the world economy in recent years has been that while countries may pay careful attention to the design of macroeconomic policy in terms of its effects on their own economies they very rarely give any thought to the repercussion effects on the rest of the world. The need for such recognition of interdependence was noted by Williamson (1982).

> The international spillover effects of macroeconomic policy are too strong for it to be sensible for individual countries to believe that they can rationally plan their actions independently of what is happening elsewhere.

The literature on macroeconomic interdependence originates with the contribution of Mundell (1968). This analysis was confined to a basically static framework, though as with all comparative static Keynesian models it contained hidden dynamics in terms of the effects of investment on the capital stock and the balance of payments on the stock of foreign exchange reserves. Hamada and Sakurai (1978) use a two-country model under fixed and flexible exchange rate regimes to examine the transmission of economic fluctuations between countries. Commodity arbitrage ensures purchasing power parity in their model and so it is deviations of output from its natural rate which causes terms of trade fluctuations which are the channel of interdependence under flexible exchange rates. Miller (1982) presents a two-country model in which the exchange rate is determined in the asset market and goods prices are sticky, therefore permitting persistent deviations from PPP.

There has also been a small literature on optimal policy design with interdependent economies. Hamada (1974 and 1976) uses a game theoretic framework to analyse the problems arising from uncoordinated decision making. Miller and Salmon (1985) extend this framework to deal with problems wth a dynamic structure.

This chapter attempts to distinguish inefficiencies which arise because of fundamental disagreement between countries over macroeconomic targets and those which arise because of failure to coordinate the approach to a mutually desirable steady state. The first category we term steady-state inefficiency (SSI) and the second dynamic inefficiency (DI).

The plan of the chapter is as follows. Section 2 considers that SSI problem and gives a particular economic example. Section 3 goes on to consider the DI case. The economic example given here is that of optimal disinflation policy. Section 4 contains conclusions.

2. STEADY-STATE INEFFICIENCY

The world is assumed to consist of two economies and to be describable by the following set of differential equations

$$\dot{\mathbf{x}} = f(\mathbf{x},\mathbf{u}_1,\mathbf{u}_2) \tag{10.1}$$

where $\mathbf{x}$ is a vector of states and $\mathbf{u}_1,\mathbf{u}_2$ are vectors of the control variables available to the policy authorities in the two countries. Each country is assumed to have a loss function of the form

$$\int_0^{\infty} (\mathbf{x},\mathbf{u}_i)\, e^{-\rho_i t} dt \tag{10.2}$$

The most popular formulation of this problem in the macroeconomic control literature has been to treat (10.1) as linear and (10.2) as quadratic in deviations of states and controls from target values. It is well known that given this formulation and assuming $\rho_i = 0$ we can derive a pair of linear, time-invariant steady-state Nash reaction functions as in (10.3)

$$\mathbf{u}_1 = \phi_1\mathbf{u}_2 + \Omega_1\mathbf{x}_1^* \qquad (10.3)$$

$$\mathbf{u}_2 = \phi_2\mathbf{u}_1 + \Omega_2\mathbf{x}_2^*$$

With suitable restrictions on the ϕ_1, ϕ_2 matrices it can also be shown that there is a unique Nash equilibrium pair of control vectors such that each player is simultaneously playing his best response strategy to the other. However if the target vectors $\mathbf{x}_1^*$, $\mathbf{x}_2^*$ are incompatible this will be inefficient in the sense that policy coordination could generate Pareto improvements.

Let us consider a specific economic example. The model used is a version of the Mundell (1968) two-country fixed-price model with flexible exchange rates and internationally mobile capital. Output in the two countries is given by

$$x_1 = \alpha_1 e + \alpha_2 m_1$$

$$x_2 = -\beta_1 e + \beta_2 m_2 \qquad (10.4)$$

where x, e and m are the natural logarithms of output, the exchange rate and the money supply respectively. These can be thought of as reduced form expressions of the *IS/LM* systems for the two countries. The exchange rate is determined by relative monetary policies

$$e = \gamma(m - m^*) \qquad (10.5)$$

Each country is assumed to have a loss function defined on deviations of output and the exchange rate from target values.

$$L_1 = \frac{1}{2}(x_1 - x_1^*)^2 + \frac{\delta_1}{2}(e - e_1^*)^2$$

$$L_2 = \frac{1}{2}(x_2 - x_2^*)^2 + \frac{\delta_2}{2}(e - e_2^*)^2 \qquad (10.6)$$

The justification for the inclusion of the exchange rate in the loss functions is that countries not only care about the

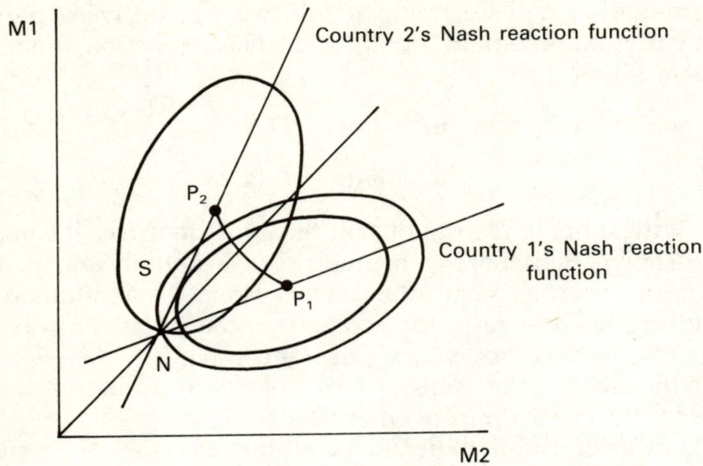

Figure 10.1

level of output but also its composition (i.e. the division between traded and non-traded goods sectors). A higher value of *e* will tend to increase the output of the traded goods sector in country 1 and reduce that in country 2. The Nash reaction functions can be derived as

$$m_1 = \frac{1}{\Delta_1}[(\alpha_1^2\gamma^2 + \delta_1\gamma^2)m_2 + \alpha_1 x_1^* + \delta_1\gamma e_1^*]$$

$$m_2 = \frac{1}{\Delta_2}[(\beta_1^2\gamma^2 + \delta_2\gamma^2)m_1 + \beta_1 x_2^* + \delta_2\gamma e_2^*]$$

$$\Delta_1 = \alpha_1^2\gamma + \alpha_1\alpha_2 + \delta_1\gamma^2$$

$$\Delta_2 = \beta_1^2\alpha + \beta_1\beta_2 + \delta_2\gamma^2 \tag{10.7}$$

If each country has similar but incompatible targets (e.g. both countries desire too low a value of *e*) then the Nash equilibrium will be of the form shown in Figure 10.1 by point *N*.

In this case the Nash equilibrium shows a deflationary bias. However, if both countries set too low a target on *e* then the resulting equilibrium would have an inflationary bias.

One suggestion is that inefficient Nash solutions can be improved on if there is a recognized leader in the world economy (see Kindelberger, 1976). If country 1 is leader then it has a free choice of points on country 2's reaction function and chooses the one which generates minimum loss (i.e. *S* in Figure 10.1).

In the case analysed the reaction functions are upward sloping, as shown in the diagram, and the Stackelberg leader solution unambiguously results in a Pareto improvement. However Turner (1983) has shown that this result is not robust since in cases where the reaction functions are downward sloping the follower's welfare deteriorates relative to the Nash solution.

So far all our discussion has been in terms of a single play or one-shot game. Much recent research has been devoted to the implications of repeated games. Suppose we consider a situation in which the game we have set up simply repeats itself indefinitely. Solutions superior to Nash can be sustained by the use of conditional strategies where each player threatens to punish the other if he deviates from cooperative behaviour by himself withdrawing cooperation. Unfortunately there is no unique solution to the infinitely repeated game. Indeed what has become known as the folk theorem of repeated games states that in an infinitely repeated game with undiscounted loss functions any solution superior to and including the one-shot Nash solution can be justified as a Nash solution by an appropriate pair of strategies.

The folk theorem result stems from the assumption of infinite repetitions. If there is a known terminal date to the game (e.g. in the case of national policy authorities this could be an election date) then the equilibrium is simply for the one-shot Nash solution to be repeated at every stage. This result was first shown by Selten (1978) who entitled it the 'chain store paradox', it can easily be proved by backward induction. Kreps and Wilson (1982) show that cooperative solutions can still be achieved in finite horizon games if there is some uncertainty attached to players' behaviour.

Recent theory therefore leaves us in a position of not being able to say much about the outcome of a repeated game. However, in the particular situation we are concerned with, it seems likely that non-cooperation will tend to dominate. This is because national policy authorities frequently have short horizons set by election dates. In the run up to elections the incentive to renege on cooperative policies becomes very strong and it is therefore likely that any tacit cooperation will break down.

3. DYNAMIC INEFFICIENCY

To illustrate DI we abstract from problems of SSI assuming that targets are compatible. The model we use is analysed more thoroughly in Turner (1984). It consists of a two-country world in which each country is attempting to bring down inflation subject to a Phillips curve in which core inflation reacts sluggishly. The equations for the home economy are

$$\dot{p} = \psi x + \pi + \delta(p^* + e - p) \tag{10.8}$$

$$(p^* + e - p) = \eta(x - x^*) \tag{10.9}$$

$$(\dot{p}^* + \dot{e} - \dot{p}) = -\phi(p^* + e - p) \tag{10.10}$$

$$\dot{p}_c = \dot{p} + (1 - \alpha)(\dot{p}^* + \dot{e} - \dot{p}) \tag{10.11}$$

$$\dot{\pi} = \gamma(\dot{p}_c - \pi) \tag{10.12}$$

A similar set of equations describe the foreign economy. All foreign variables are indicated by a^*. (10.8) is the Phillips curve, the terms of trade enter because an improvement in them increases real wages and therefore dampens nominal wage inflation. (10.9) and (10.10) describe the behaviour of the terms of trade. A cut in output causes a real appreciation. If capital is immobile then this is simply due to the reduced amount of the country's product on world markets. In the case of mobile capital it is because a rise in real interest rates is necessary to engineer the fall in output. (10.11) gives the rate of increase of the consumer price index, which is a weighted average of the rates of increase of domestic goods prices and the domestic price of foreign goods. (10.12) describes the adjustment of core inflation π.

If the policy authorities in the home economy have loss function

$$\int_0^\infty \frac{\pi^2}{2} + \frac{r}{2}x^2\,dt \tag{10.13}$$

Then it is possible under Nash behaviour to regard this as a control problem with one state variable π and one control x. The constraint subject to which (10.13) is minimized can be derived from (10.8)–(10.12) as

$$\begin{aligned} \dot{\pi} &= b_1 x - b_2 x^* \\ \pi(0) &= \overline{\pi}(0) \\ b_1 &= \gamma[\psi + \delta\eta - (1-\alpha)\phi\eta] \\ b_2 &= \gamma[\delta\eta - (1-\alpha)\phi\eta] \end{aligned} \tag{10.14}$$

Solving this problem for both countries by means of the Pontryagin minimum principle yields a 4×4 dynamic system in the rates of core inflation and the costate variables.

$$\begin{bmatrix} \dot{\pi} \\ \dot{\pi}^* \\ \dot{\lambda} \\ \dot{\lambda}^* \end{bmatrix} = \begin{bmatrix} 0 & 0 & \dfrac{-b_1^2}{r} & \dfrac{b_1 b_2}{r} \\ 0 & 0 & \dfrac{b_1 b_2}{r} & \dfrac{-b_1^2}{r} \\ -1 & 0 & 0 & 0 \\ 0 & -1 & 0 & 0 \end{bmatrix} \begin{bmatrix} \pi \\ \pi^* \\ \lambda \\ \lambda^* \end{bmatrix} \tag{10.15}$$

In cases where the economies are structurally similar Aoki (1981) has shown that the order of dynamics can be reduced by taking averages and differences of the variables. Taking averages of (10.15) yields

$$\begin{bmatrix} \dot{\pi}_a \\ \dot{\lambda}_a \end{bmatrix} = \begin{bmatrix} 0 & \frac{-1}{r}(b_1^2 - b_1 b_2) \\ -1 & 0 \end{bmatrix} \begin{bmatrix} \pi_a \\ \lambda_a \end{bmatrix} \tag{10.16}$$

To compare this with a coordinated policy regime we assume a single controller who minimizes a weighted average of the individual countries' loss functions. This becomes a problem in two state variables and two controls. Again solving by Pontryagin's minimum principle yields a dynamic system of the form

$$\begin{bmatrix} \dot{\pi} \\ \dot{\pi}^* \\ \dot{\lambda} \\ \dot{\lambda} \end{bmatrix} = \begin{bmatrix} 0 & 0 & \frac{1}{r}(b_1^2 + b_2^2) & \frac{2b_1 b_2}{r} \\ 0 & 0 & \frac{2b_1 b_2}{r} & \frac{-1}{r}(b_1^2 + b_2^2) \\ -1 & 0 & 0 & 0 \\ 0 & -1 & 0 & 0 \end{bmatrix} \begin{bmatrix} \pi \\ \pi^* \\ \lambda \\ \lambda^* \end{bmatrix} \tag{10.17}$$

which yields the following system in averages

$$\begin{bmatrix} \dot{\pi}_a \\ \dot{\lambda}_a \end{bmatrix} = \begin{bmatrix} 0 & \frac{-1}{r}(b_1 - \beta_2)^2 \\ -1 & 0 \end{bmatrix} \begin{bmatrix} \pi_a \\ \lambda_a \end{bmatrix} \tag{10.18}$$

To compare the two we take the eigenvalues of (10.16) and (10.18). These are: $w_{OLN} = \pm\sqrt{[\gamma^2/r(\psi^2 + \psi(\delta y - (1 - \alpha)\phi y))]}$; $w_{PE} = \pm\sqrt{(\gamma^2\psi^2/r)}$.

In each case transversality conditions require that the system be driven only by the negative root. The source of inefficiency can clearly be seen. Under Pareto efficient (PE) control the controller behaves as if he were in charge of a single closed economy while under open-loop Nash (OLN) control each country perceives gains to the made in controlling inflation by variations in the real exchange rate. However these gains are achieved only at the cost of imposing an externality on the other country. As a rough guide to the difference that coordination makes Table 10.1 gives some numerical calculations of the stable roots under OLN and PE control.

Table 10.1

Parameter values	$\gamma = \psi = \delta = \phi = 0.5$ $y = 1.0 \quad \alpha = 0.75$		
	$r = 1.0$	$r = 2.0$	$r = 3.0$
OLN	−0.3307	−0.2338	−0.1909
PE	−0.25	−0.1767	−0.1443
PE/OLN	0.7559	0.7557	0.7559

4. CONCLUSIONS

In this chapter we have shown that uncoordinated policy can result in avoidable welfare losses both because countries disagree about targets or because they fail to coordinate the approach to agreed targets. Although some examples of policy coordination do exist, for example the European Monetary System can be seen as a means by which EEC members attempt to achieve some cooperation in macroeconomic policy design, there are important cases in which it could still prove beneficial. Obvious examples of this are interaction between the US and European economies and between the industrialised Northern economies and the primary producers of the South.

ACKNOWLEDGEMENT

This chapter derives from my doctoral thesis to be submitted to the University of Warwick and financed by an ESRC grant. Thanks are due to Marcus Miller and Mark Salmon for supervision and comments.

REFERENCES

Aoki, M. (1981) *Dynamic Analysis of Open Economies*. Academic Press, London, New York.

Hamada, K. (1974) 'Alternative exchange rate systems and the interdependence of monetary policies', in Aliber, R. Z. (ed.), *National Monetary Policies and the International Financial System*, University of Chicago Press.

Hamada, K. (1976) 'A strategic analysis of monetary interdependence', *Journal of Political Economy*, **84**, 677–700.

Hamada, K. and Sakurai, M. (1978) 'International transmission of stagflation under fixed and flexible exchange rates'. *Journal of Political Economy*, **86**, 877–895.

Kindelberger, C. (1976) 'Systems of international economic organisation', in Caleo, D. F. *et al. Money and the Coming World Order*. New York University Press.

Kreps, D. and Wilson, R. (1982) 'Reputation and imperfect information', *Journal of Economic Theory*, **27**, 253–279.

Miller, M. H. (1982) 'A theoretical analysis of feasible policy measures under high US interest rates'. Mimeo, University of Warwick.

Miller, M. H. and Salmon, M. (1985) 'Dynamic games and the time inconsistency of optimal policy in open economies', *Economic Journal* Conference Supplement, **95**, 124–137.

Mundell, R. A. (1968) *International Economics*, Macmillan, London, New York.

Selten, R. (1978) 'The chain-store paradox', *Theory and Decision*, **9**, 127–159.

Turner, P. M. (1983) 'Interdependence and optimal fiscal policy in a two-country model'. Mimeo, University of Southampton.

Turner, P. M. (1984) 'Real wage resistance and optimal disinflation in open economies', *University of Southampton Discussion Papers in Economics and Econometrics* No. 8410.

Williamson, J. (1982) in *Promoting World Recovery A Statement on Global Economic Strategy*: by twenty-six economists from fourteen countries. *Institute for International Economics*.

Index